EDUCATING

*for a Culture
of Peace*

EDUCATING
for a Culture
of Peace

Edited by

RIANE EISLER *and*
RON MILLER

Foreword by NEL NODDINGS

HEINEMANN
Portsmouth, NH

Heinemann
A division of Reed Elsevier Inc.
361 Hanover Street
Portsmouth, NH 03801–3912
www.heinemann.com

Offices and agents throughout the world

The author and publisher wish to thank those who have generously given permission to reprint borrowed material:

"Education for Integrity: Connection, Compassion and Character" by Rachael Kessler. Copyright © 2004 by Rachael Kessler.

"Creating a Culture of Peace with Nonviolent Communication" by Sura Hart. Copyright © 2004 by Sura Hart.

"Music: A Culture of Peace" by Raffi. Copyright © 2004 by Raffi. Reprinted by permission of the author.

Library of Congress Cataloging-in-Publication Data
Educating for a culture of peace / edited by Riane Eisler and Ron Miller.
    p. cm.
  Includes bibliographical references.
  ISBN 0-325-00726-8 (alk. paper)
    1. Peace—Study and teaching.   2. Education—Philosophy.   I. Eisler,
Riane Tennenhaus.   II. Miller, Ron, 1956–
JZ5534.E373 2004
303.6'6—dc22   2004008604

Editor: Lois Bridges
Production: Lynne Reed
Cover design: Night & Day Design
Typesetter: Kim Arney Mulcahy
Manufacturing: Steve Bernier

Printed in the United States of America on acid-free paper
08 07 06 05 04 VP 1 2 3 4 5

to our children and grandchildren

CONTENTS

PART FOUR: MOVING FROM DOMINATOR TO PARTNERSHIP CULTURE

FOREWORD

NEL NODDINGS

E ducating for a Culture of Peace invites educators to think about the most important topics to be addressed in education today: peace and nonviolence, cooperation and partnership in both individual and national relations, cultivation of the moral sentiments, concern for nonhuman animals and plants, conservation and just distribution of the earth's resources, and the promotion of democratic character. It suggests ways in which teachers might approach these vital issues, and it encourages us to make it possible for teachers to do so.

When we look at the world around us—plagued by war and terror, many of its people suffering disease and deprivation, the earth itself threatened with perhaps irreparable damage—the usual school curriculum seems misguided, even trivial. Students are expected to know which amendment gave women the right to vote (the question appears on standardized tests), but they may know little about women's struggle to obtain legal protection against domestic violence and to control their own bodies and finances. They must learn key dates associated with wars, battles, and treaties, but they do not often learn about what war does to the moral responses of otherwise decent young people. I have come to believe that it is a major moral responsibility of schools to help students understand the morally corrupting influence of war. Again, students are tested on the parts and structure of plants but rarely learn anything about growing them or protecting species. Popular textbooks describe the Dust Bowl as a "natural catastrophe" when, of course, it was a human-made disaster.

Today's schools are increasingly authoritarian—characterized by coercion and control. In the name of democracy, they force all students—regardless of interest or ability—into the same so-called academic studies, and they use rigid rules and penalties to control unhappy teenagers. Too many of us have forgotten what John Dewey told us so clearly: To maintain a democracy, we must allow our children to participate democratically in the activities designed to educate them. It would be hard to exaggerate the damage we

ix

are doing to our children, teachers, and schools through the current mania for testing, standardization, and corrupt forms of accountability.

Educating for a Culture of Peace describes a better way to educate. The way is more democratic, more vital, more intellectually honest, and more relevant to the human condition. Thoughtful educators will welcome a book that says what must be done to achieve and maintain a truly democratic society and a culture of partnership. Even more, they will appreciate the invitation to join in a vigorous campaign to return education to its proper focus on human flourishing.

EDUCATING

*for a Culture
of Peace*

PART ONE

The Urgent Need
to Educate for Peace

INTRODUCTION

RON MILLER

The essays in this book challenge the reader to examine basic assumptions about the purpose and task of education. The authors believe that humanity is living in a precarious time, a time of crisis, which demands more of education than the narrow-minded and short-sighted goals currently driving public policy in many parts of the world. Education, we assert, cannot afford to be obsessed any longer with goals that are more petty and more limited than the urgent task of building a culture of peace. We believe it is now necessary to replace the culture of war and injustice that pervades so many societies and nations with a culture of peace and compassion, if we are to survive, let alone thrive, on this planet. Education, we assert, must serve a purpose beyond economic productivity or personal triumph in the competitive marketplace: Our young people must learn how to create a culture of peace in the world.

It is not easy to shift one's basic understanding of education, for education embodies a people's vision of the future. In tradition-bound cultures, where the rhythms of social life flow surely and steadily from generation to generation, education is a relatively simple endeavor, a matter of imbuing the future with the trusted cultural patterns of the past. Formal learning, whether it occurs in the routines of daily life or in schools, consists primarily of the *transmission* of inherited knowledge, ideas, and values. The adult generation tells its youth what they must learn, and the cost of youth failing or refusing to learn these things is to become outcasts. The cultural pattern being transmitted has remained coherent for generations, and therefore, in the eyes of adult society, it works. If there are inherent limitations in an ancient tradition, such as unexamined prejudices or injustices toward whole classes of people or a habitual resort to violence, these are not to

1

be questioned in the educational process, for this culture's view of its future remains determinedly rooted in its history. Young people are taught to respect inherited beliefs, to conform to conventional norms, to obey authority. This is the taken-for-granted meaning of *education* that we have inherited from the past.

But it is obvious that we can no longer dwell in the past. The institutions and cultural values associated with the rise of modernity have had momentous effects, both positive and negative, on traditional social organization. Individualism, democracy, and material prosperity have opened up new vistas of equality and opportunity for many millions of people. Yet they have also shattered communal relationships and sense of responsibility toward local environments (Oliver, Canniff, and Korhonen 2002), exacerbating social inequality and ecological degradation. The modern, technologized world has uprooted the stability of traditional cultures. Modern people face wrenching choices and radical dislocations, not only from generation to generation, but often from one month to the next. Every aspect of our culturally mediated identity—from our economic activities and religious understandings to our food preferences and courtship rituals—is challenged or altered by the hypnotic power of mass media, the dizzying speed of technological innovation, and outbursts of mass violence, both sudden (for example, September 11) and endemic (in many parts of the world), all of which have pervasive global influence.

Consequently, the way *education* has been understood for many centuries, as the transmission of a shared social reality, is obsolete and inadequate for addressing the severe challenges of our time. As John Dewey observed more than a century ago, the challenges of modernity ought to cause us to radically rethink the purpose and process of education. To sustain a democratic culture in the face of rapid change and extreme conflict, he argued, requires the cultivation of critical, not merely technical, intelligence. Rather than instilling obedience and conformity, education for modern times must enable individuals to think deeply and creatively, and to work collaboratively as students and citizens to alter social practices that hinder their freedom or welfare. Education, he asserted, cannot simply look to the past but must be responsive to the pressing issues and dilemmas of a changing world. An education that is relevant to our time cannot simply aim for *transmission*, but must support cultural *reconstruction* or *transformation*.

Unfortunately, in these troubling times many societies are choosing reactionary responses to the unsettling consequences of modernity. This is most evident in the various forms of religious and cultural fundamentalism that have arisen from the Middle East to the American heartland, and in attempts by ruling elites, religious hierarchies, and male-dominated institutions to maintain their control in the face of moral confusion and psychological disorientation that modernity has brought in its wake. Yet even the most advanced forces of modernization, otherwise so disdainful of traditional restraints, have adopted the educational mode of *transmission* to instill and reinforce a semblance of cultural stability. Ignoring the need for critical intelligence in sustaining a democratic culture, the leaders of government, business, and other powerful social institutions have forged authoritarian educational systems intended to mold a national—indeed, global—consensus in support of their own economic and political fundamentalism.

By defining learning reductionistically as quantifiable performance on academic tests, these "standardistos" (as teacher-author Susan Ohanian aptly calls them) have isolated education from any meaningful engagement with the disturbing moral, political, and economic realities of our age and made schools training grounds for mindless conformity and quiescent citizenship. By repeatedly threatening that young people, local communities, and even national economies will fail—that is, become outcasts—if their standards are not worshipped, the elites have persuaded whole populations to maintain, indeed to rigidify, the familiar, old-fashioned ways of teaching that rely on the forcible transmission of approved facts, beliefs, and attitudes.

The construction of this educational empire (which is, in fact, an education *for* empire) is wrong for many reasons, according to those of us who envision a more caring and democratic culture than the one now unfolding. When education-as-transmission is transplanted from its heritage within the archaic, local, tradition-bound community to the modern nation-state and multinational corporation, powerful elites obtain compelling influence over the ideas and attitudes of huge masses of people. A pervasive academic monoculture seriously restricts opportunities for creative exchange of diverging intellectual, ethical, or ethnic perspectives. Teachers become technicians rather than mentors; students become workers (or customers) adhering to prescribed tasks (or consuming an endorsed product) rather than curious, critical thinkers in search of wisdom and meaningful identity.

There is another major reason why present educational regimes are dangerously inadequate, and it is the focus of this book: The world is in crisis, suffering from insane violence, degradation of nature, rampant greed and commercialization, and loss of meaning and community, but the consuming goal of our schools is to train young people to compete in the job market, reinforcing the domination of the global corporate economy, which fuels many of these problems. Moreover, modern schooling, like any transmission-oriented model, prevents young people from recognizing or addressing critical problems in the world around them. So long as they are made to memorize the so-called facts presented in authorized textbooks, students are isolated from the difficult choices they will need to make, and the complex issues they will need to understand, if they are ever to respond effectively to this suffering world. If we do not involve young people in reconstructing our societies, in building a culture of peace, justice, and compassion, their future looks bleak indeed, no matter what marketable skills their schooling provides them. If education embodies a people's vision of the future, what future do we wish for our own children?

The authors in this collection stand with other visionary educators who, for the past forty years at least, have passionately decried the failure of modern schooling to address the crisis of our age. During the period of intense cultural critique in the 1960s, opponents of the expanding technocracy such as Paul Goodman, John Holt, George Dennison, Ivan Illich, and A. S. Neill clearly saw the need to free education from the grip of corporate interests and standardized, bureaucratic management (Miller 2002). More recently, writers such as Douglas Sloan (1983), David Purpel (1989), Nel Noddings (1992), James Moffett (1994), Deborah Meier (1995, 2000), and various others have rejected the dominant emphasis of the professional education literature on standards and testing to argue that educating for a democratic and humane society requires qualities such as freedom, creativity, social responsibility, and commitment to moral and ethical ideals that transcend self-interest and corporate profits.

The increasingly rigid and constricted scope of present-day schooling is a key component of the destructive global technocratic monoculture now emerging, and it needs to be addressed just as urgently as the economic and environmental challenges that concern so many activists. In recent years, a growing number of astute critics and visionaries (identified by sociologist Paul Ray as "cultural creatives" [Van Gelder, Ray, and Anderson, 2001]) have stepped forward to alert the industrialized world to the dangerous, possibly fatal course it is pursuing. Human rights activists, environmental scientists, spiritual teachers, peace workers, holistic health professionals, and investigators of sustainable economics and agriculture have been warning that there is not a great deal of time left to turn from cultural practices that destroy communities and ecosystems toward more nourishing, egalitarian, compassionate, and life-affirming ways of treating human beings and the biosphere at large. However, only a few of these visionaries (notably, Theodore Roszak [1978] and Michael Lerner [2000]) have offered any specific, coherent insights into the vital role that education will need to play in any such transformation.

Riane Eisler, author of the international bestseller *The Chalice and the Blade* (1987), is perhaps the best known of the *cultural creative* writers to focus on the importance of education in reversing the destructive tendencies of both authoritarian traditions and modern technocracy. After exploring the broad sweep of cultural history and identifying the ruinous effects of a dominator cultural orientation on modern social institutions, Eisler concluded that her vision of a partnership-oriented culture could be achieved, in large part, through a deliberate change in educational practices. *Partnership education* is a coherent cluster of attitudes, goals, teaching approaches, design elements, and curriculum decisions meant to awaken young people's compassionate awareness of the huge moral and cultural choices that lie before them. In her book *Tomorrow's Children* (2000), which spelled out the approach of partnership education, Eisler used the phrase "caring for life" to describe its essential underlying moral orientation: Where a dominator culture gives priority to top-down control, power, and authority, whether in intimate or international relations, a partnership culture seeks to protect the delicate variety, interdependence, and integrity of living beings, human and nonhuman. An attitude of reverence for life is the fundamental basis for a partnership culture, a caring and humane culture, a culture where peace rather than violence prevails. And this attitude can be cultivated, and must be cultivated, in the adult society's interactions with its children—that is, through education.

Partnership education, as I understand it, is not a method to be slavishly practiced, nor is it a brand name like Montessori or Waldorf. Rather, it is a philosophical attitude, a specific expression of an educational orientation that has been called "progressive" and "holistic" at various times over the last century. The theme, if not the exact phrase, of *caring for life* appears commonly in the work of educators within this philosophical tradition, for they understand that to *educate* (literally, to call forth) a human being is to nourish the mysterious life forces that give birth to our existence—exactly the opposite intention of drumming in obedience to stale cultural programming. I did find this evocative phrase in the early work of Parker Palmer, one of the most widely respected advocates of holistic education; he wrote in a Quaker publication in 1978 that the moral goal of mature development is to "commit ourselves to being authentic adults—that is, persons whose lives are built around caring for new life. . . ." I found this summarization of the purpose of holistic education to be so apt that I used the phrase as the title for my own collection of essays on this theme (Palmer 1978; Miller 2000).

This volume, *Educating for a Culture of Peace*, contains writings of sixteen educators and visionaries who insist that in a world suffering from obscene violence and wanton desecration of the precious web of life, it is time for us to act as *authentic adults* by nourishing our young people's lives rather than teaching them entrenched patterns of prejudice and injustice or burdening them with the demands of our grossly competitive and materialistic society. It is time for us, as adults, teachers, and policymakers, to let go of the dominator cultural programming that was inflicted upon us, long enough to give our children a glimpse, and a hope, of a more peaceful, joyful, and caring world.

Eisler and I invited our colleagues, both practitioners and scholars, to share their thoughts about educating for a culture of peace. Some of them have adopted the conceptual framework of partnership education in their thinking, while others are considerably less familiar with Eisler's work. The intention here is not to promote a particular educational model, but to urge readers to recognize that *it is possible to build a culture of peace*—it is possible to make a cultural shift from dominator to partnership values, from violence and exploitation to compassion and collaboration—if we begin to make more conscious decisions about the education we provide to our young people. We want readers to recognize that contemporary schooling is failing our children and ultimately damaging their lives by bequeathing to them a society that gives free rein to greed and shrugs at murderous hatred and chronic violence as being an unavoidable aspect of human nature. We urge readers to act upon this recognition by asking hard questions of the standardistos and demanding more nourishing learning experiences than their harsh regime of testing and authoritarian control.

The authors in this volume repeatedly call for a fuller recognition of our common humanity. Prejudices that we learn from our culture, often directly through formal education, divide us from each other according to gender, race, religion, class, nationality, sexual orientation, and numerous other categories. In a culture of domination, these divisions become excuses for ranking groups of people into those who are superior over those who are inferior, deserving over undeserving, privileged over marginalized. A culture of peace, on the contrary, honors the essential needs and aspirations of all human beings and recognizes, also, that our needs must be seen in the context of the fragile and interconnected web of life. A culture of peace nurtures strivings for mutual understanding, tolerance, and cooperation, rooted in empathy and compassion. Surely this must become the primary goal of education in our time.

ABOUT THE BOOK

In the first section, "The Urgent Need to Educate for Peace," Riane Eisler, David Loye, and I are attempting to establish the historical and philosophical context for examining the educational issues raised throughout the book. Eisler explains the nature of partnership-oriented cultures; this is the moral framework all the authors in this volume address. Loye, a leading theorist in contemporary evolutionary science, explains how modern education rests on a dangerously faulty scientific foundation and shows how a revised understanding of humanity's place in nature would lead to new possibilities in educational practice.

The next group of essays, "Education as a Human Connection," address the theme of *human connection*, and we present inspirational writings by four remarkable educators: Rachael Kessler, the late Thomas Gordon, Doralice Lange de Souza Rocha, and Sura Hart. All of them emphasize that the *quality* of the teaching encounter is an essential element of educating for peace. Partnership education, peace education, holistic education—whatever we call it—is not a technique, nor is it a curriculum package. It is an encounter among human beings rooted in caring and compassion, and ultimately in love. Without a relationship deeply rooted in respect and care, there can be no culture of peace.

The third section of the book, "How Schools Would Be Different in a Culture of Peace," suggests ways that educational practice would change once we begin to apply partnership values and engage in caring relationships. Lisa Goldstein, Dierdre Bucciarelli, Chip Wood, and the beloved children's troubadour, Raffi, each portray a transformational vision of teaching and learning. This collection of writings is not meant to be a systematic manual for restructuring schools, but a source of inspiration to parents, educators, and policymakers—a call to action. Schools *can* be joyful, nourishing, as well as challenging environments for learning when we choose to serve humane and democratic purposes. This is not an impossible dream; progressive and holistic educators, like those contributing to this book, have demonstrated for many years that these ways of teaching are effective.

The final group of chapters, "Moving from Dominator to Partnership Culture," demonstrates that education for a culture of peace must directly take on some of the tough issues of modern society. Caring for life is not a neutral stance, but a profound moral critique of the prejudice, exploitation, and violence that characterize a dominator culture. Our colleagues Paulette Pierce, Linda Bynoe, Carl Grant, and LaVonne J. Williams write passionately about our responsibility as educators to challenge attitudes that dehumanize entire classes of people. These essays describe teaching encounters with older students—young adults—because this direct confrontation with injustice requires a certain level of experience and maturity of judgment. Educating for a culture of peace does not involve proselytizing or colonizing young minds, programming them to hold correct opinions. As we argue throughout this book, our goal is to encourage compassion, genuine dialogue, and reflective awareness. We believe that peace emerges through listening and collaboration, not through imposition or control. As Eisler has written, partnership education must involve a partnership *process* of learning, a more respectful and caring relationship between teachers and learners, as well as between peers—both adults and children. Without this essential element, bringing peace education into schools as an isolated unit of curriculum is self-defeating.

These four sections, while highlighting different aspects of a holistic education for peace, inform and expand upon each other. They describe the social and moral context of education, explain the essential features of a caring learning environment, provide examples of partnership and holistic education in practice, and return, full circle, to the social and moral issues from which education derives its meaning and purpose. It is our hope that this collection of visionary writings will inspire readers to demand a new sense of moral purpose in education, commensurate with the unnecessary violence and suffering that plague our beautiful planet.

REFERENCES

Eisler, R., 1987. *The Chalice and the Blade: Our History, Our Future.* San Francisco: Harper & Row.

———. 2000. *Tomorrow's Children: A Blueprint for Partnership Education in the 21st Century.* Boulder, CO: Westview Press.

Lerner, M. 2000. *Spirit Matters: Global Healing and the Wisdom of the Soul.* Charlottesville, VA: Hampton Roads.

Meier, D. 1995. *The Power of Their Ideas: Lessons for America from a Small School in Harlem.* Boston: Beacon Press.

———. 2000. *Will Standards Save Public Education?* Boston: Beacon Press.

Miller, R. 2000. *Caring for New Life: Essays on Holistic Education.* Brandon, VT: Foundation for Educational Renewal.

———. 2002. *Free Schools, Free People: Education and Democracy After the 1960s.* Albany: State University of New York Press.

Moffett, J. 1994. *The Universal Schoolhouse: Spiritual Awakening Through Education.* San Francisco: Jossey Bass.

Noddings, N. 1992. *The Challenge to Care in Schools: An Alternative Approach to Education.* New York: Teachers College Press.

Oliver, D., J. Canniff, and J. Korhonen. 2002. *The Primal, the Modern, and the Vital Center: A Theory of Balanced Culture in a Living Place.* Brandon, VT: Foundation for Educational Renewal.

Palmer, P. 1978. And a Little Child Shall Lead Them. Pamphlet. Philadelphia: *Friends Journal.*

Purpel, D. 1989. *The Moral and Spiritual Crisis in Education: A Curriculum for Justice and Compassion in Education.* Granby, MA: Bergin and Garvey.

Roszak, T. 1978. *Person/Planet: The Creative Disintegration of Industrial Society.* Garden City, NY: Anchor Press/Doubleday.

Sloan, D. 1983. *Insight-Imagination: The Emancipation of Thought and the Modern World.* Westport, CT: Greenwood.

Van Gelder, S., P. Ray, and S. Anderson. 2001. "A Culture Gets Creative." *Yes! A Journal of Positive Futures* 16 (Winter): 15–20.

EDUCATION FOR A CULTURE OF PEACE

RIANE EISLER

I was seven when the Gestapo came to drag my father away. My parents and I miraculously escaped the Nazis. But only by a hair's breadth were we spared the violence that cost millions their lives.

Today violence threatens not millions but billions—indeed, all of our lives. In our age of nuclear and bacteriological weaponry, nothing less than human survival may be at stake.

In recognition of the gravity of our situation, the United Nations declared the years 2001 to 2010 the International Decade for a Culture of Peace and Non-Violence for the Children of the World, and has highlighted the importance of educating for a culture of peace.[1] Even before this, peace researchers and educators recognized that a fundamental cultural shift is urgently needed.[2] Thousands of nongovernmental organizations working for a more peaceful and equitable world also reflect the growing consciousness that we stand at an evolutionary turning point. Some schools have introduced nonviolent conflict resolution programs. Some universities offer peace studies. Some teachers and a few schools, particularly those following Montessori, Waldorf, and other progressive, holistic, or social justice approaches, have teaching non-violent and caring behaviors as core goals.[3] A variety of programs—from Teaching Tolerance to the Lion and Lamb Project—offer hands-on resources for teaching caring and reducing the marketing of violence through toys and the mass media.[4] A few programs enlist families, schools, and community agencies in violence prevention and peace promotion strategies.[5] On a more global level is UNESCO's "Declaration on a Culture of Peace" and its "Education for a Culture of Peace" program.[6]

These are all encouraging developments. But at the same time, violence and the terrible suffering it wreaks continue to afflict our globe. Terrorism and warfare are on the rise. Violence against women and children is endemic. And rather than countering this violence, both informal and formal education often exacerbate it. The mass media unleash a daily barrage of violent "entertainment." The news highlights violence, as in the journalism motto "if it bleeds, it leads." Boys are systematically taught violent habits through toys, games, and stories of "manly" violence. In some world regions, children are taught that killing, even deliberately killing civilians, will be rewarded by God. And almost everywhere, the educational canon—from grammar school to graduate school—still idealizes "heroic" violence.

Why is this? And what can we do to change it?

This chapter addresses these urgent questions drawing from a cross-cultural and historical study of many cultures. It identifies the configurations of beliefs, behaviors, relations, and institutions that, regardless of other differences, support a peaceable or violent culture. It also shows how education can help develop and maintain a culture of peace—or rather, the core configuration of such a culture in a wide variety of cultural contexts.

HUMAN POSSIBILITIES

We are often told that violence is in our genes, that it's just human nature. Certainly the human capacity for violence is genetically based; otherwise we would not be capable of violence. But our capacity for caring and peaceableness is also genetically based. This too is human nature.

All these capacities are part of our genetic repertoire. But genetic capacities are not automatically expressed. Even genetic predispositions are not automatically expressed. For example, Jean-Louis Gariépy and his colleagues bred mice to be aggressive. They then reared the mice in isolation, which tended to reinforce aggressive tendencies. But when the high-aggression mice were brought out of isolation upon reaching puberty (about forty-five days old) and placed in groups between forty-five and sixty-nine days, many of the mice genetically bred for aggression became nonaggressive (Gariépy et al. 1996, 1998).

These kinds of experiments verify what we know from psychology and sociology: Gene expression or inhibition is a function of the interaction of genes with experience (Eisler and Levine 2002). Human behavior is of course much more flexible than that of mice. Humans rely far more on learning than mice. Hence, for humans, experience is even more important. And since for humans experience is primarily shaped by culture, to understand what genetic possibilities will be expressed or inhibited we have to move to an examination of what kinds of cultures produce experiences that facilitate or inhibit our genetic potential for caring and creativity or for cruelty and destructiveness.

We all know that some cultures and subcultures are more war-like and others are more peaceful. For example, in the samurai culture of medieval Japan—as in many societies today—"real" masculinity meant being a "heroic" warrior. By contrast, the Hopi Indians of North America—like an increasing number of men today—did not define manliness in terms of a warrior ethos. Here men were honored for being peaceful and nonaggressive.[7]

Every culture will have some violence. But, as the above examples illustrate, the real issue is whether a culture institutionalizes, systematically teaches, and even idealizes, violence.

This raises the question of why some cultures institutionalize, systematically teach, and idealize violence, and others do not. Conventional cultural classifications do not address this crucial question. To answer it, we need new cultural categories.

A NEW SYSTEM OF CULTURAL CLASSIFICATION

We are taught to classify cultures as ancient or modern, technologically developed or undeveloped, Eastern or Western, religious or secular, capitalist or communist. But these categories only describe particular features of a social system rather than its underlying character. They do not tell us how key institutions such as the family and education are structured. They do not deal with the primary human relations without which there would be no human societies: the relations between parents or other caretakers and children, and between women and men.

Most critically, conventional categories fail to describe an essential feature of all societies: the kinds of relations—from intimate to international—its institutions and systems of belief support or inhibit. Are they relations based on mutual respect or on domination and submission? Even more specifically, do they in reality, rather than rhetoric, tend to inhibit the human capacity for violence or do they actually support its expression?

Based on a multidisciplinary study of human societies over the long span of both history and prehistory, my research introduced a new system of cultural classification that addresses these questions. Focusing on patterns or interactions between the key components of societies, this system of classification identifies two underlying possibilities for structuring relations, institutions, and systems of beliefs: the *partnership* model and the *domination* model (Eisler 1987/1995).

No society orients completely to one or the other of these models. It is always a matter of degree. But where a society falls on the *partnership-domination continuum* affects every social institution—from the family and education to politics and economics. It also affects the society's guiding system of values. And it particularly affects whether or not violence is socially supported, indeed required.

The Domination Model

Cultures orienting to the domination model first arose in marginal world regions where resources were scarce, while cultures orienting more to the partnership model arose in the more hospitable regions of the globe. For example, in the technologically developed Minoan civilization that sprang up on the fertile Mediterranean island of Crete, we find no images idealizing violence or signs of destruction through warfare. By contrast, the Indo-Europeans or Aryans who overran Europe and India in successive waves were chronically at war, as reflected in European and Indian mythologies where fierce deities constantly fight one another.

On the surface, cultures orienting to the domination model may seem completely different. But they all share the same core configuration. The first component of this configuration is rigid top-down physical, emotional, and economic control in both the family and the state or tribe. The second core component is the ranking of the male half of humanity over the female half. The third is institutionalized, socially idealized violence. (See Tables 1 and 2 on pages 15–16.)

We see this core configuration in stark relief if we look at theocracies such as the Taliban of Afghanistan. Here personal, economic,

Table 1   Blueprints for the Domination/Control and the Partnership/Respect Models

Component	Domination Model	Partnership Model
One: Social Structure	Authoritarian structure of rigid ranking and hierarchies of domination.*	Egalitarian social structure of linking and hierarchies of actualization.*
Two: Gender Relations	Ranking male half of humanity over female half. High valuing of traits and activities such as control and conquest of people and nature associated with so-called masculinity,** with negative consequences for men and women.	Equal valuing of female and male halves of humanity. Values and activities that promote human development and welfare, such as empathy, nonviolence, and caregiving, are highly valued in women, men, and social policy.
Three: Violence and Fear	High degree of fear and socially accepted violence and abuse—from wife and child beating, rape, and warfare, to emotional abuse by "superiors" in family, workplace, and society at large.	Mutual trust and low degree of fear and social violence, since these are not required to maintain rigid rankings of domination.
Four: Belief System and Education	Relations of control/domination presented as normal, desirable, and moral in all relations—from families to the family of nations	Relations of partnership/ respect presented as normal, desirable, and moral in all relations—from families to the family of nations.

From Riane Eisler, *The Power of Partnership* (New World Library, 2002)

* What I have called a *domination* hierarchy is the type of hierarchy based on fear of pain and/or force. This kind of hierarchy is different from the hierarchy I have called an *actualization* hierarchy, where leadership and management are empowering rather than disempowering, and the goal is higher levels of functioning.

** "Masculinity" and "femininity" in this context correspond to gender stereotypes appropriate for a dominator society and *not* to any innate female or male traits.

and political top-down control, rigid male dominance, family violence, holy wars and brutal public killings of so-called criminals, such as women accused of sexual transgressions, are considered normal and moral. We find the same configuration in the European

Table 2   Interactive Dynamics

As the diagrams that follow indicate, the relationship between four major systems components is interactive, with all four mutually reinforcing one another.

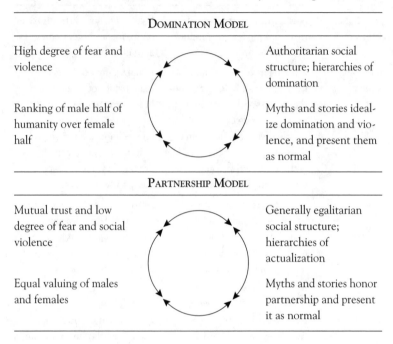

DOMINATION MODEL		
High degree of fear and violence		Authoritarian social structure; hierarchies of domination
Ranking of male half of humanity over female half		Myths and stories idealize domination and violence, and present them as normal

PARTNERSHIP MODEL		
Mutual trust and low degree of fear and social violence		Generally egalitarian social structure; hierarchies of actualization
Equal valuing of males and females		Myths and stories honor partnership and present it as normal

From Riane Eisler, *The Power of Partnership* (New World Library, 2002)

Middle Ages. Here again we see personal, economic, and political top-down control, rigid male dominance, and legally condoned violence—be it against children and women in families, against religious or political dissent, or against disempowered out-groups such as Jews. We also find incessant feuds and wars, including the holy wars of the Crusades, as well as the medieval Church's Inquisition and witch burnings, where by conservative estimates 100,000 women were killed—a slaughter of major proportions considering the small European population of the time.

These are both religious examples. But the cultural configuration characteristic of the domination model can also be found in secular societies. For example, Nazi Germany was a sharp regression to the domination model in its rigid top-down control, its call to return women to their "traditional" place, and its brutal, institutionalized, socially idealized violence.

We can see the same pattern in a leftist rather than rightist context. In the early days of the Soviet Union, in accordance with the Marxist ideal, some progress was made toward a more equitable distribution of economic resources and more equality between women and men. But the rise to power of Stalin brought a brutal dominator regression: strong-man rule, a return to the "traditional" family, and massive violence, including the killing of millions of Russian small-farm owners.

All cultures and subcultures that orient closely to the domination model require violence or fear of violence to maintain rigid rankings of domination—whether man over woman, man over man, or nation over nation. Hence, in these cultures we find a high degree of culturally accepted violence, from child and wife beating to violent scapegoating of out-groups and chronic warfare. Violence is customarily used by rulers to control their subjects and by men to control women. Childrearing is heavily based on the use of fear and force by both mothers and fathers. Teachers often use physical punishments, such as the canings common in European schools a few hundred years ago, and still lawful in some U.S. states today.

Dominator childrearing and education habituate children to the psychological and often physical abuse required to function in the rigid hierarchies of domination they are taught is "reality." Children chronically subjected to threats and aggression tend to become more vigilant and defensive-aggressive and to numb themselves so as to not feel pain. In addition, as happened to their caretakers, these children are also taught to suppress or at least compartmentalize feelings of empathy for others (Perry et al. 1996).

All these are ways of surviving in a hostile environment, and could thus be said to be adaptive in rigid dominator contexts. Not everyone adapts this way, of course. But those who do then tend to unconsciously replicate, from generation to generation, precisely the kinds of behaviors that make us feel bad, hold back our development, and perpetuate uncaring, unempathic, and violent behaviors across the board. Moreover, people with this kind of background often find it extremely hard to believe there is an alternative to either dominating or being dominated (Eisler 1995/ 1996 [Chs. 9 and 10], 2003; Eisler and Levine 2002).

Education for Violence

Some degree of empathy and caring are needed for human survival. So in societies that orient primarily to the dominator model there still has to be some empathy and caring. Moreover, in dominator-oriented societies violence is only intermittent, since this is all that is needed to maintain rankings of domination and submission backed up by fear and force.

However, to maintain their basic character, cultures and subcultures that orient to the domination model have to systematically teach violence to boys and men. In these cultures and subcultures, "soft" traits and behaviors such as empathy, nonviolence, and caring are considered appropriate only for women and "effeminate" men—that is, for those who are barred from power. "Real" masculinity is equated with domination and violence. Women are considered inferior to men, and male control over women, if "necessary" through violence, is considered normal.

Of course, these are dominator gender stereotypes rather than traits and behaviors inherent in men. There are obviously differences between women and men. But women are capable of violent behaviors, and men are capable of caring, as evidenced by the many men today redefining fathering to include "feminine" tenderness and caregiving. Girls in domination-oriented cultures and subcultures generally are not taught violent behaviors through toys or role models in stories. But there is one role model they too often have for violence: mothers who have learned that to use violence against children is part of the parenting role.

The socially accepted use of violence in intimate relations has been a training ground for habits of violence across the board. Until recently, even wife beating was dismissed as a personal rather than criminal matter. And still today, force-based childrearing is advocated as moral, integral to education "God's way."[8]

It is generally accepted that male education for violence is needed for defense. And it is true that in a world that still orients heavily to the domination model, self-defense is an important issue. However, the socialization of men for violence—indeed the equation of "real" masculinity with "heroic" and "manly" violence—sets up a self-fulfilling prophecy of violence, be it in intimate or international relations.

We are also often told that men are hormonally more predisposed to violent behaviors than women. But if this is the case, it is all the more reason not to systematically teach boys and men violent behaviors. Nonetheless, to this day male socialization still follows this pattern even in many cultures where peace and equity are normative ideals.

Boys are given swords, guns, and other violent artifacts to play with. Stories idealize "heroic" violence. Even peer group initiations tend to focus on violence, either submitting to pain inflicted by older boys and men or following orders to inflict pain on members of "inferior" out-groups.

All this is obviously not education for a culture of peace. But these values are still passed on from generation to generation through both informal and formal education in many cultures and subcultures, be they Western or Eastern, religious or secular, technologically developed or undeveloped.

Despite important educational reforms, little attention has been given to the gender-specific socialization that helps maintain dominator institutions, beliefs, and relationships in place. Even in cultures that have moved in a partnership direction, it is still unthinkingly replicated, particularly in periods of regression toward the domination model.

This socialization is inherent in the domination model, where the male half of humanity is to control the female half and where anything associated with men or "masculinity" is considered superior to women and anything considered "feminine." This lesson is learned not only by boys, but also girls, who are likewise socialized to value men and masculinity over women and femininity—as most starkly evidenced by the male preference that leads to female infanticide and/or nutritional and healthcare neglect by a child's own parents in cultures and subcultures that still orient closely to the domination model.[9]

The Partnership Model

Education has also failed to give attention to an underlying theme of modern history: It has been characterized by a succession of organized challenges to traditions of domination—whether man over woman, man over man, or nation over nation. These challenges have ranged from the challenge to the "divinely ordained" rule of kings over their subjects to the challenge to the "divinely ordained" rule of men over the women and children in the "castles" of their homes; from challenges to the once "normal" rule of race over race and religion over religion to challenges to economic and environmental exploitation.

As a result of these organized challenges, at least in some world regions, the cultural orientation to the domination model is not as severe. There have been major changes in consciousness in large segments of the population, as illustrated by the twentieth-century civil rights, anticolonial, human rights, women's rights, children's rights, peace, and environmental movements. These are all steps toward more partnership-oriented cultures worldwide.

Once again, societies orienting primarily to the partnership model can be very different from one another. For example, this orientation is found today in some tribal and agrarian societies as well as in the industrialized Nordic nations. We also see this orientation in some Western and Eastern prehistoric societies, as described in my work and in the work of scholars at the Chinese Academy of Social Sciences (Eisler 1987/1995; Min 1995). Most important, there is grassroots movement in all world regions toward family and social structures that are closer to the partnership than domination model.

The core configuration of the partnership model is a democratic and egalitarian social structure, an equal partnership between women and men, and no institutionalization or idealization of violence. The guiding principle for partnership relations is linking based on mutual respect and caring. However, there are also hierarchies. Every organization, whether familial or social, requires lines of responsibility. There are still parents, teachers, managers, leaders. But rather than *hierarchies of domination* backed up by fear and force, we see *hierarchies of actualization*.

In hierarchies of domination, power is defined as *power over*: a means of imposing and maintaining top-down control. It is the power to give orders that must be unquestioningly obeyed. In hierarchies of actualization, power is defined as *power to* and *power with*. Parenting, teaching, and leading are designed to empower rather than disempower, to inspire others to realize their potentials. Accountability and respect not only flow from the bottom up; they also flow from the top down.

As we read in the contemporary organizational development literature, the normative ideal for management is moving toward hierarchies of actualization. The manager is no longer to be a "cop" or "controller" but someone who elicits from others their best capacities, treats them with respect, and encourages teamwork rather than rankings of control. Likewise, the normative ideal for leadership is beginning to shift from the "strong" leader who uses fear, threats, or force to resolve conflicts to a leader who inspires others and develops policies that can resolve conflicts nonviolently.

I again want to emphasize that cultures and subcultures that orient closely to the partnership model are not completely violence-free. But the difference—and it is a critical difference—is that violence does not have to be institutionalized and idealized to impose and/or maintain rigid rankings of domination.

Examples of Partnership-Oriented Cultures

The argument is sometimes made that the way order is maintained in some species is through rankings of domination in which the alpha male uses violence and the threat of violence, not only to maintain his position, but to ensure that there is not constant violence among other members of the group. This is still the "law and order" argument made by some people who believe that only "strong man" leaders can maintain order.

While this kind of approach is appropriate, indeed necessary, for a dominator society, a society that integrates into the socialization of both boys and girls the universal teaching of empathic and goal-oriented self-regulation skills can maintain order through different means, and thus avoid or at least drastically reduce violence, whether intimate or international.

In the more partnership-oriented Teduray tribal culture of the Philippines, the anthropologist Stuart Schlegel found elaborate social mechanisms for the avoidance of violence as well as for the prevention of cycles of violence. The Teduray recognized that violence will occasionally erupt. But violence is not integral to male socialization. The Teduray do not rank men over women. Nor do they have economic and political tribal hierarchies of domination. Instead, there are elders—both female and male—who are highly respected because of their wisdom and who play an important role in mediating disputes (Schlegel 1998).

The Minangkabau of East Sumatra, a population of more than four million people, are also a culture where mediation for violence prevention and nonescalation are important mechanisms for maintaining a peaceable way of life. Again, the Minangkabau do not rank men over women. On the contrary, women play a major social role (Sanday 2002). Here nurturance is also part of the male role. And, as among the Teduray, violence is not part of Minangkabau childraising.

The anthropologist Peggy Reeves Sanday, who has studied this culture for many years, writes: "Childcare is not authoritarian or punitive. I have never seen any child hit or even slapped. . . . The socialization techniques fit what one would expect from the peacefulness of Minangkabau interpersonal relations: Children aren't hit, I never heard mothers screaming at their children, children get their way frequently and no one seems to mind much. The idea is that they will learn sooner or later to behave as proper Minangkabau. Shunning of naughty children may be practiced— all kids know when they have taken things beyond local expectations. Sooner or later they conform." [10]

The Teduray and Minangkabau are Eastern societies with an agrarian and/or gathering and hunting technological base. But the same partnership cultural templating can be seen in the highly technologically developed Western Nordic world.

Nordic countries such as Sweden, Norway, and Finland have created societies with both political and economic democracy. These nations have a mix of free enterprise and central planning that did not result in another domination system, as happened in the former Soviet Union. They were the first nations to move toward industrial democracy, pioneering teamwork by self-directed groups to replace assembly lines where workers are cogs in the industrial machine. And they succeeded in creating a generally good living standard for all.

It is sometimes argued that the secret of Nordic nations is that they are smaller and more homogeneous. But small is not always beautiful. Nor is large always ugly if partnership principles of organization are utilized.

Small, homogeneous nations, as well as small, homogeneous tribes, can be extremely inequitable and violent. We need only look at tribal societies where brutal chiefs control their people and the economic resources through fear and force, or at small homogeneous oil-rich nations where royal families that control enormous multinational resources still rule through fear and force, and where, as is characteristic of the domination model, women are rigidly controlled by men.

By contrast, in Sweden, Norway, Finland, and Iceland, women have held the highest political offices and a larger proportion of legislators (35 to 40 percent) are female than anywhere else in the world. And—as among the Teduray and Minangkabau—the higher status of women in the Nordic world has important conse-quences for how men define masculinity as well as for social and fiscal policies.

As the status of women rises, so also does the status of traits and activities such as nonviolence and caregiving that are in domination-oriented cultures unacceptable in men because they are stereotypically associated with "inferior" femininity. It is therefore not coincidental that these more partnership-oriented nations pioneered such caregiving social policies as government-supported childcare, universal health care, and paid parental leave. And it was these more "feminine" social policies that, as Hilkka Pietila documents, helped make Nordic countries such as Norway (which had earlier suffered from terrible famines) prospe-rous (Pietila 2001).

Neither is it coincidental that laws prohibiting violence against children in families were pioneered by Nordic nations. Or that they have a strong men's movement against male violence toward women[11] and pioneered nonviolent conflict resolution, establish-ing the first peace academies when the rest of the world only had war academies.

These are not random, unconnected developments. They are all connected with the fact that the Nordic world orients more to the partnership rather than domination model—a way of struc-turing relations, social institutions, and systems of belief that, regardless of other cultural differences, supports peaceableness. (See Tables 1 and 2 on pages 15–16.)

The Nordic nations are not pure partnership societies. There is no such thing as a pure domination model or partnership model in practice. Most families, organizations, and societies lie some-where between these two poles. But these examples show how more partnership-oriented social structures, beliefs, and relations support more caring, less violent ways of living.

EDUCATION FOR PARTNERSHIP OR DOMINATION

Cultures are not transmitted biologically. They are transmitted through both formal and informal education, starting in early childhood and continuing throughout life.

A basic question for our future is therefore what kind of culture is education transmitting today. Is it education for a culture of partnership and peace? Or is it education for a culture of domination and violence?

We need only look at the mass media to see how the message that dominator relations are normal, inevitable, and even fun is transmitted in program after program—from violent "action entertainment" and sitcoms where cruel and humiliating behaviors are modeled, to news where the infliction and suffering of pain are constantly emphasized. Formal education has an obligation to counter these messages. Yet much that is passed on from generation to generation as important knowledge and truth in schools and universities still bears a heavy dominator stamp from earlier times when education was designed to support authoritarian, inequitable, rigidly male-dominant, and chronically violent social structures.

Education for a violent or peaceable culture is very different. Just adding nonviolent conflict resolution to the existing curriculum is not enough.

We need to evaluate which elements of existing education offer the knowledge and skills to live peaceably and which elements reinforce beliefs, behaviors, and institutions that perpetuate violence. We also need to develop new curricula and pedagogies that can accelerate the movement from domination to partnership worldwide.

Tomorrow's Children: A Blueprint for Partnership Education in the 21st Century outlines such a systemic approach (Eisler 2000/2001).[12] Although it focuses largely on U.S. education, its guidelines for partnership education can be used worldwide. For example, *Tomorrow's Children* has been translated into Urdu for use in Pakistan and neighboring regions, as well as into Chinese.

Partnership education is composed of three interconnected elements: *process*, or *how* we teach and learn; *content*, or *what* we teach and learn; and *structure*, or *where* we teach and learn.

Many so-called traditional teaching methods stem from authoritarian, inequitable, male-dominated, and violent times. Like childrearing methods based on mottos such as "spare the rod and spoil the child," these teaching methods were designed to prepare people to accept their place in rigid hierarchies of domination and unquestioningly obey orders from above, be it from teachers in school, supervisors at work, or rulers in government. These educational methods also often model uncaring behaviors, teaching children that abuse by those who hold power is normal and right.

By contrast, partnership process shows children that partnership relations are possible—and much more pleasurable. Partnership process makes it possible for children to experience relations where their voices are heard, their ideas are respected, and their emotional needs are understood. Child-centered education, holistic education, cooperative learning, education for nonviolent conflict-resolution, and other progressive educational movements have been laying the groundwork for partnership educational process.[13] They promote learning experiences where students learn to work together, where each child's unique capabilities are honored, where children are treated with empathy and caring (Goldstein 1997; Kessler 2000; Noddings 1992).

Experiencing this treatment is particularly important for children who have in their homes, peer groups, and/or neighborhoods learned only two alternatives: you either dominate or you are dominated. Through partnership process, they experience the third alternative: partnership relations based on mutual respect and caring (Anthony and Calder 1987; Higgins 1994). In these ways, partnership process not only promotes learning and personal growth but also the shift to a less violent, more equitable and caring society.

Closely related to educational process is educational structure: the learning environment. For young people to function in a truly democratic society they need to experience democracy in action in both their families and schools. Yet worldwide families and schools are still generally top-down hierarchies in which young people have no voice and in which accountability flows only from the bottom up.

By contrast, in partnership structures there are interactive feedback loops. There are still hierarchies, but they are hierarchies of actualization where power is not used to disempower students but to empower them. Teachers facilitate learning rather than controlling and indoctrinating. Administrators consult with teachers, parents, other staff, and students. Students have a part in setting rules and standards and seeing that they are followed.

Schools that follow the partnership model are communities of learning rather than top-down, impersonal factories. This requires using the partnership model of smaller cooperative units combined with central planning to ensure that not only classrooms but schools are not so bureaucratized.

Partnership schools are resources not only for children but for adults. They offer counseling and educational opportunities for parents and other caregivers that will benefit children and further their development—for example, workshops for partnership parenting education where mothers and fathers can share challenges and explore appropriate solutions. They offer referrals to other community agencies to help children develop not only intellectually but emotionally and to ensure that basic needs such as good nutrition and healthcare are met.

But transforming *how* and *where* we teach in a partnership direction is not enough. We also need to address *what* we teach: the curriculum content. Transforming curriculum content is basic to transforming society in a partnership direction.

Partnership Curricula

Whether overtly or covertly, every educational curriculum is values-laden (O'Sullivan 1999; Sleeter and Grant 1994). Curricula communicate the prevailing cultural-academic assumptions both explicitly and implicitly. To change assumptions that we have inherited from earlier, more domination-oriented cultures, we need a new conceptual framework that does not view chronic violence as "just the way things are."

The conceptual framework that informs partnership curricula offers a more complete, accurate, and hopeful perspective on our past, present, and possibilities for our future. It includes information about the domination model as a human possibility. But it also shows that the partnership model is a realistic possibility, and that throughout modern history there has been movement in this direction—albeit countered by enormous resistance and periodic regressions.

Partnership curricula are designed to provide the information and skills children need to become competent, self-realized, responsible adults. They prepare young people to effectively address environmental issues and use technology in responsible ways that take into account long-term consequences, not just quick fixes.

Partnership curricula also prepare young people for the new information and service-oriented postindustrial economy by emphasizing problem solving and flexibility and helping them recognize patterns and think in more holistic ways. Most critically, partnership curricula prepare young people to live and work together in peaceful and equitable ways.

The narratives we teach give young people the wherewithal to form their views of the world and their place in it. Sigmund Freud, Carl Jung, Alfred Adler, Karen Horney, and other founders of modern psychology showed that how we view ourselves and others is rooted in how we are taught to perceive ourselves and the world.[14] More recently, studies on the effects of television violence on both children and adults further show how cultural narratives mold attitudes and behaviors, including abusive and violent behaviors as well as insensitivity to the pain these behaviors cause (Gerbner et al. 1994; Loye, Horney, and Steele 1997). There is also a large body of literature on the power of cultural narratives from anthropology, sociology, social psychology, the study of myth, and other disciplines.[15] The work of the social psychologist Milton Rokeach is particularly instructive because it shows that values can be changed by introducing new narratives (Rokeach 1973).

Every culture has partnership elements. These elements can be strengthened and built upon through partnership narratives.

For example, partnership narratives about evolution focus not only on competition but also on cooperation. They inform children that, contrary to prevailing beliefs, Darwin himself emphasized the importance of caring, cooperation, and what he called the moral sense when we come to the human level.[16]

Partnership curricula further show that images such as the familiar cartoon of the brutal caveman dragging a woman around by her hair are not found in early prehistoric art. They highlight that, on the contrary, images that honor the giving and nurturing, rather than the taking, of life play a central role in Stone Age art (Marshack 1991).

Partnership curricula also show that there is far more to history than wars, battles, and who won or lost in struggles for political control. Rather than asking children to memorize dates of wars, teachers focus on dates commemorating the efforts of women and men to construct a more equitable, democratic, gender-fair, environmentally sustainable, and peaceful world.

Partnership curricula highlight how nonviolent tactics have brought about social change. For example, in the United States women won the right to vote despite enormous opposition when courageous women such as Elizabeth Cady Stanton and Alice Paul used demonstrations, hunger strikes, and extensive political lobbying. In India, Gandhi used these same methods in his successful struggle for independence from British colonial rule. The same nonviolent tactics were used in the struggle against racial segregation and for civil rights, for laws against sweatshops and child labor, and other gains most people in the West today take for granted.

Partnership curricula help young people see that these efforts are not disconnected, that they are part of the movement to shift from dominator to partnership societies worldwide. They see that, despite enormous resistance and periodic setbacks, progress toward partnership has been made over the last three hundred years. Most important, they see that they too can help move our world in a partnership direction.

EDUCATION FOR VALUING DIFFERENCE

As we have seen, in the domination model people learn to automatically equate difference with dominating or being dominated. This learning starts early, with the ranking of the in-group of "mankind" over the female "other."

This basic lesson for relations is inculcated before children's brains are fully developed, before they have the mental capacity for critical reflection and evaluation. It is constantly reiterated through both family and cultural models of "proper" masculine roles of control and feminine roles of submission. And since the domination model provides only two alternatives—dominating or being dominated—this division of humans into those who control and those who are to be controlled can then be generalized to other people who are different: people of other races, religions, and ethnicities.

In cultures such as fundamentalist Iran and the Taliban that still orient closely to the domination model, students are explicitly taught that women are not only inferior but dangerous—and hence must be rigidly, and if "necessary," violently controlled by men. Not coincidentally, in these cultures violence against different religions, and even different sects of the same religion, is endemic, as is support for terrorism against other "evil" out-groups.

These are extreme manifestations of the effects of education for domination and violence. But even in societies that have been moving toward the partnership model, education for in-group versus out-group thinking persists. Consider, for example, how little literature, art, history, and philosophy texts contain about and by women. This clearly communicates the message that the male half of humanity is entitled to be dominant over the female half, who, so it would seem, contribute little worth passing on as important knowledge and truth.

The fact that most of us see nothing strange about calling any issue that affects no less than half of humanity "just a women's issue"—even though we would think it peculiar to call issues that affect the male half of humanity "just a men's issue"—indicates how profoundly we have all been influenced by this type of education.

But the splitting of humanity into a male in-group and a female out-group not only adversely affects women. Whether the roles and relations of the two halves of humanity are culturally constructed in accordance with the domination or partnership model directly affects every social institution.

It affects whether families are egalitarian or authoritarian. It affects whether they are violent or nonviolent, since the basis for domestic violence against women is establishing and maintaining male control. Although we are not taught this either, the social construction of gender roles and relations directly affects economics. If half of humanity is put on this Earth only to serve the other half, this provides a model for economic exploitation that can be easily generalized to other castes, races, or classes. And if the life-giving and supporting services of women are accorded no real economic value—as is the case in so-called traditional economic models—the same is true of the life-giving and supporting services of nature.

Moreover, if women's reproductive capacities are to be controlled by men—individually as heads of families and politically as heads of tribes or states—there is no hope of stemming the global population explosion. Indeed, as long as women are viewed as male-controlled technologies of production and reproduction, as they are in world regions that orient more closely to the domination model, women will continue to "choose" to breed as many children as possible—regardless of the damage to their health, their communities, or their planet.

The cultural construction of gender roles and relations also profoundly affects systems of values—and hence both domestic and foreign policies. As the Nordic nations illustrate, it impacts whether activities stereotypically associated with men, such as making and using weapons and fighting wars, or activities stereotypically associated with women, such as caring for children and maintaining a clean and healthy physical environment, are, or are not, valued (Eisler, Loye, and Norgaard 1995). It impacts whether unempathic and uncaring policies, such as the structural adjustment policies imposed by the World Bank and International Monetary Fund (IMF)—requiring debtor nations to cut health, nutrition, and other caregiving social services—continue, causing enormous suffering worldwide.

We need to educate both boys and girls to value and adopt traits and activities in domination-oriented cultures relegated to women: nonviolence, empathy, and caregiving. This will profoundly affect policy priorities, funding, and our real chances for a world of peace.

Our curricula need to recognize what should have been obvious all along: Because women and men are the two halves of humanity, lessons about proper masculine and feminine identity teach us what it means to be human. Masculinity and femininity are core components of identity for men and women. How boys and girls are brought up to view themselves and the world is central to the formation of habits of feeling, thinking, and acting. Therefore, what young people are taught about their respective roles and relations, and about the relative value of traits and activities assigned to either gender, is a fundamental issue for education—and for society.

Of course, even though it is foundational, the male-superior/dominant and female-inferior/subordinate model of gender relations is not the only obstacle to a more equitable society. Partnership curricula reveal how dominator economic and political structures profit from violence and exploitation, promoting war and environmental destruction. They point to the structural changes needed to create partnership institutions, from more democratic families to more truly democratic political structures. In these and other ways, partnership education addresses the interaction of social structures, cultural values, and individual relations and actions worldwide.

In addition to being gender-balanced, partnership curricula integrate materials on peoples of all races and many cultures. They also give visibility to people who are "different" in other respects, including people who are blind, deaf, or otherwise physically or developmentally challenged.

But by including and giving value and visibility to women and traits and activities such as nonviolence and caregiving stereotypically associated with femininity, partnership curricula help young people acquire values in which empathic relations and essential activities, such as caring for children and maintaining a clean and healthy environment, which are still stereotypically associated with women, are accorded the importance they merit. As Nel Noddings writes, "All children must learn to care for other human beings, and all must find an ultimate concern in some center of care: care for self, for intimate others, for associates and acquaintances, for distant others, for animals, for plants, and the physical environment, for objects and instruments, and for ideas" (Noddings 1995, 366).

CARING FOR LIFE

Children and adults need the basic requirements for life: nutritious food, adequate shelter, and freedom from violence in both their homes and communities. They need to be valued and to feel valuable and loved. They need an education that at a minimum offers basic skills such as the three Rs of reading, writing, and arithmetic. They also need to learn a fourth R: relational skills appropriate for partnership rather than dominator relations. Partnership-oriented cultures and education meet these needs (Eisler 2000).

Partnership-oriented cultures invest heavily in good nutrition and healthcare for women so that the children they bear are not robbed of their birthright of full physical and mental development. They invest national resources in adequate childcare— both in education for partnership childcare and in policies that support this socially and economically essential work, whether it is performed by women or men, inside or outside families.

Partnership-oriented cultures offer partnership education through both schools and continuing education programs for adults. Integral to this education is learning relational skills, including caregiving skills.

I have proposed that a thread running through the entire curriculum from preschool to graduate school should be *caring for life*: caring for self, for others, and for our natural habitat (Eisler 2000).

A key component of teaching caring for life is education for partnership parenting: parenting that is authoritative rather than authoritarian, caring rather than coercive, respectful rather than repressive. We know from neuroscience that the kind of care— material, emotional, and mental—a child receives, particularly during the first years of life, affects nothing less than the neural pathways of the brain. Positive caregiving that relies on praise, caring touch, affection, and lack of violence or threats releases the chemicals dopamine and serotonin into particular areas of the brain, promoting emotional stability and mental health (Perry et al. 1996).[17] By contrast, if children are subjected to negative, uncaring, fear, shame, and threat-based treatment or other aversive experiences such as violence or sexual violation, they develop responses appropriate for dominator environments. They tend to become abusive and aggressive or withdrawn and chronically depressed, defensive, hypervigilant, and numb to their own pain and to that of others.

These children often lack the capacity for aggressive impulse control. Neuroscientists such as Dr. Bruce Perry of Baylor College of Medicine and Dr. Linda Mayes of the Yale Child Study Center have found that regions of the brain's cortex and its limbic system (responsible for emotions, including attachment) are 20 to 30 percent smaller in abused children. These scientists have also found that children exposed to chronic and unpredictable stress will suffer deficits in their ability to learn (Perry et al. 1996). They often lack the capacity for long-term planning.

Yet education for partnership parenting is still generally ignored worldwide. Dominator parenting habits continue to be passed on from generation to generation, constricting not only individual development but economic development—not to speak of the real possibility for creating a global culture of peace.

Education for caring and mutually respectful relations between women and men is another key component of partnership education. Nordic nations already offer education for mutually fulfilling and responsible romantic relations in their educational systems. Links to resources for caring and nonviolent intimate relations, both between adults and between parents and children, are available from Internet sites such as the Spiritual Alliance to Stop Intimate Violence of the Center for Partnership Studies (www.partnershipway.org).

Introducing education for caring for life in curricula worldwide will help ensure that children learn habits of empathy and caring while they are still young and more receptive. These habits can then carry over into partnership childcare and parenting based on praise, caring touch, rewards, and lack of threat. They can also carry over into more equitable and empathic domestic and foreign policies.

Learning the skills for caring for life offers a positive rather than negative approach to violence prevention. If children are taught they should not hit other children because if they do they will be hit by a parent or teacher, they are taught that violence inflicted by a "superior" upon an "inferior" is acceptable—and that they need only grow up to get away with it. Not only is violence as a means of imposing one's will on others modeled; empathy is suppressed or compartmentalized. These are prerequisites for the ability to deliberately cause pain.

Teaching caring for life is different from teaching children to do what they are told through fear that if they don't obey they will be punished. It shifts the learning emphasis from suppression and control to development and actualization; from extrinsic punishments to intrinsic rewards.

We know from neuroscience that by the grace of evolution humans are biochemically rewarded with sensations of great pleasure not only when we are cared for but also when we care for others—be it for a child, a friend, a lover, or a pet.[18] Most of us have experienced this pleasure, even though science and evolution classes do not teach us that is it biologically based—which they would through partnership curricula.

Helping young people learn skills and habits of caring for life is essential for a truly democratic rather than authoritarian society. It is also essential for building partnership cultures of peace.

CONCLUSION

At our level of technological development, the domination model is not evolutionarily adaptive. Hence the urgent need for the fundamental changes envisioned by the United Nations International Decade for a Culture of Peace and Non-Violence for the Children of the World. In the language of chaos and nonlinear dynamics theory, we stand at a bifurcation: a turning point in human cultural evolution.

On one side lies the road of regression to even more rigid domination and control—familial, educational, religious, economic, and political. We see movement in this direction all around us: the increasing economic, political, and media control of giant multinationals, the widening gap between haves and have-nots, the growing threats to civil liberties, the push to return women to their "traditional" subservient place, the backlash of violence against women's rights and children's rights, the use of religion to justify rankings of "superiors" over "inferiors," and the escalation of intertribal and international terrorism and war.

On the other side lies the road to a more equitable, less violent, more caring partnership future. This movement toward partnership has been escalating for several centuries, largely due to the destabilization of existing habits and institutions by the technological changes entailed in shifting from a primarily agrarian to industrial world. Today, the rapid shift from industrial to postindustrial technologies is still further destabilizing entrenched beliefs and institutions—opening up further opportunities for positive change.

As a mother and grandmother, I feel a passionate urgency to help accelerate the global shift toward partnership. I know from my research that in a world still orienting heavily to the domination model, peace can be no more than an interval between wars. In such a world, there is no realistic way of ending the glaring disparities between haves and have-nots—the over-consumption and wastefulness of the haves and the poverty, malnutrition, inadequate healthcare, and overpopulation that afflict the have-nots worldwide.[19] Nor is there any way of ending the intimate violence and abuse that is schooling for relations of domination and submission across the board.

Any realistic hope of peace requires that we join hands to accelerate the cultural shift from domination to partnership worldwide. But building more partnership-oriented cultures worldwide requires attention to matters that are not usually examined in connection with violence prevention. We certainly have to address political and economic institutions and practices that perpetuate dominator structures and beliefs. But we also have to give much more attention to the relations between children and parents or other caregivers and between women and men. Building a more peaceful and equitable world requires movement toward a new kind of economics where the life-sustaining work of caring and caregiving is no longer operationally devalued (Eisler 2003). It requires that peace initiatives address ending culturally entrenched traditions of intimate violence, as these are integrally connected with intranational and international violence. And it requires a fundamental reexamination and revision of educational systems worldwide.

I know from both my life and my research that making fundamental changes is not easy. But I also know it can be done. Indeed, it has been done, or we would all still be living in a world where every woman and most men knew "their place" in rigid hierarchies of domination, a world where slavery was legal, extreme poverty was considered normal, and advocating children's rights would have been viewed as immoral, indeed, insane.

Cultures are human creations. They can and have been changed. Fundamental changes will not happen overnight. There will continue to be resistance. Shifting to partnership cultures will take ingenuity, courage, and persistence. But working together we can create cultures that support rather than inhibit the realization of our highest human potentials: our great capacities for caring, empathy, and creativity.[20] We can all help build these cultures through partnership education.

NOTES

1. See *www.unesco.org/cpp/uk/declarations/2000.htm*. See also the website of David Adams, former Director of the UNESCO Unit for the International Year for the Culture of Peace at *www.culture-of-peace.info/*.

2. See, for example, Eva Nordland, Betty A. Reardon, and Robert Zuber (1994) and Linda Lantieri and Janet Patti (1996). See also *www.peaceed .org/what/whatbr.htm* and Ingeborg Breines, Dorota Gierycz, and Betty Reardon (1999).

3. For information on Montessori, see Tim Seldin and Paul Epstein (2003) *The Montessori Way: Education for Life* (*www.montessori-foundation-books.org*) and the journal *Tomorrow's Child*; the Rudolf Steiner Foundation (*www.rsfoundation.org*) offers information on Waldorf schools; *Rethinking Schools* (*www.rethinkingschools.org,*), the Holistic Education Press (*www.great-ideas.org*), and journals such as *Encounter* and *Paths of Learning* are some sources on holistic/progressive/social justice education.

4. Teaching Tolerance (*www.teachingtolerance.org*) is a program of the Southern Poverty Law Center, and offers powerful teaching tools such as the CD "I Will Be Your Friend" and the magazine *Teaching Tolerance*. The Lion and Lamb Project (*www.lionlamb.org*) offers manuals such as "Toys for Peace: A How-to Guide for Organizing Violent Toy Trade-Ins."

5. An example is the Chicago-based Violence Prevention Peace Promotion Strategy (*www.vppps.org*).

6. See *www.unesco.org/education/ecp/index.htm*. The 1998 UNESCO "World Education Report" and the 1995 UNESCO "Our Creative Diversity Report" also pave the way for a broader report on education in terms of support for a culture of peace.

7. For a discussion of these differences, as well as the important role of the women's movement in democratizing society, see Riane Eisler (1995), published on the occasion of the United Nations Conference on Women held in Beijing in 1995.

8. See, for example, Hanna Rosin (1999), for a harrowing account of the damage done to children and parents by this approach.

9. Despite the well-known fact that women as a group have longer life spans than men, there are in some countries fewer than ninety-five women for every one hundred men. In China and South and West Asia, there are only ninety-four females for every one hundred males. The Nobel prize–winning economist Amartya Sen has estimated that more than one hundred million women across the globe are "missing." According to statistics released in 1995 (the year of the Fourth United Nations Conference on Women), deaths per year per thousand in Bangladesh were 15.7 for girls age one to four versus 14.2 for boys. In Pakistan, the ratio was 9.6 for girls versus 8.6 for boys. In Guatemala, it was 11.3 for girls versus 10.6 for boys. In Egypt, it was 6.6 versus 5.6. And even in Singapore, which at that time had a strong economy, the ratio was 0.5 for girls versus 0.4 for boys (United Nations 1995, 35). This U.N. report, published for the year of the United Nations Conference on Women in Beijing, is unfortunately unique in its wealth of statistical data focusing on gender discrimination. For a study looking at the systemic effects of gender discrimination, see Riane Eisler, David Loye, and Kari Norgaard (1995).

10. Peggy Reeves Sanday, personal communication to author, January 30, 2002.

11. As two Nordic men, Jorgen Lorentzen and Per Are Lokke wrote in the paper they presented at the international meeting "Promoting Equality: A Common Issue for Men and Women," held in Strasbourg in June 1997, "Many men have come to believe that violence against a woman, child, or another man is an acceptable way to control another person. By remaining silent about the violence, we allow other men to poison our environments. We also allow the picture of men as dangerous to stay alive. . . . Domestic violence is a problem within existing masculinity and it is we, as men, who have to stop it" (Lorentzen and Lokke 1997, 4).

12. See also Dee Buccarelli and Sarah Pirtle (2001). The video and DVD "Tomorrow's Children" (Media Education Foundation 2001) is another good resource also available from the Center for Partnership Studies (www.partnershipway.org).

13. For a good overview of some of these approaches, see Ron Miller (1997). There are other excellent books on collaborative learning, including Vera John-Steiner (2000) and Jeanne Gibbs (1994).

14. A good source on the psychoanalytical literature is Calvin Hall and Gardner Lindzey (1978).

15. An early classic from anthropology is Ruth Benedict (1934); from sociology, Max Weber (1961); David Loye (1971/1998) shows the power of racially biased narratives. Feminist writings, including classics such as Dale Spender (1983), show the attempts by women over many centuries to contradict sexist cultural narratives. Joseph Campbell (1974) is well known in the area of myth.

16. For an account of this ignored side of Darwin's work, see David Loye (2002) and (2004).

17. Excellent videos on parenting are: "I Am Your Child: The First Years Last Forever," hosted by Rob Reiner and produced by the Reiner Foundation and "Begin with Love," narrated by Oprah Winfrey. See www.iamyourchild.org and www.civitasinitiative.com.

18. Emotions occur when molecules called *neuropeptides* (amino acids strung together like pearls in a necklace) make contact with receptors (complicated molecules found in almost every cell in the body, not just the brain). Although there is still much work to be done to identify the exact nature of these chemicals, it is clear that different emotions involve different neuropeptides, which are essentially information-carrying molecules. (For an accessible account of this, see Bill Moyers [1993, 177–193]. See also Riane Eisler and Daniel Levine [2002, 9–52].)

19. Two thirds of the earth's more than six billion people live in its very poorest regions. Ninety-seven percent of the nearly eighty million people added to the planet annually are born in these regions, condemning them to a daily struggle for survival. Three hundred and fifty million of the neediest women worldwide did not want more children. Yet family planning as well as other life options than breeding men's sons are still not available to these women, with U.S. support for United Nations family planning programs totally eliminated from President George W. Bush's 2002 budget (Fornos 2002, 2).

20. For a collection of articles on this issue, see David Loye (1971/1998) and Riane Eisler (1998).

REFERENCES

Anthony, E. J., and B. Colder, eds. 1987. *The Invulnerable Child*. New York: Guilford.

Benedict, R. 1934. *Patterns of Culture*. New York: Houghton Mifflin.

Breines, I., D. Gierycz, and B. Reardon, eds. 1999. *Towards a Women's Agenda for a Culture of Peace*. New York: UNESCO.

Buccarelli, D., and S. Pirtle, eds. 2001. *Partnership Education in Action: A Companion to Tomorrow's Children*. Pacific Grove, CA: Center for Partnership Studies, in collaboration with the Foundation for Educational Renewal.

Campbell, J. 1974. *The Mythic Image*. Princeton, NJ: Princeton University Press.

Eisler, R. 1987/1995. *The Chalice and the Blade: Our History, Our Future*. New York: HarperCollins.

———. 1995. "A Time for Partnership." *UNESCO Courier*, September.

———. 1995/1996. *Sacred Pleasure: Sex, Myth, and the Politics of the Body*, San Francisco: HarperCollins.

———. 1998. "Building a Just and Caring World: Four Cornerstones." *Tikkun* 13(3).

———. 2000/2001. *Tomorrow's Children: A Blueprint for Partnership Education in the 21st Century*. Boulder, CO: Westview Press.

———. 2003. *The Power of Partnership*. Novato: New World Library.

———. 2003. "Work, Values, and Caring: The Economic Imperative for Revisioning the Rules of the Game." *www.partnershipway.org/html/subpages/articles/changingrules.htm*.

Eisler, R., and D. Levine. 2002. "Nature, Nurture, and Caring: We Are Not Prisoners of Our Genes." *Brain and Mind* 3 (1): 9–52.

Eisler, R., D. Loye, and K. Norgaard. 1995. *Women, Men, and the Global Quality of Life*. Pacific Grove, CA: Center for Partnership Studies.

Fornos, W. 2002. "Budgetary Priorities for War on Terrorism." *Popline* 24 (January/February): 2.

Gariépy, J., P. L. Gendreau, R. B. Cairns, and M. H. Lewis. 1998. "DI Dopamine Receptors and the Reversal of Isolation-Induced Behaviors in Mice." *Behavioral Brain Research* 95: 103–11.

Gariépy, J., M. H. Lewis, and R. B. Cairns. 1996. "Genes, Neurobiology, and Aggression." In *Aggression and Violence: Genetic, Neurobiological, and Biosocial Perspectives*, eds. D. M. Stoff, R. B. Carins, et al. Mahwah, NJ: Earlbaum.

Gerbner, G., L. Gross, M. Morgan, and N. Signorielli. 1994. "Growing Up with Television." In *Media Effects*, eds. J. Bryant and D. Zillman. Hillsdale, NJ: Erlbaum.

Gibbs, J. 1994. *Tribes: A New Way of Learning Together*. Santa Rosa, CA: Center Source Publications.

Goldstein, L. S. 1997. *Teaching with Love*. New York: Peter Lang.

Hall C., and G. Lindzey. 1978. *Theories of Personality*. New York: Wiley.

Higgins, G. O. 1994. *Resilient Adults: Overcoming a Cruel Past.* San Francisco: Jossey-Bass.

John-Steiner, V. 2000. *Creative Collaboration.* New York: Oxford University Press.

Kessler, R. 2000. *The Soul of Education.* Alexandria, VA: Association for Curriculum Supervision and Development.

Lantieri, L., and J. Patti, eds. 1996. *Waging Peace in Our Schools.* Boston: Beacon Press.

Lorentzen, J., and P. A. Lokke. 1997. "Men's Violence Against Women: The Need to Take Responsibility." Paper presented at the international seminar "Promoting Equality: A Common Issue for Men and Women," Palais de l'Europe, Strasbourg, France, June 17–18.

Loye, D. 1971/1998. *The Healing of a Nation.* New York: Norton; *www.iuniverse.com.*

———. 1998. *The Evolutionary Outrider: The Impact of the Human Agent on Evolution.* Twickenham, England: Adamantine Press; Westport, CT: Praeger.

———. 2002. *Darwin's Lost Theory.* *www.iuniverse.com.*

———. 2004. *The Great Adventure: Toward a Fully Human Theory of Evolution.* Albany: SUNY Press.

Loye, D., R. Gorney, and G. Steele. 1977. "Effects of Television: An Experimental Field Study." *Journal of Communication* 27 (3): 206–16.

Marshack, A. 1991. *The Roots of Civilization.* Mt. Cisco, NY: Moyer Bell.

Miller, R. 1997. *What Are Schools For?* 3d ed. Brandon, VT: Holistic Education Press.

Min, J. 1995. *The Chalice and the Blade in Chinese Culture: Gender Relations and Social Models.* Beijing: China Social Sciences Publishing House.

Moyers, B. 1993. "The Chemical Communicators: Candace Pert." *Healing and the Mind.* New York: Doubleday.

Noddings, N. 1992. *The Challenge to Care in Schools.* New York: Teachers College Press.

———. 1995. "A Morally Defensible Mission for Schools in the 21st Century." *Phi Delta Kappan* (January): 366.

Nordland, E., B. A. Reardon, and R. Zuber, eds. 1994. *Learning Peace: The Promise of Ecological and Cooperative Education.* Albany: SUNY Press.

O'Sullivan, E. 1999. *Transformative Learning.* New York: Zed Books.

Perry, B. D., R. A. Pollard, R. L. Blakley, W. L. Baker, and D. Vigilante. 1996. "Childhood Trauma, the Neurobiology of Adaptation, and 'Use

Dependent' Development of the Brain: How 'States' Become 'Traits'." *Infant Mental Health Journal* 16: 271–91.

Pietila, H. 2001. "Nordic Welfare Society: A Strategy to Eradicate Poverty and Build Up Equality: Finland as a Case Study." *Journal Cooperation South* 2 (2): 79–96.

Rosin, H. 1999. "A Tough Plan for Raising Children Draws Fire: 'Babywise' Guides Worry Pediatricians and Others." *Washington Post,* February 27, A01.

Rokeach, M. 1973. *The Nature of Human Values.* New York: Free Press.

Sanday, P. R. 2002. *Women at the Center.* Ithaca, NY: Cornell University Press.

Schlegel, S. 1998. *Wisdom from a Rainforest.* Athens: University of Georgia Press.

Seldin, T. and P. Epstein, eds. 2003. *The Montessori Way: Education for Life.* Sarasota, Florida: the Montessori Foundationn (*www.montessorifoundation.org*).

Sleeter, C. E., and C. A. Grant, eds. 1994. *Making Choices for Multicultural Education.* Columbus, OH: Merrill.

Spender, D., ed. 1983. *Feminist Theorists.* New York: Pantheon.

United Nations. 1995. *U.N. Development Programme 1995 Human Development Report.* New York: Oxford University Press.

Weber, M. 1961. "The Social Psychology of the World's Religions." In *Theories of Society,* eds. T. Parsons et al. New York: Free Press.

DARWIN'S LOST THEORY AND THE HIDDEN CRISIS IN WESTERN EDUCATION

DAVID LOYE

Here in the West it often seems obvious to us that the greatest threat to a world of peace is the kind of education the Islamic terrorists are getting. What could be worse than the picture we now have of these hordes of angry young males being taught, within societies still mired in the ignorance and the ethos of the Middle Ages, to kill in the name of Allah?

But what if it should turn out that with the best of intentions, in all innocence, we ourselves have also been a threat to world peace? Indeed, what if the very institution we have pinned our hopes on for the advance of enlightenment, democracy, and every other good thing—namely our huge investment in our schools and every other form of education—should in effect be acting as an engine of our world's destruction? In other words, what if cumulatively far more devastating than any howling mob of Taliban is what has been going on for more than a century under the supposedly wholly enlightened auspices of modern science, in supposedly the most advanced countries of the West?

This is the unsettling question I faced on stepping back from a decade of research to ponder the implications of its single most striking discovery. It was the fact that Charles Darwin went on from what we have been told for a century was the be-all and end-all for his theory of evolution to develop a "higher" theory of evolution. In *The Descent of Man*, for example, almost entirely ignored for a century, he specifically tells us he is going on beyond the "survival of the fittest" theory of *Origin of Species*, which pertains mainly to prehumans, to complete his theory with a look at *human* evolution—that is, what pertains most specifically to us, and our children, and their children on into the future.

Because of what we have been told by mainstream established authority for evolution theory throughout the twentieth century we have assumed—and those of us who are teachers have routinely taught—that in *The Descent of Man* Darwin simply goes on to show how "survival of the fittest" works at our level. That is, we assume he tells us that the process of natural selection gobbling away at the least fit of variations—namely ourselves in all our differences and everything we think or do—drives us to ever greater heights of achievement in business, in government, and in every other aspect of our culture.

Many of us do not particularly like this idea but because of the prestige of Darwin and science we accept it as the linchpin fact we must believe and teach. It is, we may feel, the core idea that historically freed us from the grasp of regressive religion. In face of the mounting threat to education of right-wingers and creationists, it is further, we may feel, the core fact for the Darwinian theory of evolution that is crucial to the drive of progressive science as our liberator.

But now a curious fact emerges. In this supposed textbook or guidebook on how we may best evolve at *our* level, I found Darwin actually writes only twice of "survival of the fittest"—and one of these times is to apologize for exaggerating the importance of this idea in *Origin of Species*. I further found that in this book of 848 pages in fine print, he writes only twelve times of selfishness, which by now hordes of sociobiologists, evolutionary psychologists, and best-selling books have assured us is the central survivalist motivation for human evolution high and low. Instead, what Darwin was actually writing about in *The Descent of Man* is *love* (which he mentions ninety-five times), *moral sensitivity* (ninety-two times), and *mind* (ninety times). It seems that he was saying what educator and moral theorist Nel Noddings has been emphasizing more than a century later—that caring and the search for meaning are at the heart of human life and should comprise the core of our work in education.

In essence, what I found is that Darwin developed not just the one theory of evolution, which as teachers in high school through college most of us have routinely taught, or otherwise believed, for more than a century. He actually developed four important theories, all of which bear on our evolution. But the one of greatest importance—which I identify as his "lost" theory—has been ignored, bypassed, and otherwise overlooked in a truly astounding way. To paraphrase Darwin briefly, this "lost" theory holds that beyond the basic drive of natural selection, which began to drop off in importance 100,000 years ago with the emergence of Homo sapiens, *our* species, lie the higher drives of moral sensitivity, love, and the effects of education and otherwise caring for one another. In other words, for more than a century we have been learning and teaching only the first half of what Darwin wanted to see put to use as a socially liberating scientific theory of human evolution in tune with the greatest of our species' earlier spiritual and philosophical visionaries.

In an extensive analysis of relevant books over the span of the twentieth century, I found only four people sufficiently aware of the lost theory to begin to recognize and adequately write of its importance. Yet what emerges from bringing into the picture the findings of a huge body of modern biology, brain research, systems science, and practically all the social sciences—most of it similarly ignored by mainstream evolution theorists—is the pivotal bearing of this "lost" theory on both the nature and the potential destiny of our species.

Neo-Darwinian biologists and their successors introduced a paradigm that explained, or seemed to explain, many of their observations of the natural world. But then as the "survival of the fittest" idea was seized up by the social, economic, and political powers-that-be to legitimize policies of domination, exploitation, and predation, the scientists were unable to stop what spread throughout the Western world to become the overriding and undermining mind-set I decided might best be called "Pseudo-Darwinian Mind." It is haunting today, for example, to read of how key scientific creators of neo-Darwinism, such as Julian Huxley and Theodosius Dobzhansky, tried to qualify or expand neo-Darwinian evolution theory in ways that could have checked or slowed the spellbound spread of the paradigm of Pseudo-Darwinian Mind, but like the sorcerer's apprentice were unable to stop what was happening.

THE IMPACT OF THE IDEA OF "SURVIVAL OF THE FITTEST"

Ask any serious evolution theorist today and they will generally discount survival of the fittest as a popularized distortion of the basic Darwinian theory of natural selection. In terms of systems dynamics, however, this is an academic smoke screen. Seized up originally by the British to justify their rule and exploitation of the "less fit" people of the colonies of their empire, as well as by the old and new robber barons to justify their seizure of enormous wealth from and exploitation of the "less fit" of Americans, the popular reading continues to accurately capture the function within and impact of the idea on our social, economic, and political systems.

How this works can be shown in countless instances that—in regard to the title for this volume—are driven by the implication of "survival of the fittest" that a culture of peace is not only unnatural but impossible. Implicit in the "survival of the fittest" idea from the beginning, the neo-Darwinian doctrine of selfishness as the primary motivation for everything including the evolution of our species became explicit with the rise of sociobiology and then evolutionary psychology in the latter part of the twentieth century. "True selfishness is the key to a more nearly perfect social contract," wrote sociobiology's prestigious originator, Harvard's E. O. Wilson (1975). British biologist Richard Dawkins then locked the mind-set in place with his engaging book *The Selfish Gene*. Here he tells the avid readership for this best-seller that in a world generated by successful genes driven by a "ruthless selfishness," "much as we might wish otherwise, universal love and the welfare of the species as a whole are concepts that simply do not make evolutionary sense" (1976, 2).

And what is the impact of the supposedly scientific certification that ultimately we are all driven solely by selfishness and thus out to get everything we can grab for ourselves and to hell with everybody else? Most fundamentally, it destroys the basis for the belief in *love* or *trust* on which everything—from the health and viability of friendship, marriage, and families to peace among nations—is built. The enraging fact here is that over his entire adult lifetime, Darwin considered selfishness to be—and wrote down clearly for all to see—a "base principle" accounting for the "low morality of savages."

A firmly held conviction for many twentieth-century evolution theorists and matter of equivocation for the rest still today is the idea there is no discernible direction to evolution other than an increase in complexity. Indeed, in many quarters, to suggest otherwise is to invite not merely the raised eyebrow but academic cold shouldering. This requirement for membership in the evolution theorists' "club" came from the pivotal incorporation into neo-Darwinian theory of the idea of *random* variation, or blind chance. If this were true—if who we are and where we are headed is all up to chance—obviously there could be no discernible direction to evolution. This idea has been popularized through books such as sociobiologist Richard Dawkins's *The Blind Watchmaker* and by the declarations of Nobel Prize–winning molecular biologist Jacques Monod. "Anything can be reduced to simple, obvious, mechanical interactions. The cell is a machine; the animal is a machine; man is a machine, " Monod said in 1970. Along this line, variation, he said in 1971, was an "accident" drawn "from the realm of pure chance" (1971, p. 114).

At first this idea was productively explored with dizzying feats of statistical magic and the interbreeding of hundreds of thousands of fruit flies. But then because of the monopoly on evolution theory established by biologists, it gradually also became routinely applied to everything bigger and more complex than a fruit fly, including ourselves. The old idea that runs through hundreds of years of evolution theory prior to the twentieth century that there might be anything one might call "progress," "direction," "purpose," "higher" or "lower," "up" or "down," "right" or "wrong," or even "meaning" in evolution was routinely dismissed.

And what are the consequences of being taught to believe there is no progress, no direction, no up or down, high or low, right or wrong, no predictability or even any meaning in evolution? From all we know of how the mind works in its search for meaning, it is evident this breeds the stupefying confusion that comes from being forced to try to believe something your own good sense tells you makes no sense. At the psychiatric extreme, these are the dynamics for what is known as the *double-bind* cause for schizophrenia. If there is no direction to evolution or meaning in life, why not then of course turn to drugs, insanity, antiques, or trivial pursuits ranging from collecting bottle caps to blowing away your neighbor, or gangster movies, as year in, year out the most reliable of moneymakers for Hollywood?

But what in fact did Darwin have to say? By simply pointing to some obvious key differences between past and present that he emphasizes along the line for moral evolution we may reconstruct for his lost theory the case for direction in evolution. Staring everyone in the face prominently in print in *The Descent of Man* for more than 100 years, he tells us: "The birth both of the species and of the individual are equally parts of that grand sequence of events that our minds refuse to accept as the result of blind chance. The understanding revolts at such a conclusion."

By automatically excluding all questions of norms, values, or more generally moral sensitivity and morality that enter into life with the emergence of our species—which thereby *must* figure in the logical shaping of a theory of evolution that might also apply to humans—the stage was set for what I am by now convinced were the worst of consequences for the rampage throughout the twentieth century of the paradigm of Pseudo-Darwinian Mind. With the exception of the protests of Julian Huxley and a few others and a well-intentioned but fatally flawed attempt by sociobiologists to remedy the situation, the prevailing mind-set for neo-Darwinian science was that through the liberation of science, the moral concern was now irrelevant, even pathological. To most of Darwin's successors, moral sensitivity, or concern about right versus wrong, was seen as old-fashioned, something perhaps for religious nuts, but definitely outside the discourse of science. All that mattered now was the heady new liberated "no-nonsense" and "only the facts, ma'am" world of modern times.

In the world beyond the test tube and the microscope of the biologists and their tidy theorizing, however, there escalated all the things that raise the questions that trouble us today—the sexual predation of children by priests, the slaughter of school children by their fellow students, the Nazi Holocaust ending six million Jewish lives alone, the obliteration of 165,000 Japanese civilians with our own test for the first atom bombs, the blessing of burglary and perjury and goodness knows what now at the highest levels by U.S. presidents, the rise of terrorism globally, and war after war after war.

And what did Darwin have to say? In the lost theory he outlines a theory of *human* evolution keyed to the emergence of love and moral sensitivity in tandem, or running parallel, to the brutality of natural selection, but ultimately transcendent. In one of many passages indicating how the thrust of moral evolution driving human evolution is shaped by education as a process not simply of imposing morality from *outside*, but rather in response to and to shape what is already motivational *within* us, Darwin wrote, "We have seen how, with the aid of active intellectual powers and the effects of habit, the social instincts—the prime principle of our moral constitution—lead over our evolution to the golden rule 'As ye would that others should do unto you, do ye to them likewise.' Here lies the foundation of morality" (Darwin, 1871/1997, p. 107).

THE HIDDEN CRISIS IN WESTERN EDUCATION

I came to Darwin and evolution theory by an unconventional route. Rather than going straight into science out of college, my formative early career years were as a newsman trained in the school of hard knocks to dig for the facts before trusting authority. Gaining my doctorate in social psychology in middle age, I taught briefly at Princeton and for the better part of a decade I worked at the Educational Testing Service, or ETS, in Princeton, in what at the time was one of the largest and most advanced educational research centers in the world. I then went on to the UCLA School of Medicine faculty.

Coming to Darwin and evolution theory in this way, out of left field so to speak—as, most vitally, an outsider rather than via the pattern of intimidation by authority to which, in order to gain one's doctorate or publication, the traditional Darwininian or evolutionary scholar is trained to repeat the word of prior authority—I now see this gave me the independence of mind that made it possible to avoid the blinding and see beyond or around the paradigm. I saw how pseudo-Darwinian beliefs were driving the destruction of our species, if not possibly all life on this planet. Through the intricate ways that systems science reveals, I saw how the neo-

Darwinian science of the half-truth gave rise to the pseudo-Darwinian ethos of survival of the fittest, selfishness above all, the belief there is no direction to evolution, no meaning to life, that one must submit without question to higher authority, and that amorality reigns, there is no right or wrong. I further saw how, in the powerful way that belief shapes history, pseudo-Darwinian beliefs were major hidden drivers of environmental devastation, the devastation of war, the widening of the gap between rich and poor, the violence-oriented domination of stereotypical male or "macho" values, the devaluing of more peaceful female and "feminine" values, overpopulation, terrorism, and nuclear overkill.

Out of my involvement in education and teaching at Princeton and the UCLA School of Medicine came the horrified realization of what I and all the rest of us had been and were unwitting parties to. Here we all were—all these fine, dedicated teachers, responsible schoolboards, able administrators, supportive parents, funding foundations and federal and state agencies, educational researchers, textbook publishers, the generators of tons of teaching and testing materials, and above all, the millions of children we were variously "processing" in all the nations of the Western world, and in pockets of Westernism within Eastern culture worldwide. And generation after generation for a whole century—still ongoing—we have been and are the dutiful and conveniently blinded people who comprise what functions as a vast global machine dedicated to teaching the destructive half-truth of a theory and story of human evolution perpetuating the power over us of Pseudo-Darwinian Mind.

It wasn't and isn't just the teaching of the half-truth in high school biology or science courses that was and is directly doing this to us. As the story of evolution is the central "hat rack" upon which history, civics, English literature, and the rest of the humanities are hung, the tenets and implications of Pseudo-Darwinian Mind slip in automatically as the "given" whenever the discussion or lesson strays to the question of evolution or basic human motivation. And beyond the school lies the even more powerful reinforcement of the media that in its din of venality and banality, along with the rare dart here and there of decency and intelligence, from cradle to grave shapes us for better or worse. A glance at the weekly TV schedule in the newspaper is surely all the verification one needs. Who could deny the impact of Pseudo-Darwinian Mind when the top shows on television for the 2001–2002 season were virtual orgies of the paradigm—*Survivor, Fear Factor,* a show openly called *Greed* to directly cater to the celebration of selfishness, and NBC-TV's *The Weakest Link,* which circled the earth with replicas in seventy nations and even subjected sixth-grade students to the humiliation of being branded losers before millions of viewers?

That the vast complex of newspapers, books, magazines, movies, radio, and music plus television has, through the gut-cutting dynamics of the ethos of "survival of the fittest," already become concentrated within the ownership of fewer than a dozen corporations globally is one of numerous portents of the authoritarian world toward which we in the West are headed without vast change in our educational system.

TOWARD A CULTURE OF PEACE

To counteract the cultural influence of pseudo-Darwinism, we need to revision education in four ways advanced by leading scientists and educators through the Darwin Project (*www.thedarwinproject .com*).

First we need to switch at all levels of education, K–12 through graduate studies and beyond, including the media, from only teaching the "old" story and the "old" theory to the liberating and hopeful new kind of education about evolution that the key aspects of Darwin's lost theory offer. It isn't just what Darwin said or the fact he said it that matters. Rather, as eleven other members of the General Evolution Research Group, including Riane Eisler, join me in spelling out in *The Great Adventure: Toward a Fully Human Theory of Evolution* (2004), we should emphasize the findings of recent scientific studies and interpretations that corroborate the validity of Darwin's lost vision—which in turn in its emphasis on love and moral sensitivity is the old, old vision of the better human and the better future for humanity that goes back to its earliest roots in the greatest of the spiritual visionaries and later in the greatest of moral philosophers.

In his lost theory Darwin clearly anticipates, for example, the work of Abraham Maslow and the field of humanistic psychology and the human potentials movement. Offsetting the compart-mentalizing of science that led to the biological monopolizing of evolution theory, he anticipates the establishment of the systems science of Ludwig von Bertalanffy, Kenneth Boulding, and Kurt Lewin. Obviously he anticipates the new biology of love being developed by Humberto Maturana and Mae-Wan Ho and the psychology of love of Robert Sternberg and others. In brief but key passages, he also expresses the spirit of progressive education that runs from Pestalozzi through Montessori, Dewey, Piaget, Nod-dings, and Eisler into our time.

Second, we need to clear up what not only constitutes the mess but verges on a national scandal for the teaching of evolu-tion in our schools. Here the creationists come into the picture. In a time of the greatest right-wing influence on the presidency, Congress, and even the Supreme Court, the creationist, and now the "intelligent design" threat to the teaching of evolution is no longer a peripheral matter but must be taken seriously.

Part of the problem is that if we consider the nature and impli-cations of the lost theory it becomes apparent the creationists are justified in complaining they do not want to see their children taught the bleak and brutal doctrine of first-half Darwinism. Who in their right mind would want to see their child marched off into the never-never land of Pseudo-Darwinian Mind? So far nationwide the effect of their attacks, along with their proposals to teach creationism instead of or on par with evolution, has been to frighten many schoolboards and teachers into what are no more than token efforts at teaching evolution. Evolution light, it might well be called—the objective being to confine the hot potato of the most important of subjects for our species to the most innocuous and essentially meaningless unit of study possible, to be given to the football coach if no one else will touch it, but in any case tossed into the curriculum without relating the subject to anything else.

But what if creationist parents were presented with the science of this new teaching of evolution emphasizing love and moral sensi-tivity? Would it not rob the worst of their demogogues of much of their fire while attracting the borderline creationist, or intelligent designist, to a science still independent of but now consonant with, rather than the purported enemy of, morality, and spirituality?

Third, by moving out of the box of a truncated perspective on biology into the full-spectrum wonder of the relevant social and system science, the needed updating of theory and the telling of the new story can provide the central storyline to which all else relates. This may sound a bit mystical at first glance. But the necessity for this can be seen if we consider the fact that prior to the rise and diversionary scatter of twentieth-century science every culture has nourished its own version of a unifying story of some purpose and meaning to evolution at the core. This comes from the fact we are a species that finds sanity and purpose by pulling what is otherwise confusing and even frightening into stories to stabilize and give meaning to our lives. The teaching power of relating all subjects to a central storyline for what she terms "meaningful evolution" can be seen in the exceptionally important pioneering of Riane Eisler in this direction in *Tomorrow's Children: A Blueprint for Education in the 21st Century* (2000).

Finally, we ought to recognize and respond to the urgent need for Western educators to pursue the implications of the central thrust for Darwin's lost theory. This is his conviction and emphasis on moral sensitivity as the central driver of human evolution. It is no coincidence, but largely forgotten today, that John Dewey and Jean Piaget were also among the twentieth century's most notable moral theorists. Nor is it coincidence that moral theorists Lawrence Kohlberg, Carol Gilligan, and Nel Noddings were and are also notably innovative educators.

Recognition of this long-known requirement for an adequate education bumps up against two roadblocks in America today. One is the fact of the rightist and conservative coopting of morality as "their" issue and the drive to impose their version of morality on everyone else. The other is the critically important barrier of the requirement of the separation of church and state that offers us our chief constitutional protection against the rightists and all others similarly motivated. But what is the consequence of this situation? The machine-gunning and bombing by students of their fellow students and attempts by students to knife or poison teachers make the headlines. But more widely corrosive are the cheating, lying, bullying, and everything else today considered being "cool," along with elevation of the word *bad* to mean *good*, according to the chic new ethic of depravity. There is something seriously wrong with an educational system spending millions for the production of literacy that automatically turns out moral illiterates.

A great advantage of the new holistic or fully human Darwinian theory and story of evolution is that it makes moral sensitivity and the requirement of ethics a matter of *science* rather than religion. Working out the details for this expansion for both public and private education—vital to the evolution, if not indeed the very survival of our species—will take thought and time. But the hopeful fact is that the scientific alignment for the new story and theory puts it on course toward a working partnership, rather than conflict, with the United States constitutional requirement of separation of church and state.

In short, recovery of the lost top-half of Darwin's theory reveals not just the poorly understood, almost universally ignored, and certainly insufficiently rewarded power of teachers, but also something that many of us have long suspected, but for which we have never before had thrice-blessed scientific proof: *the incredible power of teachers to advance human evolution.* Considering the millions of us spread around the globe in all the nations of this earth—as explored in detail in the global outreach of the new Darwin Project website (www.thedarwinproject.com)—we are in fact now looking at the potential for and call to action of a revolutionary power for building the culture of peace our species has sought for thousands and thousands of years.

REFERENCES

Boulding, K. E. 1978. *A New Theory of Societal Evolution.* Beverly Hills, CA: Sage.

Darwin, C. 1871/1981. *The Descent of Man.* Princeton, NJ: Princeton University Press (first edition).

———. 1871/1997. *The Descent of Man.* San Francisco, CA: Lightbinders, Inc. (second edition published in CD-ROM, Pete Goldie, editor).

———. 1874/1952. *The Descent of Man.* Chicago, IL: Encyclopedia Britannica-Great Books (fourth edition).

Dawkins, R. 1976. *The Selfish Gene.* New York: Oxford University Press.

Doubzhansky, T. 1964. *Genetics and the Origin of Species.* New York: Columbia University Press.

Eisler, R. 1987. *The Chalice and the Blade.* San Francisco: Harper & Row.

———. 2000. *Tomorrow's Children: A Blueprint for Partnership Education in the 21st Century.* Boulder, CO: Westview.

Gilligan, C. 1982. *In a Different Voice.* Boston: Harvard University Press.

Goldie, P. *Darwin.* 2nd ed. San Francisco, CA: Lightbinders.

Greene, J. C. 1996. *The Death of Adam.* Ames: Iowa State University Press.

Ho, M. W. 1998. "Organism and Psyche in a Participatory Universe." In *The Evolutionary Outrider: The Impact of the Human Agent on Evolution,* ed. D. Loye. Westport, CT: Praeger.

Huxley, J. 1964. *Essays of a Humanist.* New York: Harper.

Keynes, R. 2001. *Darwin, His Daughter, and Human Evolution.* New York: Riverhead.

Kohlberg, L. 1984. *The Psychology of Moral Development.* San Francisco: Harper & Row.

Lewin, K. 1951. *Field Theory in Social Science.* New York: Harper & Row.

Loye, D. 1971. *The Healing of a Nation.* New York: Norton.

———. 2000. *Darwin's Lost Theory of Love.* New York: iUniverse.

———, ed. 2004. *The Great Adventure: Toward a Fully Human Theory of Evolution.* Albany: SUNY Press.

Loye, D., and M. Rokeach. 1960. "Ideology, Belief Systems, Values, and Attitudes." *International Encyclopedia of Neurology, Psychiatry, Psychoanalysis and Psychology.* New York: Van Nostrand.

Maslow, A. 1991. *The Farther Reaches of Human Nature.* New York: Viking.

Maturana, H., and V. Verden-Zoller. 1998. *The Origins of Humaness in the Biology of Love.* Durham, NC: Duke University Press.

Miller, R. 1990. *What Are Schools For?* Brandon, VT: Holistic Education Press.

Monod, Jacques. 1971. *Chance and Necessity.* New York: Vintage.

———. 1974. Quote from BBC Interview, July 1970. In *Beyond Chance and Necessity,* John Lewis, ed. London: Teilhard Centre for the Future.

Noddings, N. 1992. *The Challenge to Care in Schools.* New York: Teachers College Press.

Piaget, J. 1965. *The Moral Judgement of the Child.* New York: Free Press.

Rachels, J. 1998. *Created from Animals: The Moral Implications of Darwinism.* New York: Oxford University Press.

Richards, R. J. 1987. *Darwin and the Emergence of Evolutionary Theories of Mind and Behavior.* Chicago: University of Chicago Press.

Sternberg, R. J. 1998. *Cupid's Arrow: The Course of Love Through Time.* New York: Cambridge University Press.

von Bertalanffy, L. 1976. *General System Theory.* New York: George Brazilier.

Wilson, E. O. 1975. *Sociology: the New Synthesis.* Cambridge: Harvard University Press.

PART TWO

Education as a Human Connection

EDUCATION FOR INTEGRITY
Connection, Compassion, and Character
RACHAEL KESSLER

Across America, parents, educators, and civic leaders are concerned about the destructive behavior that continues to increase among our adolescents. I recently awoke to this news in my local newspaper:

> The fourth hit list in five months was reported at a . . . district school, sheriff deputies said Wednesday.
>
> The latest list . . . was an email message allegedly written by an eighth-grade girl that named three students, a teacher, and a para-educator.
>
> Two twelve-year-old girls were turned in last week by students at [another school] who accused them of writing a hit list that included the names of forty students and teachers. Both girls were arrested.
>
> In January, a hit list was discovered in a student's notebook at [an additional middle school]. The boy said he made the list because he was "bored" and decided to include the people in his class he didn't like. (Reid 2002, 1A–2A)

As I read further, I saw that in the fourth incident, one boy had been found guilty and faced up to two years in a juvenile detention center. *What happened?*

"It's about communication with the kids about what we will tolerate and what we won't," said the administrative official concluding the report.

Is that all this is about—communicating what we will tolerate and what we will not? Incidents like these and those with more fatal consequences are becoming alarmingly typical across the country, often in our most privileged communities (Powers 2002). State legislatures and the federal government are passing legislation to urge educators to undertake so-called character education

57

so our young people can be taught the difference between right and wrong, between what is tolerable and what is not. Certainly the transmission of ethics and the structure of discipline are essential to fostering character in our children. But there is more.

As you hold in your mind and heart the disturbing news item above, hold also this letter from Leah, an eighteen-year-old girl who knew firsthand the kind of hate we see erupting in our youth.

> Remember all those times I said I hated everyone at my high school and that none of them were worth my time? Well, suddenly, I didn't hate anyone anymore. That's one of the things I learned that has impacted me the most—that we are all the same. We all have fears and pains and some good sides and some bad sides. I judged people so easily before, I felt hate so easily. Senior Passage showed me a whole new way to look at people. I discovered the beauty of an open mind.

What might happen if all of our students had the support to open their minds and hearts in this way?

In this chapter, I offer another piece of the puzzle—another analysis of "what this is all about." I explore another approach to how educators can meet the challenge to prepare children for a compassionate and democratic society.

PREVENTION: A BRIEF HISTORY

I began my work with adolescents in the late 1970s, when we were just beginning to understand the concept of "a generation at risk." In education and social service, we began to see that alarming numbers of American teenagers across the lines of class, race, and geography were hurting themselves and others. We began to develop strategies for prevention for *all* of our kids.

"Let's inform the mind," was the first approach, growing out of a traditional educational model: "If their minds understand the dangers (of substances, pregnancy, and sexually transmitted diseases) students will make the right choices." But the field of prevention began to demonstrate what I had learned from my own adolescence: The mind can be well informed, but the being of the teenager chooses danger and destruction in a moment when something other than the mind is in charge.[1]

What, then, is in charge? Whence arise the decisions, the behaviors, the actions that bring harm?

A clue to this essential question can be found in what Gandhi called "the will to do no harm." For Gandhi, this was the essence of nonviolence. It was not the knowing in the mind of what is right and what is wrong. That knowing is necessary but not sufficient. What makes the difference is the deeper wanting to cause no harm to self or others.

This wanting is not the stuff of obligation and "shoulds." It comes from a place beyond reason, a place we might locate in the heart, or in the soul. It arises from the feeling of meaningful connection.[2] Connecting deeply to oneself and to others gives rise to feelings of empathy. Empathy can grow into compassion and even communion. This chapter is about how we can help adolescents form those meaningful connections that lead to compassion, and how compassion, in turn, can lead to character. What climate, principles, and practices can we provide in our schools so students experience "a convergence between what I feel I am supposed to do and what I want to do" (Mayeroff 1990, 11)?

But to understand how to promote peaceful and caring behavior in our youth, we must also explore the deeper roots of what leads them to harm. I learned from my own self-destructive behavior as a teenager that such acts rarely come from a thoughtful decision-making process. Instead, these behaviors often spring from what Daniel Goleman (1995) has called the "emotional hijacking" that suppresses rational thought. And they arise as misguided coping strategies to deal with a variety of deeper conditions that have become increasingly common for American children and youth: social isolation, unrelieved stress, eroded self-worth, inability to learn, and poor decision-making skills. These are the root causes identified by the field of prevention as it searched for an alternative to the failed strategy of providing information and even skills to reduce destructive behavior. Looking further, social scientists agreed these root causes arose from the breakdown of the family and of community, from economic changes that lead to more mobility and a dramatically widening gap between rich and poor, and from media messages that convey that joy and intimacy can be found through alcohol and sexuality, conflicts resolved through violence, and meaning found in what is external.

While these were key factors, they did not fully address the roots of pain and destructive behavior of young people. I added to this analysis in the 1980s and early 1990s three root causes that emerged from my own work with adolescents as I tried to understand this generation at risk: fear, unexpressed grief, and a spiritual void.

Grief is a normal reaction to both traumatic loss and the ordinary losses of human development. In the dominant American culture we have never really known how to grieve and to support the grief of others. Our young people today experience a great deal of traumatic loss—a high incidence of relocation required by our economy, a high divorce rate, and a higher exposure to violent death personally and in the media. When grief is not expressed, the young person becomes numb. It is much the same with fear (Kessler 2003).

We are also afraid to feel our own fear. *Anxiety*—a vague, generalized sense of dread or agitation that overtakes us when we avoid a direct confrontation with the sources of our fear—is the disease of our adult culture. Often hidden and unexpressed, fear permeates the lives of children. John Holt writes:

> What is most surprising of all is how much fear there is in school. Why is so little said about it? Perhaps most people do not recognize fear in children when they see it. They can read the grossest signs of fear; they know what the trouble is when a child clings howling to his mother; but the subtler signs of fear escape them. It is these signs, in children's faces, voices, and gestures, in their movements and ways of working, that tell me plainly that most children in school are scared most of the time, many of them very scared. Like good soldiers, they control their fears, live with them, and adjust themselves to them. But the trouble is, and here is a vital difference between school and war, that the adjustments children make to their fears are almost wholly bad, destructive of their intelligence and capacity. The scared fighter may be the best fighter, but the scared learner is always a poor learner. (1964, 49)

Giving students opportunities to express their fear is the first step in helping them learn to deal with it without going numb. Even before the tragic events of September 11, young people I worked with expressed fear of the future—or fear of having no future. "Will I die when I wake up? I've been thinking a lot about that lately," said a young woman in Washington, DC, explaining why she was drawn to the symbol of the coffin as students chose between primarily positive images to represent their feelings that day. "I wonder about nature—are we doing irreparable damage with our lack of concern?" wrote a high school senior in the 1980s. Other students have written questions such as, "How do I know the world around me is safe and not going to end any minute?" "Will the environment survive for my children and their children?" A seventh-grade student writes, "I wonder about war, earthquakes, my family, peace, AIDS."

Natural numbing mechanisms that set in during early adolescence bury the fear and grief but mark it with a tombstone labeled *despair*.[3] If the natural mechanisms are not enough protection, young people are drawn to the powerful numbing quality of addiction. "The future is uncertain, so eat dessert first" becomes the watchword of many teenagers gobbling up experiences their bodies and souls are not ready to digest.

Another cause of numbing related to this fear for the future was suggested by a young colleague of mine. "Do you know what it's like to grow up in a generation where everyone around you is telling you that the world you've been born into—the only world you know, is flawed and the worst the world has ever been?" writes Katia Borg, a teacher, artist, and visual communications consultant in her early thirties (personal communication). "The media is *so* full of make-wrong about everything, and then there is the constant lack of interest in the new generations for all the creativity and newness they bring. Where do we honor youth for the brilliance they bring us?"

Beyond fear and unexpressed grief is another critical root of youth violence: a spiritual void. Not until the tragic events at Columbine High School in 2000 did the social scientists and political leaders wake up to see "the spiritual emptiness so many young people feel"[4] When the spiritual void is not filled with authentic nourishment and guidance from responsible elders, many young people seek connection, joy, creativity, and transcendence through sexuality and drugs; they seek meaning and beauty in what can be bought and sold; they seek initiation through self-designed rituals and badges of adulthood.

Only recently have I been able to recognize an additional factor producing numbness for adults and children alike. It is the force of speed that has overtaken our culture—the impact of moving too fast and doing too much.

Our young people today grapple with too much emptiness and too much fullness. They are too empty of the resources that sustain the human spirit—devoted love, a sense of meaning and purpose, a feeling of ongoing connection to something larger than themselves, adults who model integrity, serenity, and peace. And they are glutted with sensationalism, stuff, and speed. The result of both the spiritual void and this toxic overload that our culture promotes to fill that void is often numbness.

Numbness begets violence—to the self and to others. Feeling nothing, the young person can feel no empathy, no compassion for herself or for another. When the heart walls off, or closes down, it becomes increasingly difficult to access the desire to care and protect—the "will to do no harm." Many young people are living through a perpetual cycle of loss, grief, and numbness that generates more loss, grief, and further numbness. Numbing leads inevitably to implosion, or to explosion when an unexpected trigger unleashes all the pent-up feeling.

An increasingly pervasive source of numbness in both adults and youth is speed. "Too much, too fast, too soon." This is the hallmark of our current generation at risk, according to a colleague who uses the lens of trauma to understand what is happening for so many youth today:

"The signs we see in so many of our youth are the signs of trauma," says Melissa Michaels, a teacher and healer who has developed an approach that uses movement and other expressive arts to help young and old move from trauma to dynamic wellbeing. "Why do we see so much trauma in our adolescents today? They've had to deal with too much, too fast, too soon."

Trauma, she explained, occurs when "energy gets activated in the system and has no way to complete."

> With our fast pace, our children don't have time to digest, assimilate, and to practice that which they're ingesting . . . to eliminate or to metabolize life. Or to build a relationship with a musical instrument, a friend, themselves, or their families.
>
> With the strong imprinting of media, and the fast pace of our culture, our kids have not had the opportunity to organically develop. Instead of discovering life, it is being given to them in ways that are not necessarily beautiful or good—in the sense of modeling virtue or being life-giving.

Melissa calls this the "ghetto of too much."[5]

Some of my colleagues argue that the increased pace, particularly via technological innovation, is fostering evolutionary growth. "Rapid activity can increase spatial and visual learning," says Katia Borg. "We also have to be more present in the moment—we don't have as much time to prepare. And, it's teaching us to be comfortable with ambiguity and the unknown." Viewing the changes through the lens of my aging body, mind, and spirit, I am constantly reexamining my own assumptions as I dialogue with the students and young teachers who inspire me.

My own experience tells me that when I move too fast, my capacity to feel deeply will often dull or shut down. But speed, for me, is also a by-product of numbness because when I am unconsciously shutting down my emotions to protect myself from vulnerability, I often slip into overdrive. Like me, many of the adults today who are guiding the growth and development of children are infected by this cycle of speed and numbness. And, as Melissa points out, for our children, the fast pace can also produce another by-product—apparently the opposite of numbness—overstimulation. A state of heightened sensitivity and unmanageable stress can lead to hair-trigger responses not easily controlled by an ethical framework.

On top of the excesses of stimulation and expectations for performance that often lead to unmanageable stress, Melissa comments on our young people's excessive exposure to violence.

> Our children have seen more violence in an up close way than ever before. Yes, we have had war throughout time, but there's a different quality now to the exposure. My daughter said to me recently, "In my high school years, I have seen the president have an affair, I saw the Oklahoma City bombing, I witnessed Columbine and 9/11." And now, up close, in the last few weeks, she has known one of the "good boys" from our community shoot two girls and then kill himself.

The violence, says Melissa, is a cry for help, a way of saying *I don't know what to do with all this energy in my system.* "It explodes," she says, "Or implodes with eating disorders or cutting. Our kids have all this energy in their system—we call it ADD and ADHD and anxiety. They don't have a way of dealing with it."

Talking about good behavior is not going to change people's behavior. We have to give them tools for unwinding their tightly wound systems. They haven't even grown their bones yet; their brains are still developing. We want them to make good choices but they are so stressed out. So amped.

We have to give them tools for unwinding and for repatterning. For developing healthy communications and authentic expression.

What are these tools for developing healthy communication and authentic expression? How can we create the safety that makes it possible to speak in meaningful ways? How can we offer students experiences that help them unwind their nervous systems?

PASSAGEWAYS: A DEEPER APPROACH TO PREVENTION

For twenty years, I have worked with teams of educators and youth development specialists around the country in both private and public school settings to create curriculum, methodology, and teacher development that can feed the awakening spirit of young people as part of school life. I call this approach "The Passage-Ways Program"—a set of principles and practices for working with adolescents that integrates heart, spirit, and community with strong academics. This curriculum of the heart is a response to the "mysteries" of teenagers: Their usually unspoken questions and concerns are at its center.

I first discovered this approach at the Crossroads School in Santa Monica, California, where I worked for seven years as chair of their department of human development, building the team that created the Mysteries Program. In the 1990s, I began to take the gifts of Mysteries into schools around the country—adapting, refining, and expanding the curriculum to include what I learned from colleagues in the new and growing field of social and emotional learning. In those first years, I could not explain how our classes invited soul into the room. We were not—and are not—practicing religion or even talking about religion. Yet the students reported that there was something spiritual about our classes.

Classrooms That Welcome Soul

When soul is present in education, attention shifts. We listen with great care not only to what is spoken but also to the messages between the words—tones, gestures, the flicker of feeling across the face. We concentrate on what has heart and meaning. The yearning, wonder, wisdom, fear, and confusion of students become central to the curriculum. Questions become as important as answers.

When soul enters the classroom, masks drop away. Students dare to share the joy and talents they have feared would provoke jealousy in even their best friends. They risk exposing the pain or shame that might be judged as weakness. Seeing deeply into the perspective of others, accepting what has felt unworthy in themselves, students discover compassion and begin to learn about forgiveness.

How Can Classroom Teachers Invite Soul?   Safety in the classroom is the essential first step in welcoming soul into a classroom and in helping students make the choices that build and sustain a life of compassion and integrity. Students need to feel safe to:

- feel and know what they feel;
- tolerate confusion, uncertainty;
- express what they feel and think;
- ask questions that feel "dumb" or "have no answers";
- take risks, make mistakes, and grow and forgive;
- wrestle with the "demons" inside that lead us to harm.

To achieve this safety and openness, students and teachers in a classroom informed by PassageWays work together carefully for weeks and months to build the healthy relationships that lead to authentic community. "Creating community," writes Ruth Charney in *Teaching Children to Care*, "means giving children the power to care." She offers a perspective on discipline that speaks to the dual challenge we face in helping students cultivate the will to do no harm: "Teaching discipline requires two fundamental elements: empathy and structure" (1994, 14–15).

Early in the semester, we collaboratively create *agreements*—conditions that students name as essential for speaking about what matters most to them.[6] In classroom after classroom, across the country and the age span, students call for essentially the same qualities of behavior: respect, honesty, caring, listening, fairness, openness, and commitment. As teachers, we add "the right to pass" and the willingness to learn about forgiveness when we make mistakes.

PassageWays uses *play* to help students focus, relax, and become a team through laughter and cooperation. In addition to strengthening community and helping students wake up to be fully present, games and *expressive arts* engage students in moving their bodies—essential for the unwinding of the nervous system, which can help students deal with overstimulation and stress.

Symbols that students create or bring into class allow teenagers to speak indirectly about feelings and thoughts that are awkward to address head on. In PassageWays, we find that symbols are a powerful way to help students move quickly and deeply into their feelings. "Take some time this week to think about what is really important to you in your life right now," we ask the high school seniors in a course designed to be a rite of passage from adolescence to adulthood. "Then find an object that can symbolize what you realize is so important to you now."

> This raggedy old doll belonged to my mother. I have been cut off from my mother during most of high school. We just couldn't get along. But now that we know I'm going to leave soon, we have suddenly discovered each other again. I love her so much. My relationship to my mother is what is really important to me now.

> I wear this ring around my neck. It belongs to my father, but he has lent it to me. It's his wedding ring, and my parents are divorced. My father travels a lot and I worry about him. It feels good to have his ring close to my heart. And it reminds me of how precious relationships are. And how fragile.

A principal in Canada shared a story from her days of teaching of a first- and second-grade class where she also worked with symbols.

> I talked with my students about life being like a journey. As little as they were, they seemed to understand. They drew pictures about their journey. We talked about their journeys. Then I asked them to look for an object in nature that reminded them of themselves and of their journey.
>
> A first-grade girl brought in a tiny pine cone. She said, "This pine cone is at the beginning of its life as a tree. It reminds me of me because I'm at the beginning of my journey as a person."

A second grade boy brought in two jars filled with shells. "I call these 'brain shells,'" he said, pointing to the first jar. "They remind me of me because I'm very smart."

Then, he held up the jar in which the same shells were crushed. "These crushed shells remind me of me too. They remind me of how hard I am on myself when I don't do things just right."

While symbols are particularly important for adolescents because they allow an indirectness of expression at a time when young people need to create a separate sense of self, we can see that even for young children symbols lead to profound self-awareness. Self-awareness, what Goleman (1995) considers the foundation skill of emotional intelligence, is essential to deep connection to the self and to meaningful communication that allows deep connection with others.

Symbols can also be used as a private exercise in self-awareness. "Draw or sculpt a symbol of what you are feeling right now. You don't need to show it to anyone else. It's just for you." Or, "Write a metaphor about what friendship means to you. You can share it with the group or keep it for yourself, putting it in your folder to look at when the semester ends."

Questions of wonder or *mysteries questions* are another tool in PassageWays for encouraging students to discover what is in their hearts. Once trust and respect has been established in the classroom, we give students the opportunity to write *anonymously* the questions they think about when they can't sleep at night, or when they're alone or daydreaming in class.

Why am I here? Does my life have a purpose? How do I find it?
I have been hurt so many times, I wonder if there is God.
How does one trust oneself or believe in oneself?
How can I NOT be a cynic?
Why this emptiness in this world, in my heart? How does this emptiness get there, go away, and then come back again?
Why am I so alone? Why do I feel like the burden of the world is on my shoulders?
Why do I feel scared and confused about becoming an adult? What does it mean to accept that this is *my* life and I have responsibility for it?
Why was I given a divorced family?

These are some of the thousands of questions I have gathered from teenagers twelve to eighteen years of age since the mid-1980s. After September 11, we began to hear some new ones:

Why do I feel helpless?
How do I make a difference?
What does this mean for the future?
Does it serve me to listen to the media?
What is the lesson we are being forced to learn?
Should I remain in the anger that is consuming me or let go and *give up*?
Do I have a say in "my" country's actions?
How can I hold strong when the world gets chaotic, angry, and fearful?
Why are we so hated?

When students hear the collective mysteries of their own classroom community read back to them in an honoring voice by their teachers, there is always one student who says, "I can't believe I'm not alone anymore." And then another will say, "I can't believe *you* people wrote *those* questions." Sharing their deep concerns, their curiosity, wonder, and wisdom, students begin to discover a deep interest in their peers—even the ones they have always judged to be unworthy of their attention and respect. The capacity for empathy has been stirred.

Into this profound interest in their peers, we introduce the practice of council, the core of the PassageWays approach and of several other programs as well.[7] With everyone sitting in a circle where all can see and be seen, the council process allows each person to speak without interruption or immediate response. Students learn to listen deeply and discover what it feels like to be truly heard. As each student reflects on the same theme, or tells a story from their life that illustrates how they currently think or feel about the theme, students who listen deeply find themselves "walking in another person's shoes." *Multiple perspective-taking* is a skill and an experience that leads not only to critical and creative thinking but to the development of empathy and compassion as well.

"I remember you guys, and I bet you remember me," said Richard, his voice quavering as he said his good-byes to the students in his Senior Passage course.

I was the guy you threw food at in the lunchroom. I was the kid you hurled insults at—like *geek* and *dork*. Well, you know what? I'm still a geek. I'm still a dork. I know that and so do you. But I also know something else.

In the weeks and months of listening to your stories, and you listening to mine, I've seen that even the most beautiful girls in this class—the most beautiful girls in the world—have suffered with how they look or how others see them. I've shared your pain and you've shared mine.

You guys have really taken me in. You've accepted me and respected me. I love you guys, and I know you love me.

"Apprehending the other's reality, feeling what he feels as nearly as possible," says Nel Noddings in *Caring: A Feminine Approach to Ethics and Moral Education*, "is the essential part of caring from the view of the one caring. For if I take on the other's reality as possibility and begin to feel its reality, I feel also that I must act accordingly" (1984, 16). In Richard's story, we can see clearly the possibilities for compassion and caring that arise when students have the opportunity to meet as a group in ways that go beyond civility, beyond cooperation to discover a genuine communing heart to heart, soul to soul. Even students who are estranged, alienated, or who see themselves as enemies have experienced through PassageWays the joy of transcending mistrust, stereotypes, and prejudice that felt like permanent barriers.

In her book *Turning to One Another*, Meg Wheatley beautifully describes the practice of "bearing witness" that captures the experience many young people discover as they sit in a council circle, silently supporting their peers.

> A few years ago, I was introduced to the practice of "bearing witness." This is not a religious practice. Rather, it's a simple practice of being brave enough to sit with human suffering, to acknowledge it for what it is, to not flee from it. It doesn't make the suffering go away although it sometimes changes the experience of pain and grief. When I bear witness, I turn toward another and am willing to let their experience enter my heart. I step into the picture by being willing to be open to their experience, to not turn away my gaze. (2002, 82)

As our students learn to keep their hearts and minds open to both the suffering and joy of their schoolmates, the "will to do no harm" is awakened or strengthened. "You cannot harm a man whose story you have heard," says my colleague, Toke Moller, a Danish leadership educator, quoting an unnamed Kenyan poet (personal communication). A sixth-grade student in a Passage-Ways class put it this way: "When I really get to know someone, I just can't be mean to them any more."

Our emphasis in PassageWays on the learning that comes through relationships built on deep listening and authentic speaking runs counter to current trends and values in education. For example, it is difficult to see how "cyber learning" can help students develop a willingness to heal the breach of fundamental, even enduring differences, or learn to slow down long enough to feel and meaningfully express those feelings. In her article "Embodied Learning," Janet Emig challenges cyber learning as a poor substitute for children and adults being supported to form positive, healthy, whole relationships with themselves and each other.

> Our high-speed (and still accelerating) society is developing a population of people who cannot tolerate ambiguity, and who think that the solution to any problem with another individual is to "press a button." In other words, we are becoming less and less capable of exercising patience with ourselves, each other, and our work. We are less capable of working through difficult times, because we want things to change "right now." (2001, 279)

Emig's assessment of the importance of "embodied learning" highlights the importance of the kind of meaningful encounters between young people that we have made central to the Passage-Ways approach.

> I truly believe that for many of our students and for subsequent generations of students, the embodied classroom remains one of the last sites for socialization available in our society. The embodied classroom is a site where students are required to acknowledge human complexity, situational ambiguity, vexed, even unanswerable questions about self and society. The embodied classroom is a place to learn tolerance while coping with the shock of diverse and alien opinions tightly held, eloquently defended, and to attend to the other who will not go away with the press of a button, who stays relentlessly, inescapably there. (2001, 279)

For some students, however, learning online may be an opportunity for quiet, reflection, and moving at their own pace. In a time when children are programmed into social situations full-time from an early age, young people today also yearn for solitude. In PassageWays, we offer students an opportunity to experience stillness and silent reflection practiced in the company of others. Silence becomes a comfortable ally as we pause to digest one story and wait for another to form or when teachers call for moments of reflection or when the room fills with feeling at the end of a class.

In the weeks before we introduce council, we offer many activities designed as building blocks for learning deep listening and authentic speaking—listening and speaking from the heart. Learning to tolerate and enjoy silence, to communicate in ways that allow us to be truly seen and heard, students gain further tools for unwinding their nervous systems from the trauma of too much, too fast, too soon. Numbing begins to melt as their feelings are called forth in the mirror of other students' stories or in the silence and stillness that slows the busy mind.

Initiation—or rites of passage—is the final core principle and set of practices included in the PassageWays approach. We provide teachers the tools for creating curriculum that support and mark the critical and vulnerable transitions students make as they navigate the losses, challenges, and thrill of moving from one stage of development to another. Some American teenagers are blessed with meaningful confirmations, bar and bat mitzvahs, quinzienara ceremonies in the Mexican community, or initiation journeys offered by the Buddhist or African American communities. But most of our youth today have no opportunity to be guided by responsible adults through the loneliness and confusion of the adolescent journey. Not only the youth but the entire community suffers. "Because of the unhappy loss of this kind of initiatory experience, the modern world suffers a kind of spiritual poverty and a lack of community," says Malidoma Some. "Young people are feared for their wild and dangerous energy, which is really an unending longing for initiation" (1994, 68). Students who have had the opportunity to experience the support of a school program designed to be a rite of passage learn that they can move on to their next step with strength and grace. "A senior in high school must make colossal decisions whether he or she is ready or not," writes Carlos, describing the meaning of the program for his life. He adds:

> The more people can be honest about and aware of their own needs when making these decisions, the healthier the decisions will be. This class has provided me with an environment that allows me to clear my head, slow down, and make healthy choices for me.

A young woman from Colorado described it this way:

> It is difficult for me to express the depth and meaning of this group in a way that does it justice. It has taught me that I have the power to control my destiny, but also to let it guide me when necessary. I have learned to see the beauty in myself, others, the world. Along with this I have become more accepting of my weaknesses. The group has created an environment for all of us to see and learn things that have always been present, just not recognized.

One of the most moving prevention strategies I ever witnessed was a circle of parents honoring their eighth-grade daughters in a ceremony to culminate the rite of passage program designed to prepare these young women for the transition to high school. As their mothers and fathers reflected out loud on the growth and strength they saw in their daughters, tears streamed down the faces of the girls, melting the veneer of sophistication of these "popular girls" whose parents had been so afraid of the dangers that lay ahead. Witnessing this circle, I felt these young women were being inoculated with a strong dose of self-worth and love that would protect them against the "lure of risk" awaiting them in ninth grade (Elias et al. 1997, 9). One girl (who later became a leader in her high school) spoke through her tears: "I always thought that you saw me the way I do when I think the worst of myself. I had no idea you saw all these good things in me." Similarly, I listened to a teacher describe a day-long ceremony she arranged recently with mothers and fifth-grade daughters to mark their initiation into puberty. Listening to the details of that day of honoring the feminine in themselves and each other, I knew in my heart that those girls would be protected against some of the cruel sniping, scapegoating, and rumor-mongering we are seeing in so many of our middle school girls.

Michael Meade captures the dire consequences to our society when elders neglect the responsibility for initiating our youth. "If the fires that innately burn inside youths are not intentionally and lovingly added to the hearth of community, they will burn down the structures of culture, just to feel the warmth" (1993, 19).

What does it take for teachers to claim the role of elders who will intentionally and lovingly shepherd the energies of adolescents so their journey becomes one of awakening to their own responsibility, caring, and integrity?

Teachers Who Welcome Soul

Since "we teach who we are" (Palmer 1997), teachers who invite heart and soul into the classroom also find it essential to nurture their own spiritual development. This may mean personal practices to cultivate awareness, serenity, and compassion, as well as collaborative efforts with other teachers to give and receive support for the challenges and joys of entering this terrain with their students.

We can have the best curricula available, train teachers in technique and theory, but our students will be unsafe and our programs hollow if we do not provide opportunities for teachers to develop their own souls, their own social and emotional intelligence. Students are reluctant to open their hearts unless they feel their teachers are on the journey themselves—working on personal as well as curriculum integration. One of those dimensions is an open heart, or the willingness to care.

The capacity of the teacher to *care* deeply for students is the foundation of all of the classroom practices described above. When students don't trust adults—a common phenomenon in today's society—they are not motivated to learn from us. And they will certainly not embrace our values or ethical beliefs. "The bonds that transmit basic human values from elders to the young are unraveling," write Larry Brendtro, Steve Van Bockern, and John Clementson in an article about why so many youth are wary of adults. "If the social bond between adult and child is absent, conscience fails to develop and the transmission of values is distorted or aborted" (1995, 35–43).

In their classic book *Reclaiming Youth at Risk*, these same authors assert that "research shows that the quality of human relationships in schools and youth service programs may be more influential than the specific techniques or interventions employed."

> Relationship-reluctant children need corrective relationships to overcome insecure attachments. The helping adult must be able to offer warm, consistent, stable, and non-hostile attachments. . . . Long before science proved the power of relationships, pioneers in psychology and education discovered this on their own. (1990, 71–72)

Nel Noddings adds another dimension to understanding the crucial role of the caring bond between teachers and students:

> Kids learn in communion. They listen to people who matter to them and to whom they matter. . . . Caring relations can prepare children for an initial receptivity to all sorts of experiences and subject matters. (1992, 36)

Because his teacher cared deeply for his subject matter and for his students, my youngest son fell in love with physics after hating it for weeks and struggling with a failing grade. Inspired and supported by the extra care from that teacher, he took with him not only the A for achievement, but an attitude of openness to science and to all sorts of things that might not be appealing on first glance. The receptivity Noddings speaks of that grows out of authentic caring from adults is critical not only to academic learning but to the transmission of values, the willingness of our students to embrace the values and caring behavior we practice and preach.

Caring deeply for our students is essential, but it is not enough if we are to become the elders who can guide them through the confusions and complexity of living and choosing from a place of integrity and compassion. I believe that teachers and parents who are best able to lead adolescents on this journey are those who have been willing to wrestle with their own obstacles to a compassionate life: What are the conditions that bring out the worst in us? What triggers our own impulses to harm ourselves or others? When have we been hurt so deeply that our minds and hearts filled with thoughts of revenge and hate? How have we learned to forgive and what do we know about that journey?

When have we acted in ways that produced suffering and how do we relate to those moments in our history? Can we take responsibility, make amends, express remorse and accountability, while still bringing love and compassion and forgiveness to ourselves? It may or may not be appropriate for us to speak directly to our students about these questions. The boundaries of their develop-ment as well as the boundaries of our own privacy may require us to keep the answers to ourselves. But the quality of our being with students, especially with adolescents, will reflect the degree to which we have lovingly and honestly reflected on our own moral development and the challenges and mistakes we have made along the way. The more that we can ride the paradox of being a person who is committed to living with integrity at the same time that "nothing human is alien to me," the more our students will instinctively trust our guidance.

Dr. Rachel Naomi Remen describes the process that adults must undergo to discover the authentic wholeness that is, I believe, essential for a teacher seeking to guide the development of character in children: "Reclaiming ourselves usually means com-ing to recognize and accept that *we have both sides of everything*," she writes in *Kitchen Table Wisdom*. "We are capable of fear and courage, generosity and selfishness, vulnerability and strength. . . . It is not an either/or world. It is a real world" (1996, 37).

No one, at no time, has an ear more tuned to what is real and what is pretense, what is character and what is hypocrisy in a teacher or parent than an adolescent with whom we are engaged in the enterprise of educating for character.

CONCLUSION: CHARACTER EDUCATION OR EDUCATION FOR INTEGRITY

I have had more than an intellectual interest in the subject of promoting peace. While my mother carried me in her womb, she learned that her three sisters and their entire families had been buried alive in the Ukraine by German soldiers. My father was told that both his parents were lost in the concentration camps in Poland. They named me for two of these women. The legacy of violence was in my marrow.

My professional mission has been to discover, cultivate, and share with as broad an audience as possible the tools for educating a generation of children who would come to adulthood with the capacities and the motivation to create lives of compassion, peace, and meaning.

Students who have discovered a sense of meaning in their lives, who have a deep sense of belonging, faith, and reverence for life are protected from the self-destructive and violent impulses that ravage so many of their peers. They often have the will and the incipient tools for building social structures that can foster peace and justice at a larger scale.

In almost twenty years of working with the principles and practices of PassageWays, I have watched with deep satisfaction how students and their teachers begin to develop the fundamental capacities for inner peace and harmony with others:

- understanding and expressing their own feelings;
- empathy and compassion for others;
- managing the stress, which unrelieved, becomes a hair trigger for conflict or the erosion of health;
- decision-making skills that are responsible to their own health and well-being,
- conflict-resolution skills and group problem solving;
- sensitivity to, tolerance for, and appreciation for diverse cultures, learning styles, and beliefs.

Education is not enough to build and sustain a culture of peace. But there is an inextricable link between this type of education and the social and political changes that are so essential: "There is a two-way street here that gives us hope," write Linda Lantieri and Janet Patti in *Waging Peace in Our Schools*. "While the education of the heart requires changes in society in order for its most revolutionary ideals to be realized, emotionally literate people are exactly the kind of people most likely to bring about that change." These young people, they write, who have "learned to de-escalate violence and turn conflict into opportunity, to value each unique individual" will be "building a future full of hope and gentleness" (1996, 243).

The movement for character education is finding a strong voice today in our schools and in our legislatures. All of us, across the spectrum of belief, are hungering for a way to build strong character in our youth. The word *character* comes from to *engrave*; surely there is value when character education seeks to engrave in the minds of students a set of virtues, a capacity for moral discern-ment. But imprinting at the cognitive level is not enough. The best character education programs out there know this now.

When we are looking at character from the perspective of the soul, it is perhaps more useful to speak of educating for integrity. *Integrity* comes from the root *integer*—which means *undivided*.

The divided self is still capable of moral action. We can and should teach our children impulse control, and the ethical capaci-ties to distinguish right from wrong, and to respect the command-ments hallowed by great traditions. But we must also help young people discover an inner experience that is aligned with an outer life of action without harm. While it is not always simple and seamless, young people can develop an inner core of *being* peace, being compassion, being respect from which the *doing* and *choosing* of caring, fair, and just behaviors can flow in an undivided self.

Connection—meaningful, deep connection—is, I believe, the root of such compassion. Attachment. Bonding. Teachers can cre-ate the conditions in the classroom that allow students to dis-cover healthy relationships, meaningful attachment, and constructive bonding to people who deserve to be trusted.

Students who feel deeply connected don't need guns to feel powerful. They don't need danger and risk to feel fully alive. Out of connection grows compassion—compassion for themselves and for others. Even for "others" who have previously seemed alien and beyond the bounds of respect and care. And out of compas-sion grows character—a quality of character that recognizes in ourselves and in others the dangers of human frailty and the per-vasive threat of the degradation and dehumanization we call "evil." Out of connection and compassion comes a wanting inside that may start as a fragile whisper but matures into a loud voice determined to honor and protect life.

NOTES

1. And further, the mind of even the brightest adolescent can twist information in a logic that bears no relationship to reality.
2. "Hard-Wired to Connect," a recent study from the National Commis-sion on Children at Risk, according to William Raspberry of the *Washington Post*, "argued that the loss of connectedness is devastating

America's youth," and that "human beings may be hard-wired for transcendent connections as well."

3. When researchers studied the feelings of children and youth about the nuclear threat in the 1980s, they discovered that until the age of thirteen or fourteen, children were very conscious of their fears, but also had hope that something could be changed. At fourteen, when the mechanisms of denial set in, teenagers lost their conscious awareness of their fear. With that loss came despair. The work of Johanna Macy revealed that empowerment for change could only be reclaimed by going through the layers of numbness to feel the despair and the fear.

4. James Garborino, April 22, 2000, on National Public Radio panel commenting on the Columbine school tragedy

5. Melissa Michaels, telephone interview, March 2002.

6. In the language of adult groups, agreements would be called "ground rules" or "norms." We find the term more effectively engages students in a sense of empowerment over their classroom.

7. For an in-depth exploration of the practice of council, see Zimmerman and Coyle (1996).

REFERENCES

Brendtro, L., S. Van Bockern, and J. Clementson. 1995. "Adult-Wary and Angry: Restoring Social Bonds." *Holistic Education Review* 8 (1): 35–43.

Charney, S. R. 1994. *Teaching Children to Care: Management in the Responsive Classroom*. Greenfield, MA: Northeast Foundation for Children.

Elias, M. J., J. E. Zins, R. P. Weissberg, K. S. Frey, M. T. Greenberg, N. M. Haynes, R. Kessler, M. E. Schwab-Stone, and T. P. Shriver. 1997. *Promoting Social and Emotional Learning: Guidelines for Educators*. Alexandria, VA: Association for Supervision and Curriculum Development.

Emig, J. 2001. "Embodied Learning." *English Education* 33 (4): 279.

Goleman, D. 1995. *Emotional Intelligence: Why It Can Matter More Than IQ*. New York: Bantam Books.

Holt, J. 1964. *How Children Fail*. New York: Dell.

Jones, T. S., and R. Compton, eds. *Kids Working It Out: Stories and Strategies for Making Peace in Our Schools*. San Francisco: Jossey-Bass.

Kessler, R. 2003. "Grief as a Gateway to Love in Teaching." In *Teaching, Loving, and Learning*, eds. D. Liston and J. Garrison. New York: Routledge.

Lantieri, L., and J. Patti. 1996. *Waging Peace in Our Schools*. Boston: Beacon Press.

Macy, J. 1983. *Despair and Personal Power in a Nuclear Age.* Gabriola, BC: New Society Publications.

Mayeroff, M. 1990. *On Caring.* New York: HarperCollins.

Meade, M. 1993. *Men and the Water of Life: Initiation and the Tempering of Men.* San Francisco: HarperSanFrancisco.

Noddings, N. 1984. *Caring: A Feminine Approach to Ethics and Moral Education.* Berkeley: University of California Press.

———. 1992. *The Challenge to Care in Schools.* New York: Teachers College Press.

Palmer, P. 1997. "The Heart of a Teacher: Identity and Integrity in Teaching." *Change* (November/December).

Powers, R. 2002. "The Apocalypse of Adolescence." *Atlantic Monthly* (March):1–20.

Reid, C. 2002. "New Hit List Found: Report Is Fourth at a BVSD School in Five Months." *Daily Camera,* March 14, 1A–2A.

Remen, N. R. 1996. *Kitchen Table Wisdom: Stories That Heal.* New York: Riverhead.

Some, M. 1994. "Rites of Passage: If Adolescence Is a Disease, Initiation Is a Cure." *Utne Reader* (July/August):68.

Van Bockern, S. 1990. *Reclaiming Youth at Risk: Our Hope for the Future.* Bloomington, IN: National Educational Service.

Wheatley, M. 2002. *Turning to One Another: Simple Conversations to Restore Hope to the Future.* San Francisco: Berrett-Koehler.

Zimmerman, J., and G. Coyle. 1996. *The Way of Council.* Ojai, CA: Bramble Books.

NONVIOLENT PARTNERSHIP PARENTING AND TEACHING
Leaving Behind the Old Control Model

THOMAS GORDON

M ost of us were taught to believe that *bringing up* children means that they must be disciplined (controlled) by parents and teachers. Indeed, most of us were brought up this way, as were our parents and grandparents before us. Another belief is that children need to be spanked, and that so-called bad children need to be spanked more. This kind of approach is sometimes called "traditional" childrearing, and touted as the remedy for antisocial behaviors, including violent ones. However, recent findings show that this punitive childrearing is not only ineffective but hazardous to the mental and physical health of children. Moreover, it is not conducive to developing a truly democratic society or to creating a world of peace.

It is my strong belief that an in-depth analysis of the practice of disciplining children at home and in the schools is long overdue. Any idea so universally accepted and so rarely questioned deserves to be evaluated. As an avowed person-centered therapist, student-centered teacher, and group-centered leader, I bring strong biases to this analysis. These are tempered, however, by the findings from the many pertinent research studies I have discovered and by forty years of teaching parents, teachers, and leaders viable alternatives to discipline—effective nonpower methods. Some of these methods are rooted in the person-centered philosophy so ably championed by Carl Rogers—methods that grant children a lot of freedom but freedom within limits, methods that promote self-discipline and self-responsibility, methods that foster motivation, creativity, and emotional health.

The issue of how children are treated is of profound social importance. As Riane Eisler points out, "traditional" fear- and force-based methods of childrearing were appropriate for earlier, more autocratic, chronically violent times, but are not appropriate for democratic and peaceful societies. These methods are our heritage from earlier cultures that oriented more to what Eisler calls a dominator rather than partnership model of structuring relations (Eisler 2000). In these kinds of cultures, ranking of "superiors" over "inferiors" are maintained through controls ultimately backed up by violence, the threat of violence, or other threats of pain. Hence, if we are serious about moving toward a culture of partnership and peace, our methods of child socialization need to be reexamined.

This reexamination is not easy, as most of us unconsciously follow old patterns, even when we are trying to shift to new ones. There are in addition many external cultural obstacles to change, including a strong movement worldwide to return to traditions of top-down control, be it in the family, economics, or national and international politics. But this backward push is all the more reason that a reexamination of discipline is essential at this time.

This chapter describes alternative approaches to traditional discipline, approaches that have been developed and tested for years. These are alternatives supported by research findings. They include methods that encourage the involvement of children in family and classroom rule-setting, methods that foster participation in all phases of the learning process, skills that influence children to solve their problems themselves and regulate their behavior out of consideration for the needs of others, and a nonpower method of resolving adult-child conflicts so that neither loses—or both win.

DIFFERENT MEANINGS OF DISCIPLINE AND AUTHORITY

One of my first discoveries was that people writing about discipline were not using the same definitions of certain words they were commonly employing. This made for muddy waters and widespread misunderstanding, to say the least.

Take the word *discipline* itself. As a noun, the definition of which is "behavior and order in accord with rules or regulations," discipline provokes no controversy. Everybody appears to be in favor of discipline in the classroom or good discipline of a basketball team. The noun conjures up order, organization, cooperation, following rules and policies, and consideration for the rights of others.

As a verb, *to discipline* has two quite different meanings. The first is "to train by instruction and exercise; to drill, edify, enlighten." This variety of discipline, too, seldom causes arguments. However, the second meaning of the verb *to discipline* is what makes hot and heavy controversy. Here are some synonyms for the second kind of discipline, which is a controlling, restricting, chastising, punishing type of action:

arrest	curb	oversee
birdie	direct	penalize
castigate	govern	punish
chastise	harness	rebuke
check	inhibit	regulate
confine	keep in line	rein in
constrain	leash	reprimand
contain	make an example of	reprove
correct	manage	restrain
criticize	muzzle	restrict

Clearly, the teach-train-inform kind of disciplining is an effort to influence children, while the second kind of disciplining is an attempt to control them. Most teachers and parents want nothing more strongly than the ability to influence youngsters, but in their zeal to do so, fall into the trap of using control methods—imposing limits, making rules, sending commands, coercing, punishing, or threatening punishment. Control methods don't really influence children to choose particular ways of behaving, they merely coerce or compel them to do so.

We must also recognize two radically different kinds of the control type of discipline: externally imposed or internally imposed, other-imposed or self-imposed, discipline by others or self-discipline. I didn't find anyone against self-discipline, although most of the dare-to-discipline advocates, among whom are James Dobson and John Rosemond, fail to mention it. There is controversy, however, and it's quite widespread, over what is the best way to foster self-discipline in children and youth—a conflict over the "means" to achieve the agreed upon and valued *ends*—namely, self-disciplined children. Most teachers and parents, I suspect, take the position that children internalize adult-imposed discipline, hoping it will be eventually transformed into self-discipline, a theory championed by Freud and by most psychologists who advocate disciplining to control children. Seldom did I find anyone challenging this traditional belief, as I shall do later.

Another source of semantic confusion comes from the term *authority*. Everybody who writes about discipline uses this word, but few authors recognize the existence of the various meanings the term has. First, there is the authority derived from a person's special expertise: "She is an authority on corporate law," "He speaks with authority." This is often referred to as earned authority. I've adopted the convention of labeling it *Authority E*—for expertise.

Second, there is the authority derived from the job or role a person occupies in life. Airline pilots ask passengers to fasten seat belts, and they usually comply; a committee chairperson is given the authority to open and close its meetings and to guide and direct what goes on in between. I've termed this kind of authority *Authority J*—for job.

A third kind of authority is derived from understandings, agreements, rules, and contracts people make in their relationships with others. I agree to drive my daughter to the auto repair shop; in our family we have an understanding (policy) that we knock before entering another's bedroom; we have agreements as to who does each and every one of many jobs in our house. I call this *Authority C*—for contract.

Finally, there is the authority derived from possessing power over another—power to control, dominate, coerce, bend one's will, and so on. Call this *Authority P*—for power over. This type of authority is what people mean when they talk about "obedience to authority," "exercising your authority," "a breakdown of authority," "rebelling against authority." Understandably, it is the authority many teachers believe they need to discipline (control) children at school.

I found countless examples of cloudy thinking due to failure to recognize the difference among these four kinds of authority. Most frequent was the common assertion that teachers or parents are justified in using their authority (Authority P) to discipline youngsters because kids need and want the adult's superior wisdom and knowledge. Wisdom and knowledge obviously are Authority E, not Authority P. Another common rationalization I often found in the dare-to-discipline books is that power-based authority (Authority P) is justified because the word *discipline* was derived from the root word *disciple*, meaning a learner. A perceptive reader would see through this deception, recognizing that you use Authority E to teach and instruct disciples, not Authority P.

I also discovered that dare-to-discipline advocates try to make using Authority P sound less authoritarian and coercive than it is by using euphemisms for this type of authority. These are nice-sounding terms interchangeable with authority—such as the *leadership* of teachers and parents, *benign* authority, the *loving leadership* of one's parents, *guidance*, or *being authoritative*.

Even when using the Bible to justify adults' punishing children (Authority P), James Dobson (1970), perhaps the most widely known dare-to-discipline advocate, confuses two kinds of authority. He first cites this scriptural admonition, "Children obey your parents in all things, for this is well-pleasing unto the Lord." Then he cites another passage (Ephesians 6:4) to further justify parents using authority, but this second scriptural definition of discipline involves giving children suggestions and advice, which is clearly Authority E: *"Don't keep on scolding and nagging your children, making them angry and resentful. Rather bring them up with the loving discipline the Lord himself approves, with suggestions and godly advice"* [emphasis mine]. "Suggestions and godly advice," as I see it, are ways of instructing or teaching (Authority E) and not demanding obedience (Authority P). One might assume, as I did, that dare-to-discipline defenders at some deeper level actually disapprove of disciplining children. Why else would they need to use so many euphemisms and Biblical passages to justify using their power? And one might guess that many disciplinarians feel guilty about using their power over persons smaller than they are ("This hurts me worse than it does you.").

DEFICIENCIES AND DANGERS OF PUNISHMENT

Punishing children is endemic in most world regions. In the United States, evidence shows that more than 90 percent of American parents hit toddlers and most continue to hit their children for years (Straus, Gelles, and Steinmetz 1980). In a 1994 USA Today/CNN Gallup Poll, 67 percent of a national sample of American adults agreed that "It is sometimes necessary to discipline a child with a good hard spanking."

Punishments are still more severe in some other world regions. The incidence of severe violence against children has only recently received attention, as it was traditionally considered a family matter that brooked no outside interference (Eisler 1996). In some nations, canings are still routine in schools, as they were in the West even as late as the Enlightenment.

In United States schools, the frequency of corporal punishment has been decreasing steadily as more states have enacted laws prohibiting corporal punishment, yet the practice is still prevalent in twenty-three states (Riak 2002). Schools are the only public institution in the United States where corporal punishment is still legal. It is no longer permitted in the military, in prison, or in mental hospitals.

At this time, only Scandinavian nations have laws that prohibit physical violence against children in homes, even though studies show that children who are physically punished become more rather than less disruptive and noncompliant. Moreover, as the recent spotlight on child abuse shows, the social failure to address physical punishment often leads to escalations that cause serious injuries and in some cases death.

Even when physical violence is not employed, most parents and teachers employ other kinds of punishment, for example, deprivations, extra work, confinement, verbal abuse, the silent treatment, and staying after school. No doubt, close to 100 percent of teachers and parents regularly employ some form of punishment to control youngsters.

And all this is still considered normal and right, despite the proven deficiencies and dangers of punishment:

1. For punishment to work, it must be severe, and yet when it is severe, youngsters look for all kinds of ways to avoid it, postpone it, weaken it, avert it, escape from it. They lie, put the blame on someone else, tattle, hide, plead for mercy, and make promises to "never do it again."

2. Boys of twelve years of age whose parents scored high in restrictiveness and punishment showed strong tendencies toward self-punishment, accident proneness, and suicidal intentions (Sears 1961).

3. The more corporal punishment a person has experienced, the more likely he or she is as an adult to be depressed or suicidal, physically abuse his or her child or spouse, engage in other violent crime, have a drinking problem, be attracted to masochistic sex, and have difficulty attaining a high-level occupation and high income (Straus 1994).

4. Mothers of children with low self-esteem were found to have used less reasoning and discussion and more arbitrary, punitive discipline (Coopersmith 1967).

5. Children of punitive authoritarian parents tend to lack social competence with peers, to withdraw, to not take social initiative, to lack spontaneity (Baldwin 1948).

6. Children of controlling (authoritarian) parents who valued obedience and respect for authority showed relatively little independence and social responsibility (Baumrind 1971).

7. Less than one out of four hundred children whose parents did not hit them were found to be violent toward their parents, as opposed to children who had been hit by their parents. Half of the latter group had hit their parents in the previous year (Straus, Gelles, and Steinmetz 1980).

8. Studies of the family backgrounds of both male and female juvenile delinquents consistently show a pattern of harsh, punitive, power-assertive parental punishment, in contrast to nondelinquent youngsters (Martin 1975).

9. Schools using more physical punishment often have more vandalism, student violence, poor academic achievement, truancy, and higher dropout rates (National Coalition to Abolish Corporal Punishment in Schools 2001).

10. In a study of 230 Columbia University graduate students, those who as children had been subjected to the most pun-ishment, as compared with those who had received the least, reported more hatred toward parents, more rejection of teachers, poorer relationships with classmates, more quar-rels, more shyness, more unsatisfactory love affairs, more worry, more anxiety, more guilt, more unhappiness and cry-ing, and more dependence on parents (Watson 1943).

It is quite clear: Punitive discipline is hazardous to the mental health of children.

PARTNERSHIP ALTERNATIVES TO DISCIPLINING CHILDREN

Although the philosophy and practice of trying to control chil-dren by administering rewards and punishments is nearly univer-sal in both families and schools, promising alternatives to this ineffective method do exist, and pockets of innovation and change can be found, if one looks diligently enough.

Involvement of Children in Rule-Setting

It is a well-established principle that people are more motivated to comply with rules or limits if they have been given the opportu-nity to participate in determining what they should be. For more than forty years, in my Parent Effectiveness Training (PET) (1970) and Teacher Effectiveness Training (TET) courses (1974), our instructors have been advising parents and teachers to avoid making rules unilaterally. Via tape-recorded examples, demonstra-tions, and role-playing, we teach methods for involving children in the process of determining the policies and rules they will be expected to follow. Among such family policies and rules are those covering bedtime, TV usage, household chores, storage of playthings, use of the telephone, allowances, privacy, homework, and any other activity that has the potential for generating prob-lems or conflicts. More than a million parents have been exposed to this new way of determining family rules. Similarly, in TET we offer the same methodology for involving a class of students in the process of classroom rule-setting.[1]

Nonblameful *I-Messages*

Another noncontrolling method taught in the PET and TET is sending *I-Messages*. Typically, teachers and parents confront children with *You-Messages*, those containing heavy loads of blame, judgment, and criticism, each of which provokes resistance and lowers the child's self-esteem:

- "You're acting like a first-grader!"
- "You take your seat right away!"
- "You ought to be ashamed of yourself!"
- "You're driving me crazy!"
- "You're being naughty!"
- "You will have to stay after school now!"

In PET and TET we provide a variety of experiences for learning and practicing nonblameful I-Messages as the means for telling the child exactly why his or her behavior is unacceptable to the adult:

- "When there is so much noise, I can't hear what anyone is saying."
- "When the paints aren't put away, I have to take a lot of time to do it myself."

I-Messages are actually appeals for help, which partially accounts for their superior effectiveness in influencing children to change their behavior. In addition, they place full responsibility on the child for initiating the change, are less likely than You-Messages to injure the relationship, and do not damage self-esteem. A teacher reported this incident shortly after taking the TET course:

> I was reluctant to try an I-Message with the kids I have. They are so hard to manage. Finally, I got up my courage and sent a strong I-Message to a group of children who were making a mess with water paints in the back of the room by the sink. I said, "When you mix paints and spill them all over the sink and table, I have to scrub up later or get yelled at by the custodian. I'm sick of cleaning up after you, and I feel helpless to prevent it from happening." I just stopped then and waited to see what they would do. I really expected them to laugh at me and take that "I don't care" attitude they've had all year. But they didn't. They stood there looking at me for a minute like they were amazed to find out I was upset.

And then one of them said, "Come on, let's clean it up." I was floored. You know they haven't turned into models of perfection, but they now clean up the sink and tables every day whether they've spilled paint on them or not.

Baumrind (1971) found that nursery school children who rated high in self-control and self-discipline had parents who refrained from punitive messages or punishments and instead made extensive use of reasoning and what she termed "cognitive structuring." This academic-sounding term turns out to be our I-Message—telling children the negative effects of their behavior on others. Baumrind explains that these messages help children internalize the consequences of their behavior and develop conscience or inner control—what I call self-discipline as opposed to externally administered discipline.

Modeling

One of the most important behavioral elements of partnership parenting and teaching is modeling. Modeling is important for learning all through life, but it is particularly important with infants and toddlers, who absorb what they observe and sense long before they have words. This modeling is perhaps the hardest part of changing unconscious old habits of control. Certainly it does not mean being perfect, as none of us can be that. But it means reexamining basic assumptions about relationships, including assumptions about how parents themselves should relate to one another.

If parents model unequal relations for children between fathers and mothers, this is a major lesson for socializing children to see the world in terms of top-down rankings. Though we do not usually think of them this way, traditional gender roles where women are to serve men and men are to be served, where women are to do all the menial work, and men use loud angry voices to control, are effective ways of teaching children that the natural order of the world is one where those on the bottom obey and serve and those on top control and get served.

When these gender-based rankings are enforced through traditions of physical abuse of wives, as they still are in many cultures and subcultures worldwide, children are not being brought up for a culture of peace and equity. But even without domestic violence, these are not environments where young people learn to really value the nurturant activities of caring for children, the sick, and the elderly stereotypically associated with so-called inferior women.

No matter how much parents may tell children to be caring and empathic, if these behaviors are devalued because they are associated only with inferior women, and if children do not see these behaviors modeled in the relations of the adults around them, what they actually learn is that these behaviors are not really all that important. And learning empathy and caring for others, along with mutuality, are the essence of partnership relationships. In such environments, children also soon learn that adults say one thing and do another. It takes infants and toddlers some time to mature to the point where they understand words. But they understand actions and feelings quite early.

In short, children learn a great deal from interactions. And this includes learning what is acceptable behavior on their part and what is not.

Nonverbal Methods

Adults have available a variety of nonverbal ways of dealing with unacceptable behaviors. For example, when very young children whine or pester or throw their food on the floor or dawdle or make messes, parents can utilize some of the following approaches:

1. Guessing what the child needs or what deprivation lies behind the unacceptable behavior and then satisfying the need.
2. Substituting for the unacceptable behavior some other behavior that is acceptable to the adult—for example, giving the child a damaged pair of nylon hose as a replacement for the new pair the child pulled out of the drawer.
3. Modifying the environment to produce a change in the child's behavior—for example, childproofing the classroom or home, enriching the child's environment so as to capture the full interest of the child, providing designated areas for messing or painting, and assigning storage areas.

Participative Management in Schools

The movement toward partnership parenting and teaching is not an isolated phenomenon. The exploration of the kinds of alternatives we have been examining is part of a larger cultural move‑ ment toward the partnership model. For example, we are seeing a quiet revolution in the way many companies are being managed. This new leadership style is called "participative management" because it relies on extensive employee involvement in making decisions and solving problems related to the workplace environ‑ ment, the design of products, the methods of production, quality improvement, cost control, and the like.

More and more United States companies are instituting some form of participative management. Some have trained their man‑ agers and supervisors with our course (LET). The benefits of this more democratic style of leadership can be quite remarkable: increases in employee productivity have jumped 100 percent, grievances have fallen from three thousand per year to fifteen, absenteeism has been cut in half, 80 percent decrease in products rejected because of poor quality (Simmons and Mares 1983).

Also, we have been witnessing a growing recognition of the importance of increasing student participation in order to improve learning motivation and decrease discipline problems among teachers, school administrators, and teacher educators. This too is movement toward the partnership model. Urich and Batchelder (1979) describe how an urban school drastically changed its social climate by increasing student involvement in tackling such impor‑ tant problems as tardiness, absenteeism, apathy, and low achieve‑ ment. The students worked with teachers and administrators to come up with improvements in each of the problem areas. In other schools, students have been given the opportunity to monitor their own academic progress and identify areas of needed improvement. In one study, such students were found to make significant gains in study habits and achievement (McLaughlin 1984).

Some schools have allowed students to participate in academic goal setting and in designing their own tailor-made high school courses (Burrows 1973). Other schools have involved students in cooperative projects with peer workgroups, resulting in enhanced academic and social skills (Johnson and Johnson 2002). Students also have been given responsibility for correcting unproductive behavior of their peers (Duke 1980) and for sharing their opinions concerning the quality of their teachers' instructional skills and teacher-student relationships (Jones and Jones 1981). Student participation has been extended into some of the schoolwide administrative issues, such as school discipline, school climate, textbook adoptions, new curricula, budget cutting, and energy savings (Aschuler 1980).

Renowned psychiatrist William Glasser, author of the bestseller *Schools Without Failure* (1961), prescribed a challenging remedy for disciplinary problems in our schools in his book *Control Theory in the Classroom* (1986). Students are organized into teams of two to five students made up of low, medium, and high achievers. The high achievers help the lower ones, team members are urged to depend a great deal on themselves and their own creativity, they choose how to offer the teacher evidence of how much they have learned, and each student gets the team score.

The superiority of such cooperative learning efforts over the traditional competitive student-student relationships has been conclusively established in a comprehensive review of 122 studies, published from 1924 to 1980. The results were remarkable: sixty-five studies found that cooperation produces higher achievement than competition, only eight found the reverse; cooperation promoted higher achievement than independent work in 108 studies, only six found the reverse (Johnson, Maruyama, Johnson, Nelson, and Skon 1981).

In a study of eighteen "alternative" high schools in California, where there were personalized teacher-student relations, student participation in school governance, and a nonauthoritarian rule structure, the researchers found that both teachers and students reported fewer and less serious disciplinary behavior problems than in the conventional high schools with minutely defined adult-made rules and rigid ways of dealing with infractions (Duke and Perry 1978).

Helping Children Find Their Own Solutions to Problems

When children experience some form of deprivation or unmet needs, they often react by behaving in disruptive or noncooperative ways—both in their families and at school. Acting-up children are usually troubled children—youngsters carrying around a lot of frustration, disappointment, resentment, or anger. And troubled children also make poor learners. Consequently, it seems obvious that both discipline problems and low achievement could be reduced in schools if teachers could be taught how to be more effective as helping agents or counselors. This is precisely one of the principal objectives in the TET course.

I naturally chose the client-centered methodology of counseling as the model to be taught in both TET and PET, having been trained by Carl Rogers and having many years in private practice as a client-centered therapist. Our training has three principal objectives:

1. to show teachers and parents how their habitual ways of responding when children share their problems can act as communication blockers and convey nonacceptance. We call these nonfacilitative messages the "twelve roadblocks": ordering, warning, moralizing (shoulds and oughts), giving solutions, teaching, evaluating negatively, evaluating positively, ridiculing, psychoanalyzing, reassuring (consoling), probing, and kidding (diverting);
2. to help teachers and parents reach a reasonable level of competence in responding to children with active listening, which conveys acceptance and shows accurate understanding;
3. to influence parents and teachers to have more trust in children's ability to solve problems themselves.

By and large, I'm convinced that we have succeeded rather well in accomplishing these objectives. Considerable evidence of this can be found in some of the research studies that have evaluated the effects of PET and TET We have located more than sixty separate studies, many of which unfortunately have flawed designs or inadequate statistical procedures. Robert Cedar (1985) at Boston University took twenty-six of the more carefully designed of these studies and included them in a meta-analysis, a statistical technique for combining and analyzing the findings from many different studies. The results of his meta-analysis were as follows:

- PET had an overall effect size of 0.33 standard deviation units, which was significantly greater than the effect size for a group representing alternate treatments, such as behavior modification training or Adlerian-based parent training.
- The better-designed studies were found to show significantly greater effect sizes of PET than the less well-designed studies.
- PET was shown to have a positive effect on parent attitudes and parent behavior, and this effect endured for some period (up to twenty-six weeks) after the course was completed.

Cedar, concluded, "Most of Gordon's claims were (with qualifications) substantiated."

There is also a wealth of hard data showing conclusively that the same facilitative skills we teach in TET greatly help teachers better achieve even the traditional and commonly accepted goals of our schools, such as scholastic achievement, good attendance, creative thinking, and high motivation for learning. In one study (Aspy and Roebuck 1977), involving six hundred teachers and ten thousand students (from kindergarten to grade 12), the students whose teachers were trained in the skills of empathic understanding, acceptance, respect, and positive regard for students as persons were compared with students whose teachers were not trained. The students of the trained teachers were found to:

- miss fewer days of school (four fewer days a year);
- make greater gains on academic achievement measures, including both math and reading scores;
- be more spontaneous;
- use higher levels of cognitive thinking;
- increase their scores on ten tests;
- make more gains in creativity scores;
- show increased scores on self-regard measures;
- commit fewer acts of vandalism;
- present fewer disciplinary problems.

Another study showed a significant reduction of disruptive behaviors as a result of teachers being trained in facilitative skills. Roebuck measured the teachers' empathic understanding, respect for students, and the degree of student involvement provided by the teachers. Her findings: more disruptive behavior in classes whose teachers were low in empathic understanding, respect, accepting students' ideas, and inviting students' thoughts and opinions (Roebuck 1980).

Under the leadership and supervision of two German social scientists, Reinhard Tausch and Anne-Marie Tausch, a large number of doctoral dissertations and masters' theses produced evaluations of the effects of teachers' facilitative skills on student effectiveness. Here is a clear and beautifully worded summary of the findings:

> In all of the school studies, empathic understanding, genuineness, warm respect, and nondirective activities proved to significantly facilitate the quality of the pupils' intellectual contributions during

the lesson, their spontaneity, their independence and initiative, their positive feelings during the lesson, and their positive perception of the teacher. If we want to diminish stress, aversion, and impairment of physical and emotional health in schools and at the same time facilitate the development of personality and the quality of intellectual performance, then we will need a different kind of teacher than we seem to produce at present. Teachers are needed who can create in their classes an atmosphere in which there is empathic understanding, pupils receive warmth and respect, genuineness is encouraged, and the teacher can be facilitative in nondirective ways. (Tausch and Tausch 1980, 217–18)

The No-Lose Method of Conflict Resolution

Although getting youngsters to participate in mutual rule-setting significantly prevents a lot of adult-child conflicts in families and in classrooms, conflicts will always arise for which no rules have been previously established. Parents and teachers have to deal constructively with these situations or else their relationships will suffer. Indeed, conflict is part of human relations, as different people will have different needs and desires. The issue is how conflict is resolved. Unfortunately, most teachers and parents are locked into either-or thinking about resolving conflicts with children: They are either strict or lenient, either tough or easy, either authoritarian or permissive, either their solution in the conflict prevails or the youngster's solution prevails. In our classes we show how both of these either-or approaches to conflict resolution are win-lose methods—either the adult wins and the child loses or the child wins and the adult loses.

One father shows this either-or thinking when he describes the power struggle in the parents' relationships with their children in this excerpt from a recorded interview:

> You have to start early letting them know who's boss. Otherwise they'll take advantage of you and dominate you. That's the trouble with my wife—she always ends up letting the kids win all the battles. She gives in all the time and the kids know it.

Children, too, see their conflicts with adults as win-lose power struggles. Cathy, a bright fifteen-year-old, expressed this clearly in a recorded interview:

> What's the use of arguing? They always win. I know that before we ever get into an argument. They're always going to get their way.

After all, they are the parents. They always know they're right. So, now I just don't get into arguments. I walk away and don't talk to them. Course it bugs them when I do that, but I don't care.

In PET and TET we teach parents and teachers how to resolve conflicts with an alternative method called the no-lose method (or the win-win method), in which both the adult and the child participate in a process of six separate steps:

Step I: Define the conflict in terms of needs.
Step II: Generate possible solutions.
Step III: Evaluate the possible solutions.
Step IV: Reach an agreement on the best solution.
Step V: Determine what is required to implement the solution.
Step VI: Evaluate the effectiveness of the solution.

Readers may recognize that these six steps are similar to John Dewey's six steps for effective individual problem solving. We have found they work equally as well as steps for effective resolution of conflicts between individuals.

The no-lose method of resolving conflicts requires a firm commitment to an entirely different posture from that assumed in the traditional win-lose methods. The parent or teacher conveys this message to the child:

We have a conflict—a problem to be solved. I don't want to use power to win at the expense of your losing. But I don't want to give in and let you win at the expense of my losing. So let's put our heads together and search for a solution we can both accept.

The no-lose method derives its influence from Authority C, the authority derived from people having made a mutual commitment to an agreed-upon solution.

CONCLUSION

The alternative to the old domination/control model of parenting and teaching is not a laissez-faire, no rules approach. It is rather involving young people in creating rules and living by them in ways that model mutual respect, empathy, and caring. But to shift to this approach we have to unlearn old habits and learn new ones.

Since the early 1960s I have been deeply involved in offering training to parents and teachers in nonpower and noncontrolling methods, which I firmly believe are far more effective than discipline in influencing children to be cooperative, considerate, responsible, and, above all, self-disciplined. I have briefly described these methods, documenting their positive effects on children's mental health.

These nonpower methods add up to a new and far more effective model of parenting and teaching. By giving up using power, parents and teachers will foster self-disciplined children. By relating to children democratically and refusing to be either dictators or doormats, parents and teachers will increase children's compliance with rules through involving them in the process of making the rules. By helping youngsters find their own solutions to problems, parents and teachers will foster more independence, more control over their own destiny, and higher self-esteem. By involving children in their own learning process and in the process of governing their classrooms and schools, teachers will make schooling far more interesting, prevent disciplinary problems, and foster higher achievement motivation.

And by making a commitment to resolve all conflicts with children so nobody loses, parents and teachers will equip children with the skills to become a new species of world citizen—persons who will eschew the use of violence in dealing with conflicts between individuals, between groups, between nations. No one has expressed more clearly how power-based methods create psychopathology than Abraham Maslow (1970):

> Let people realize clearly that every time they threaten someone or humiliate or hurt unnecessarily or dominate or reject another human being they become forces for the creation of psychopathology, even if these be small forces. Let them recognize that every man who is kind, helpful, decent, psychologically democratic, affectionate, and warm is a psychotherapist's force even though a small one.

If I were called upon to find a convenient way to describe my model for effective relationships of the kind we deal with in our training programs, the word *democracy* first comes to mind. I believe we have been teaching parents, teachers, managers, and spouses how to create and maintain democratic relationships—relationships in which I help you meet your needs and you help me meet mine, relationships that are synergistic—separate persons working cooperatively together with greater total beneficial effects than the sum of their individual effects—and relationships that are equalitarian.

I happen to believe that relationships that are democratic will necessarily be therapeutic, and the more democratic, the more therapeutic.

NOTE

1. For more information about Dr. Gordon's books and programs for parents and teachers, please contact: Gordon Training International, 531 Stevens Avenue West, Solana Beach, CA 92075, phone (858) 481-8121; info@gordontraining.com, www.gordontraining.com. Editors' Note: Dr. Gordon passed away shortly after submitting this essay for this volume. His work continues.

REFERENCES

Aschuler, A. 1980. *School Discipline: A Socially Literate Solution.* New York: McGraw-Hill.

Aspy, D. N., and F. N. Roebuck. 1977. *Kids Don't Learn from People They Don't Like.* Amherst, MA: Human Resource Development Press.

Baldwin, A. L. 1948. "Socialization and the Parent-Child Relationship." *Child-Development* 1: 127–36.

Baumrind, D. 1971. "Current Patterns of Parental Authority." *Development Psychology Monograph* 4 (1): Part 2.

Burrows, C. 1973. *The Effects of a Mastery Learning Strategy on the Geometry Achievement of Four and Fifth Grade Children.* PhD. diss., Indiana University, Bloomington.

Cedar, R. B. 1985. *A Meta-Analysis of the Parent Effectiveness Training Outcome Research Literature.* PhD. diss., Boston University.

Coopersmith, S. 1967. *The Antecedents of Self-Esteem.* San Francisco: Freeman.

Dobson, J. 1970. *Dare to Discipline.* Wheaton, IL: Tyndale House.

Duke, D. L. 1980. *Managing Student Behavior Problems.* New York: Teachers College Press.

Duke, D. L., and C. Perry. 1978. "Can Alternative Schools Succeed Where Benjamin Spock, Spiro Agnew and B. F. Skinner Have Failed?" *Adolescence* 13: 375–92.

Eisler, R. 1996. "Human Rights and Violence: Integrating the Private and Public Spheres." In *The Web of Violence*, edited by Lester Kurtz and Jennifer Turpin. Urbana: University of Illinois Press.

———. 2000. *Tomorrow's Children: A Blueprint for Partnership Education in the 21st Century.* Boulder, CO: Westview Press.

———. 2002. *The Power of Partnership.* New World Library.

Glasser, W. 1961. *Schools Without Failure.* New York: Harper & Row.

———. 1986. *Control Theory in the Classroom.* New York: Harper & Row.

Gordon, T. 1955. *Group-Centered Leadership.* Boston: Houghton Mifflin.

———. 1970. *Parent Effectiveness Training.* New York: Wyden.

———. 1974. *Teacher Effectiveness Training.* New York: Wyden.

———. 1976. *P.E.T. in Action.* New York: Wyden.

———. 1977. *Leader Effectiveness Training.* New York: Wyden.

Johnson, D., and R. Johnson. 2002. *Learning Together and Alone: Cooperation Competition and Individualization.* Englewood Cliffs, NJ: Prentice-Hall.

Johnson, D., G. Maruyama, R. Johnson, D. Nelson, and L. Skon. 1981. "Effects of Cooperative, Competitive and Individualistic Goal Structures on Achievement: A Meta-Analysis." *Psychological Bulletin.* 89: 47–62.

Jones, V., and L. Jones. 1981. *Responsible Classroom Discipline.* Newton, MA: Allyn and Bacon.

Martin, B. 1975. "Parent-Child Relations." In *Review of Child Development Research,* edited by M. L. Hoffman and L.W. Hoffman. Chicago: University of Chicago Press.

Maslow, A. H. 1970. *Motivation and Personality.* 2d ed. New York: Harper & Row.

Maurer, A. 1984. *1001 Alternatives to Punishment.* Berkeley, CA: Generation Books.

McLaughlin, T. 1984. "A Comparison of Self-Recording and Self-Recording Plus Consequences for On-Task and Assignment Completion." *Contemporary Educational Psychology* 9: 185–92.

Randolph, N., and W. Howe. 1966. *Self-Enhancing Education.* Palo Alto, CA: Stanford Press.

Riak, J. 2002. www.nospank.net/eddpts.htm.

Roebuck, F. N. 1980. *Cognitive and Affective Goals of Education: Towards a Clarification Plan.* Paper presented at the annual meeting of the Association for Supervision and Curriculum Development, Atlanta.

Rogers, C. R. 1977. *On Personal Power.* New York: Delacorte.

Sears, R. R. 1961. "The Relation of Early Socialization Experiences to Aggression in Middle Childhood." *Journal of Abnormal and Social Psychology* 63: 466–92.

Simmons J., and W. Mares. 1983. *Working Together.* New York: Alfred A. Knopf.

Straus, M. A. 1994. *Beating the Devil out of Them: Corporal Punishment in American Families.* New York: Lexington Books.

Straus, M. A., R. J. Gelles, and S. K. Steinmetz. 1980. *Behind Closed Doors: Violence in the American Family.* New York: Anchor Press/Doubleday.

Tausch, R., and A. M. Tausch. 1980. *Verifying the Facilitative Dimensions in German Schools—Families—and with German Clients.* Unpublished manuscript.

Urich, T., and R. Batchelder. 1979. "Turning an Urban High School Around." *Phi Delta Kappan* 61: 3.

Watson, G. 1943. "A Comparison of the Effects of Lax Versus Strict Home Training." *Journal of Social Psychology* 5: 102–105.

ON BEING A CARING TEACHER

DORALICE LANGE DE SOUZA ROCHA

Many authors in the literature of holistic education have noted the importance of the "quality of being" of teachers. In various ways, they have remarked that who we are as persons and how we behave around children have a significant impact on our students. Rudolf Steiner, for example, commented,

> These are the things that matter the most for young children. What you say, what you teach, does not yet make an impression, insofar as children imitate what you say in their own speech. But it is what you *are* that matters; if you are good this goodness will appear in your gestures; and if you are bad-tempered this also will appear in your gestures—in short, everything that you do yourself passes over into the children and makes its way within them. . . . The inclinations that children develop depend on how you behave in their presence." (Steiner 1998, 92)

Holistic educators such as Scott Forbes (personal communication), Rachael Kessler (1991, 2001), Krishnamurti (1981), Steven Levy (1996), Ba and Josette Luvmor (personal communication), John P. Miller (1993, 1994), Ron Miller (1995), and Parker Palmer (1993, 1998) have all addressed this point. As Levy put it, "Every decision we make, every judgment we administer, every interaction with a child, demonstrates what we value and serves as a model for our students about what really counts in life, in being human. . . . The children take all this in day after day, as unconsciously as breathing. It all works in subtle ways in the formation of their character" (1996, 154–55).

These authors are implying that if we want to be true educators, we need to work on our own development and on our relationship with the people, the knowledge, and the world around us so that we can be good role models for our children and/or students. I used to think I understood this thought. However, it was only when I concluded the data analysis of a long-term research project I am working on[1] that I came to fully understand the importance of this matter. The findings of my research suggest that a school's educational philosophy is key in directing the practice of the teachers. However, I have found that if there is an inconsistency between a school's philosophy and a teacher's quality of being, the teacher is likely to be ineffective in promoting the school's goals.

While developing my research in one of the schools included in my study, I met a girl, Cleo[2] (nine years old), who used to attend a Waldorf school. According to her mother, who appreciates the Waldorf approach very much, her daughter seemed to be a "fit" for Waldorf education. However, she had to take Cleo out of the local Waldorf School. She explains:

> I don't think there is an approach to education that more consistently daily touches all of those important pieces of learning for children from developing their fine motor skills to music, to art, all the handwork they do, as well as the storytelling, the spiritual piece, it is really children coming into who they are . . . [Cleo] is a Waldorf kid! She loves music, she loves arts, she is physical, she loves stories, she is really into the imaginative world. . . . But Cleo went to first grade with this teacher who really scared her . . . he hit her with a pointer one day, and punished students in different ways. . . . No matter how much we worked on it . . . he was really glued on where he was and didn't get how to work with it. . . . So it really got to a crisis point and that's when we said we need to pull her out of this environment. She lost a lot of self-esteem last year, she was not a good learner, she would never do anything good enough.

Cleo had to go to a different school not because she or her family didn't like Waldorf education (her brother still attends the school where she used to go). She and some of her classmates left their Waldorf school because of the teacher they happened to have. This teacher, according to them, "did not live up to the school's educational philosophy."[3] It is an irony that this situation happened right in a Waldorf school, since these schools are usually quite committed to promoting the personal and professional development of the teachers. They generally not only encourage them to meditate on their practice on a daily basis, but promote activities in weekly staff meetings specially designed to foster teachers' growth and development.

Cleo, who almost completely lost her self-esteem and joy for learning because of her experience with her Waldorf teacher, regained these qualities in the new school she started to attend. Her mother comments:

> It was an incredible process to see this little girl lose her sense of self with the other teacher and now to see her with someone who she feels comfortable with. How much she loves to learn! . . . And how capable she is to take things up! *It wasn't really Waldorf that wasn't working for her, it was her relationship with her teacher which really didn't work* [emphasis mine].

Cleo came to like and do really well in the new school not only because it was a really good school, but also because of the teacher, Cynthia, who worked with her. I had the opportunity to closely observe Cynthia throughout my research and found that she was in fact an exemplary teacher.

LOOKING WITH LOVING EYES: SEEING THE BEAUTY, TRUSTING THE GOODNESS

According to Ron Miller (personal communication), an important characteristic of holistic educators—and I would say, of good teachers in general—is that they believe in the wisdom of human nature and in the "goodness" of children. They believe that children naturally want to learn, and will learn if given the opportunity to learn. Cynthia seemed not only to believe in the wisdom and "goodness" of children, but by the way she talked about her students—and also by the way she actually treated them—she seemed to like them all.

Cynthia would normally think the best she could of each child. She believed that if a child presented some kind of behavioral problem, it was not because she was bad, but because something was going wrong in her life that was leading her to the problem. Cynthia was patient, compassionate, and nonjudgmental. She tried to understand and meet each child according to her needs regardless of the difficulties the latter was going through. She would always try to look at each child with "loving eyes":

> I try as much as it is humanly possible to think the best of the situation and not put a negative judgment on something. If there is a difficulty

here, it's not that the child is bad, there is a difficulty here for us to work out and so we are going to try to understand it, and there is always a positive way to grow from it. It doesn't have to be a tragedy. I want, as much as I can, to *be patient,* to try to understand what is going on, to very calmly ask them, require them to participate with me. . . . I am always learning from them, but I am also always asking "How can I teach them?" *As I meet with them one by one, I ask "How can I be your teacher?" "Who are you?" "What is it that you need?" "What is it that I can get to you?"* And I pray I can give it, I pray I have the wisdom and a moment to respond in the best way I possibly could respond, and I won't always. But to me that's part of the spirituality of it: *That nobody is cut off, nobody is excluded. That they don't look with impatience or judgment. I want to look with loving eyes at what is going on. It is this constant process of trying to pull people back in, pull them back together, and try to reflect back over and over the wonderfulness of who they are!* [emphasis mine].

As her students went through difficult problems, Cynthia would try to help them solve these problems. Let me give an example of a situation that happened in her classroom:

I am thinking of a specific event that happened in class early in the year in which one child accused another of having stolen something. And this became a huge issue at the end of the explore time,[4] because there was denial, there was dramatization, then the class began to polarize and argue "Yes the child did it," "No that child didn't," "How do you know that child did or did not?" And so we had a meeting, a discussion, and talked about "How do you know that?" . . . and "How do you want to treat each other? . . . Let's talk about this thing from a little larger perspective." In other words, "What kind of classroom do you want to have? Do you want the kind of classroom where people can make a mistake and to be able to be brave enough to say they made a mistake? . . . Do you want the kind of classroom where if you make a mistake you hide and you continue to lie and are afraid because people are going to get you and to tease you?". . . So we had a huge discussion about this and they said they wanted a classroom where people could make mistakes. And I said: "How would you treat a child who made the mistake?" And they agreed that there would not be teasing. Then the child who was being accused asked to go outside and talk to the one who was accusing. And as the two were out, I said to everyone else: "This is about you too. Because if they come in, can you imagine how scary it is to be out there admitting that you did something wrong and then you will walk back in and then everyone will ridicule you for it? It is up to you, what do you want to do? This is your class, how are you going to handle this when they come back in?" So there was this very huge discussion and they were so loving about it. I think that was the most beautiful moment I had ever seen in teaching. They were so kind, when they came in one child who had been in the main group went and hugged the person and said: "I have made a mistake somehow like you. . . . You did the right thing!"

As Cynthia asked her students questions such as, "What kind of community do you want to build?" or "What kind of classroom do you want to be a part of?" she helped them think about and verbalize their innermost desire to build a caring community and to be a part of it. As she had this kind of attitude, she fostered a sense of community and a culture of peace in her classroom based not merely on moral stands and rules, but on love and compassion.

Presence and Openness

Cynthia seemed to be able to fully live in the moment in the situations she found herself. When she was with someone, she was with this someone as if there was not anything else more important for her to do. This made of each of her interactions with everyone in the school a special circumstance, a moment where people felt heard and cared for. As Cynthia could be very much present in the moment with the people she was with, she was also open to listen to, to take into consideration, and to address the needs of individual children and their families. In one case cited by a parent, for instance, Cynthia listened both to a child and his father discuss a disagreement over homework. As she was present to the needs of them both, she was able to help them effectively and amicably address the problem. Her attitude in situations such as this modeled to students (and to their parents) an open and healthy way to address their issues.

Calm, Yet Full of Spirit

Cynthia avoided exposing her students to criticisms. Usually, when problems came up, such as when a student would get too noisy or restless in the group, she would gently talk with the child and ask him or her to calm down. Sometimes she would also discretely call the child for a private conversation and explain that what she or he was doing didn't seem right. She usually remained so calm during these conversations that even though they often occurred in the middle of the classroom where everyone was working, many of the students wouldn't even notice these conversations were going on. Cynthia was consciously understanding, gentle, and nonpunitive and clearly modeled what Riane Eisler (2000) would call a "partnership way of being." Consequently, usually there were no heavy feelings involved between her and the children even when difficult situations occurred.

"Cynthia is calm, yet, full of spirit" is an expression that Cleo used to describe her, a viewpoint I found accurate. She is full of spirit and has a passion for life, for her work, and for her students, and she is able to be fully present in the moment with the people she is with. And yet she doesn't overwhelm her students with her presence and passion and seems not to lose control of her temper in the face of difficult situations. Her way of being allows her to solve problems in peace and in partnership with those involved in the issue at stake.

Teaching from the "Big Self" Rather Than the "Small Self"

Cynthia seemed to be able to teach from her heart, from her "big self" (higher self) rather than from her "little self" (ego), as Jack Miller (1988) would probably put it. When she faced difficult situations with students, instead of asserting her will and taking up a dominator's role, as many of us probably would—and as the aforementioned Waldorf teacher did—she seemed to be able to step back and ask herself, "What is going on here? What is the best way to go about this situation?" Her attitude helped her maintain a good relationship with students and avoid power struggles with them. Jack Miller (personal communication) explains:

> When we are teaching from the ego what happens is that we can get into these little battles with students, these little ego melodramas. . . . If we can teach more from the big person, then what happens is that we see ourselves in the students. The boundary between ourselves and the students breaks down. And then we can have these moments of connection with students.

Cynthia's priority was to meet her students' needs rather than winning "battles" and having things done her own way. An example:

> Joshua and Daniel spent most of explore time wandering around and talking to each other. It is about 9:30 and Cynthia is about to call the group for the morning meeting when these boys bring in an electric circuit-building kit. Cynthia decides to give them a few minutes to explore the kit. After about ten minutes, she calls everyone to the meeting. The boys seem not to hear her. They keep working on a circuit-building project. She patiently waits for two more minutes, approaches them and gently calls them for the meeting once more. The boys act as if they had not heard her. She goes back to the meeting area and starts the meeting. About a minute later the boys successfully complete their project, put away the materials and quietly sit at the meeting. During sharing time they proudly talk about their circuit and Cynthia and some of the students ask them many questions about why the experiment didn't seem to work at first and how it came to work later on. Cynthia comments that they should probably invest more time studying electricity since they seemed to be so interested in it.

In this example, Cynthia would not impose her will in spite of students' needs. Even though in the eyes of an outsider Joshua and Daniel perhaps didn't deserve some extra "explore time," Cynthia knew that Joshua was going through difficulties and had been dealing with serious self-esteem issues. While she believed that children need strong and meaningful boundaries, she felt that at that moment she could be flexible and give him a chance to succeed in the experiment and share his accomplishment with the group. She was open and present enough to know that the boy very much needed that kind of experience.

Throughout all my observations, never did I see Cynthia taking up a dominator's role and having students do things they did not want to do by threatening them with punishments. She seemed to always be able to convince them that they had to complete certain tasks, even against their natural inclination to do so. Cynthia's students listened to her, as they told me during interviews, because they liked her very much as a person and as a teacher (they actually mentioned many of her qualities that I discuss here).

The Art and Craft of a Way of Teaching

Cynthia was fair in terms of sharing her time and energy with all students. When she was with a child, she would be with that child. She would normally not stop working with this child because somebody else was not doing the required assignment or was misbehaving, unless this were extremely necessary (for example, if a student were doing something unsafe or disturbing other children). During one interview, I asked her how she balanced her time and energy with her students. She explained:

> Sometimes it is a matter of saying, "OK, these two people are going to goof off at this time." . . . I need to honor this other child that I am with right now. This child needs my attention right now and so I am not going to get into it. . . . Later I follow up with them. . . . I feel that it is not right, always to be focusing on those kids who are just trying to pull me around and play with me a little bit and have fun, and disrupt everybody else.

Besides being fair, Cynthia was also a good discussion leader. She would always try to make sure that everyone had an equal share of time to expose thoughts and ideas and would try to acknowledge students' viewpoints. When conversations started to drift and lose focus, she would skillfully redirect them so that they would not lose track of the issues at stake.

When Cynthia had problems with specific students, she would usually not assume that the students themselves were a problem. She had the habit of asking herself whether her teaching approach or the kind of relationship she had established with her students was really appropriate and investigating whether the students in question were eventually having difficulties she was not aware of. She would also often discuss the case with some of the other teachers, and, when necessary, would talk with children's parents or guardians to discuss strategies on how to deal with the problem. She did what she could to help her students in every possible way, so that they felt supported and successful in school.

Cynthia would not punish her students for doing something they should not do. She would always try to help them understand, in a loving and gentle way, that the choices they were making were unhealthy and could become increasingly problematic in the long run. She tended to focus on the positive, rather than on the negative, aspects of children. In other words, when she was to comment on children's work or behavior, she would usually choose to talk about the good things they had been doing rather than about the negative things. She would also avoid naming the students who were not working or behaving appropriately. For example, instead of saying that some students were not doing cursive writing as she had asked them to, she would say, "I see that a lot of people are writing in cursive, and I am really excited about that. . . ." Or, if she had been waiting for a few children to gather for a meeting, instead of calling the names of those who were not ready, she would say "so-and-so are ready, and we will start our meeting as soon as everyone is!" Cynthia's focus on children's qualities and on the positive aspects of their actions nurtured their self-esteem and was healing for those who had learning difficulties and a lack of self-confidence.

Cynthia's qualities of being made her classroom a place where children felt safe and part of a caring community. Her students absolutely loved her and looked forward to coming to school every day, as I could verify both through extensive individual interviews with all of them and with some of their parents.

CONCLUSION

I have asked all my undergraduate students in a teaching training program[5] to write about the experiences that marked them the most in school. It is interesting that none of them referred to situations in which they learned interesting things. They all focused on issues that directly related to the quality of being and behavior of their teachers (and sometimes also of their peers). They talked about things such as how the nervousness of their preschool teacher made them fearful of school; how one of their primary teachers yelled at them when they made a reading mistake and how this made them scared of reading in public; or how the kindness and support of a given teacher gave them strength and hope to face a problem they were going through in a specific period in their life. The stories told by my students confirmed to me once more that: Who the teacher is as a person, her or his qualities,[6] and how she or he behaves around students usually speaks much louder to people's hearts than what is taught them with words.

When a parent chooses a school for one's child, she or he obviously needs to look at what kind of educational philosophy it embraces. However, it is also important to look carefully at the teacher who is going to be working with the child. If he or she doesn't have certain qualities of being, and is not personally ready to promote the school's goals, the school experience is likely not to be positive for the child, as it happened with little Cleo. Words about love, trust, respect, caring relationships, and appreciation for the beauty of people and for the world around us are not enough. Teachers need to be ready to live what they believe so that their attitudes will not challenge their own discourse and the school's philosophy.

My research and the description I made here of some of Cynthia's qualities (for example, her ability to see the beauty and to trust the goodness of children, her capacity to teach from the big self rather than from the small self, her sensitivity, openness, fairness, compassion, and respect for children) provide us with good and well-grounded examples of how we as educators—parents or teachers—can promote a culture of peace and education for partnership living. We all know developing these qualities is hard and demands long-term work. Therefore, those of us who are thinking about or already dealing with the education of other human beings need to urgently start dedicating ourselves to our self-development so that we can be good models for the people with whom we are working. And those of us who directly or indirectly deal with the education of prospective and/or continuing teachers also need to start idealizing and actually implementing programs that can help them work on their qualities of being so that they too can be good models for their students.

NOTES

1. I am investigating the educational philosophy and practices of three different kinds of alternative schools with a holistic approach to teaching and learning. The fieldwork included extensive observations of school activities, interviews with teachers, parents, and students, and the study of school materials (e.g., books, handouts, students' work, pedagogical materials). This research was initially financed by the Brazilian Government (CNPq) and is currently being financed both by the Foundation for Educational Renewal and by the Universidade Tuiuti do Paraná.

2. I used fictitious names for the children and their parents quoted here in order to protect their identity.
3. It is important to note here that in Waldorf education, the teacher usually stays with the same group of students from first to eighth grade. The school where Cleo used to go to, which was the only Waldorf school close to the town where she lived offered only one class of each grade. This meant that if she and some of her classmates stayed in the school, they would probably be stuck with the same teacher whom they didn't like for eight years.
4. Explore time at the Bellwether School is a period of 1 to 1½ hours where children can freely work on individual or group projects of their choice.
5. I teach undergraduate and graduate classes on education at the Universidade Tuiuti do Paraná, Curitiba, Brazil.
6. For example, whether they are nervous or calm, patient or impatient, kind or aggressive, caring or uncaring.

REFERENCES

Eisler, R. 2000. *Tomorrow's Children: A Blueprint for Partnership Education in the 21st Century.* Boulder, CO: Westview Press.

Kessler, R. 1991. "The Teaching Presence." *Holistic Education Review* 4 (4): 4–15.

———. 2001. "Soul of Students, Soul of Teachers: Welcoming the Inner Life to School." In *Schools with Spirit: Nurturing the Inner Lives of Children and Teachers,* edited by L. Lantieri. Boston, MA: Beacon Press.

Krishnamurti. 1981. *Education and the Significance of Life.* San Francisco, CA: Harper & Row.

Levy, S. 1996. *Starting from Scratch: One Classroom Builds Its Own Curriculum.* Portsmouth, NH: Heinemann.

Miller, J. 1988. *The Holistic Curriculum.* Toronto: OISE Press.

———. 1993. *The Holistic Teacher.* Toronto: OISE Press.

———. 1994. *The Contemplative Practitioner: Meditation in Education and the Professions.* Westport, CT: Bergin & Garvey/Greenwood.

———. 2000. *Education and the Soul: Toward a Spiritual Curriculum.* Albany: State University of New York Press.

Miller, R. 1995. "A Holistic Philosophy of Educational Freedom." In *Educational Freedom for a Democratic Society: A Critique of National Goals, Standards, and Curriculum,* edited by R. Miller. Brandon, VT: Resource Center for Redesigning Education.

Palmer, P. J. 1993. *To Know as We Are Known: Education as a Spiritual Journey.* San Francisco: HarperCollins.

———. 1998. *The Courage to Teach.* San Francisco: Jossey-Bass.

Steiner, R. 1998. "The Kingdom of Childhood." In *Rhythms of Learning: Selected Lectures by Rudolf Steiner,* edited by R. Trostli. Hudson, NY: Anthroposophic Press.

CREATING A CULTURE OF PEACE WITH NONVIOLENT COMMUNICATION^{SM}

SURA HART

> There are three cornerstones for partnership education.
> These are partnership process, partnership content, and
> partnership structure: how we teach, what we teach, and
> what kinds of educational structures we build. A primary
> aim of partnership education is to show, not only intellec-
> tually but also experientially, that partnership relations are
> possible. Hence partnership process, or how we teach and
> learn, is an essential part of education.
>
> —Riane Eisler, *Tomorrow's Children*

> As teachers we can prepare students for participating in
> and creating life-serving organizations by speaking a lan-
> guage that allows us to truly connect with one another
> moment by moment. I call this language Nonviolent Com-
> munication^{SM}. By speaking this language we can make
> partners of teachers and students, give students the tools
> with which to settle their disputes without fighting, build
> bridges between former adversaries such as parents and
> school boards, and contribute to our own well-being and
> the well-being of others.
>
> —Marshall Rosenberg, *Life-Enriching Education*

If we want to educate young people so that they are capable of creating a culture of peace, we need to nourish mutual respect, caring, and compassion in our relationships; we need to model what we hope to teach.

Unfortunately, teachers' relationships with students tend to model what Riane Eisler calls "dominator" relationships (Eisler 1987). What most students learn at school, besides academic subjects, is how to be in dominator relationships: they learn to submit to authority—or rebel against it; they learn to compete for extrinsic rewards; they learn to depend on other people to know what is best for them and what they should learn. Ultimately, they learn that their desires and needs don't matter. Students also learn a language of domination—of shoulds and musts, blame and criticism, judgment and demand—that only trains them to create further dominator relationships and maintain outmoded dominator systems.

Fortunately, we have visionary educators who point the way to an education based on relationships of partnership and compassion. Riane Eisler in her book *Tomorrow's Children*, and Marshall Rosenberg in his book *Life-Enriching Education*, articulate a vision of an educational process that helps us actualize our "enormous capacity for creativity and caring" (Eisler 2000, 9) and that "educates children to be able to create organizations whose goal is to meet human needs, to make life more wonderful for ourselves and each other" (Rosenberg 2003).

There is overall agreement in what Eisler and Rosenberg suggest for how to restructure classrooms and schools to support their vision. Of the three educational components that Eisler identifies—*process, content,* and *structure*—it is in transforming the *process* of how we learn and teach that Eisler and Rosenberg most powerfully partner with each other.

In *partnership process,* "students and teachers are partners in the adventure of learning"; they interact "in caring and respectful ways that deepen rather than dampen our human capacity for empathy"; partnership relations are demonstrated "in day-to-day settings, showing children that their voices will be heard, their ideas respected, and their emotional needs understood" (Eisler 2000, 14). In these terms, Marshall Rosenberg's language of Nonviolent Communication[SM] (NVC) is a consummate partnership process.

Nonviolent Communication[SM] has one fundamental purpose: to create a quality of connection between people that inspires natural compassion and helps us find ways to meet everyone's needs. For this reason, NVC is often called a "language of compassion." It is also referred to as a "communication process" since it offers a concrete model and practical tools for partnering with ourselves and others. At its core, NVC is a life-affirming consciousness that cultivates an awareness of our interdependence and nourishes a reverence for life.

Marshall Rosenberg developed Nonviolent Communication[SM] because he wanted to see more compassion in human relations. In his early training and practice in clinical psychology, Dr. Rosenberg became acutely aware of the negative effects of diagnostic labeling, and aware in general of the power of language to shape our thinking and our consciousness. After leaving the field of psychology, he studied the teachings of the major spiritual traditions, paying attention to the language of people whose lives emanated the love and compassion at the heart of these teachings—among them, Gandhi and Martin Luther King, Jr. From his study, Dr. Rosenberg concluded that, if we are to create a peaceful world, we need to eliminate from our language blame, shame, criticism, and demands—thinking that inhibits our compassionate nature and contributes to violence. We need a language that connects us to the heart of our human experience—our values, dreams, desires, and needs; we need a language and a consciousness that inspire us to give to each other and to care about others' needs being met as much as our own.

The language Marshall Rosenberg developed, NVC, was first used in federally funded projects in the United States to provide mediation and communication skills training for racial integration in schools. Since then, he has spread this powerful peace-making process worldwide, teaching it in schools, prisons, hospitals, and government agencies and offering mediation in war-torn countries, including Palestine, Israel, Rwanda, Sri Lanka, and Croatia. In 1985, he started an international organization, the Center for Nonviolent Communication (CNVC). There are now over one hundred CNVC certified trainers, joined by thousands of individuals, teaching and sharing NVC around the world.

Education has been a particular focus for Dr. Rosenberg and for CNVC because of the importance of reaching young people with a life-affirming consciousness and the skills to create a culture of peace. Rosenberg calls the education that will provide young people with this consciousness and set of skills *life-enriching education*. This term refers to an intention to meet human needs in every action we take—in other words, to dedicate our actions to serving life. The process language of Nonviolent Communication[SM] is a key component in life-enriching education in that it trains us to focus on the needs we are each trying to meet.

In practice, NVC does this by helping us reframe how we express ourselves and how we respond to others. It offers guidelines for how to create and maintain compassionate connection through a dialogic process, a back-and-forth of honest expressing and empathic listening. The guidelines keep our attention focused on exchanging specific information: what each person is *observing, feeling, needing,* and *requesting.*

Following these guidelines, we learn to express ourselves by first making careful observations, free of any evaluation or analysis, about what is going on that is affecting us. We learn to share honestly about how we are being affected—how we feel in relation to what's going on, and what needs of ours are being met or not being met. We then identify and articulate what we are wanting to help meet our needs, expressing this in the form of a specific request. In expressing, we focus on what *we* are observing, feeling, needing, and requesting; in empathizing with others, we give our full attention to what *the other person* is observing, feeling, needing, and requesting. Empathy—the ability to be present to another person and connect with how they truly are—is at the heart of NVC practice; it is also a core feature of partnership education (Eisler 2000).

In both expressing and empathizing, we focus on the needs we are trying to meet in every action we take; since we all have the same needs, this is our strongest point of connection. When both people are connected to their own and the other person's needs, they sometimes quite suddenly and miraculously find themselves partnering in a graceful dance of mutual giving and receiving. One of the surprising features of this language is that this can happen even if only one person knows NVC.

Educators who practice NVC are blessed with countless opportunities to engage in this dance with their students. With practice, our ability to connect with the needs of our students and find ways to help meet their needs typically increases dramatically. We experience increasing trust, cooperation, and mutual respect in our relationships with students and see this reflected in students' relationships with each other. At some point we notice that we are thinking, listening, and speaking in radically different ways than before—ways that more often inspire compassionate action. As we learn new ways, there is inevitably a lot of unlearning; for teachers, in particular, we need to unlearn the dominator ways we have been taught to learn and to teach. The following story of one school's experiment in creating a life-enriching learning community points to the practice, patience, and perseverance it can take to shift from dominator to partnership ways. It also illustrates the blossoming of compassion and joyful learning that can come from our efforts. My hope is that by reading the story of Skarpnäcks Free School, your own dreams of bringing about a culture of peace will be nourished.

LIFE-ENRICHING EDUCATION IN ACTION

When I first heard Marianne Göthlin speak about Skarpnäcks Free School, the school she had started in Sweden, based on the principles of Nonviolent Communication℠, I was on the edge of my seat. Having worked in the field of education for twenty years, and practicing and teaching NVC for ten years, I was very interested to hear how her school was set up and how the teachers taught NVC to the students. I was both surprised and very excited when I heard her say: "We don't teach Nonviolent Communication℠ to the students; we try to live it in our relationships with them."

I was surprised because I had found that young people learned NVC faster than most adults, because they have so much less to unlearn. I had assumed that in a school based on the principles of NVC, teachers would naturally teach the process to students. Marianne's statement quickly exposed this assumption and struck a chord of truth in me, resonating with my deepest understanding of how we humans learn—from the inside out, and through our day-to-day relationships.

Marianne went on to explain that it was through their relationships and their intention to connect with and care for the needs of everyone in their school, using NVC, that the Skarpnäcks teachers hoped to seed a culture of trust, compassion, and peace.

Over the course of the last year, I have been in ongoing conversation with Marianne, listening to stories that inspire me and educate me as to what it requires to shed habits of dominator schooling and create a life-serving learning community. I wove together some of the stories that Marianne has shared with me, for the many teachers who have asked me, "What does an NVC school look like?" and "How long does it take to create a school culture of compassion?" I tell this story in Marianne's voice, in the first person, hoping to connect the reader more directly with her experience.

Skarpnäcks Free School: An Experiment in Life-Enriching Education

The Skarpnäcks Free School started with a conversation between some parents who were unhappy with the authoritarian structure of the schools their children attended. Their seven-year-olds were expected to sit quietly at their desks most of the day, listening to teachers lecture to them and assign work. Teachers in Sweden are often evaluated on how quiet their classroom is and how well they keep the students occupied at their desks. This encourages teachers to focus on rote learning, memorization, and independent desk exercises.

These parents wanted a different kind of school for their children—one based on democratic principles and respectful compassionate interactions, a place where their children could be more active in their learning and free to express themselves. I had taught NVC to some of these parents and I was working as an elementary classroom teacher when they asked me if I would help them start a school founded on the principles of NVC. From the moment I said "Yes" up to the present, I have been fascinated and encouraged by our journey.

Skarpnäcks began in the fall of 1998 with twenty-four children, ages six through nine, and four teachers. Years later, we have seventy-five students, ages six through fifteen, nine teachers, and one administrator. We have grown not only in size but also, and more importantly, in compassion, cooperation, and trust.

We did not set out to formally teach children NVC, nor did we set out to teach children compassion, because how can you do that? We teachers agreed that what was important was to live the consciousness of NVC: to listen to the children and care equally about children's needs and adults' needs at the school—to focus on meeting needs and creating a school environment where we are all giving and receiving in a way we enjoy.

Our teachers believe that this way of being together, this giving and receiving, is natural to human beings. Marshall Rosenberg often talks about NVC as our natural language and quotes Gandhi as saying, "Don't confuse the natural with the habitual." Since what is habitual in children's upbringing and schooling is adults telling them what to do and expecting obedience, we knew it would take some time for them to trust that we wanted to live a different way with them. We wanted to be sure that this climate of trust was established in our school, that we were living the consciousness of NVC, before we taught students the steps and technique.

From the first days of our school, we teachers did our best to model NVC with the children. It was very important to us to listen deeply to one another, and also to make requests and not demands. We all valued active learning, choosing to be outside in nature a lot and also out in our community. We had many enjoyable projects to offer the children, but we never wanted to make demands or force them to do anything. We wanted to be partners with the children, to demonstrate that their needs are of equal importance to our needs. We wanted to model democratic values. We knew that whenever we get someone to do something because we demand it, because they fear we will punish them if they don't do it, we undermine trust, respect, caring, and cooperation, and everyone suffers.

We told the children from the start that we only wanted them to do what they could agree to and what they saw as life-enriching. We expected they would be very happy with our requests; we were surprised with the variety of responses we received, which gave us a lot of practice that first year especially.

Throughout our first year, we teachers found that the children responded to our requests in three different ways, expressed in three groups of approximately the same size. The first group of about eight students were primarily the youngest children who had been raised at home with parents who shared our values of mutuality and respect. They seemed most comfortable making choices. They were the most cooperative and most creative students. There were also a few older students in that group who appreciated the difference between our requests and their former schools, where teachers told them what they had to do.

A second group of students expressed more confusion in response to our requests. We could see them furrow their brows when we asked if they were *willing* to do an activity rather than just tell them they *had* to do it. For example, we have never assigned homework, but sometimes we offer it as an option. Some students who were accustomed to having homework assignments would say to us, "Tell me I have to do homework." We teachers were not comfortable doing this, and would tell them why this was: We wanted so much for them to learn to make choices—about what they want to learn and how they want to learn it. For us, it was even more important that the students learn to make choices that serve their lives than that they learn certain facts or concepts. We also had confidence that the two were not in opposition. In fact, we believed that the more choices they had, the more they would learn.

There was a third group of students that first year that offered the most challenge for the teachers. These students, when we would make a request of them, would say, "Do I have to?" This would be their reply to most of our requests, whether we were asking them to solve a math problem or to go play outside for exercise and fun. We were so surprised by this response, at first. Each time we heard it, we explained to them that we didn't want to make them do anything and only wanted them to meet our requests if they could do it with willingness. We also empathized with their fears that if they said "No" to what we asked, we would make them do things. Since this was most often how adults had treated them in the past, we understood how little trust they might have of us. We saw that their questioning, "Do I have to?" was their way of testing us, that we would have to earn their trust and this would take time. Even with this understanding, we were often very frustrated and even discouraged when, month after month, they continued to test us in this way. We wondered what it would take for them to really trust our intention.

Their questioning and our confusion continued throughout that first year, and we approached the beginning of our second school year with apprehension along with strong hope that they would now trust us. As we soon discovered, something had changed in them, but we were, once again, surprised. Now, whenever we made a request of students, this same group responded with "No," or "I won't do it," or "You can't make me." It seemed their questioning had turned into strong resistance. But why? We wondered what we had done to have them resist so strongly. It seemed that instead of trusting us more, they trusted us less.

Because we knew that only when someone is free to say "No" can the person truly be free to say "Yes," we did our best to listen to the needs behind their "No." As we did this, we came to see their resistance as a big step forward in their unlearning process. Teachers started to celebrate that students were exercising their power of choice and wanting to see if they would receive respect for it. The previous year the students saw themselves as having no power; they questioned teachers, wanting to know if we would really make them do things as others had done in the past. This year they were testing their own autonomy as well as our intent by saying "No, you can't make me." Again, we knew that only when the students were respected for their "No" would they be free to say "Yes."

Even with this understanding, it wasn't easy to hear their "No" and listen to what they were wanting. At our school, we do a lot of our learning out in nature and in our community. When we are preparing to take a group of twenty-two students out into the woods and two students say they won't go, what can we do? This happened to me often and my most frequent response was to listen to what they wanted and empathize with their need to make their own choices in life. I also would share with them my feelings and needs: "I feel torn when I hear you say you want to stay at school and not go to the woods with the rest of the group. I want you to do what's most wonderful for you, and I would really like to have us all together. I also want to get going to the woods soon with the rest of the children. I can't leave you alone and I'm not sure what to do to meet all our needs. Do you have an idea of what could work?" With this much dialogue, sometimes the child would decide to join us, because they saw how doing so would contribute to the ease of the school day for everyone, and also because what we were doing looked like fun to them.

If the student was still not willing to come, I tried to find another group he could stay with at school. At times, I tried calling the parent to come pick him up, if he really didn't want to go. If I could find no other way, I said, "I'm very sad to not find a way to meet your need for making your own choices right now, and also meet my need to be with all the children in this activity outdoors. I am now insisting you come with us." I only remember a few times that first year when we physically moved a child against their will. This was not done for punishment but because we could see no other way to protect the children in our care.

The NVC dialogues we have with our students are not easy to describe. They have a form but don't follow a simple formula with the promise of simple solutions. They are sometimes messy with stops and starts. But our willingness to stay in these dialogues grows stronger as over and over we enjoy the results of this process. Whenever we keep the dialogue going and stay connected to both our needs and the student's needs, instead of giving in to the old way of exerting power over them, we almost always find a way to meet everybody's needs.

Our growing motivation has served us well, as it took another full school year for this group of students to test out our resolve to only make requests and to feel confident that we would listen for the "Yes" behind their "No." This was great training for us teachers, giving us a lot of practice in walking our talk. The result is that by the end of our third year, our school community was full of trust of one another.

The following year, we welcomed our new class of six-year-olds into this trust, and then watched them repeat the now familiar pattern of unlearning: at first they responded to our requests by saying "Do I have to?" and later with "No." We were pleased to see that it only took them one year until they could hear the sincere motivation behind our requests.

Challenges and Learnings   Ten new students and two new teachers joined us last year and another ten students and two teachers this year (2003–2004). As our school continues to grow, we're challenged to keep our core philosophy strong. The parents who started Skarpnäcks were passionate about NVC and the vision of a life-enriching school. Since then, more families have joined us because they hear how children blossom at our school, but now many families don't know a lot about NVC and our educational philosophy. Each year we offer NVC training for parents, and in the coming year we will offer this throughout the year hoping that more parents will come. This is a challenge for us, since our parents lead busy lives, and not as many of them as we would like find the time to understand the vision we have for the school. It seems very important for teachers to hold the vision and find more ways to share it with our school families.

Our biggest challenge is the time it takes to learn new ways of teaching and learning and to nurture relationships. As well as wanting to connect more with parents, we also want to make more time for meeting as teachers, to talk about our personal challenges in letting go of old patterns of teaching. We want to find more ways to support each other. And we also want to include students more and more in the running of the school. How will we do this and where will it take us? I can't say for sure, but I'm hopeful and encouraged by what we have learned and accomplished so far:

- We are *unlearning* to be the authority in the classroom. This is much more difficult than we thought it would be. To really partner with the students means that our voice is just one voice in the classroom, not the only or the most important one. We are learning to take our place in the classroom, not push our point of view. We're learning to spend more time listening and less time talking.

- Because our vision is so large and the changes take stretches of time, we are finding that celebrating our small successes with each other is very important. We do this now regularly in staff meetings. We also celebrate with the children. And when we go out of the school, to conferences with teachers from other schools, we're reminded of what we have here and we come back and celebrate that awareness.

- Those of us who stay on as teachers have learned to be patient. As we have seen how this patience pays off time and again, we grow more trustful of the NVC process. Two of the four original teachers left after the second year. There were personal reasons for each of them, but a common reason was that they didn't see things progress as quickly as they liked. In hiring new teachers, we now look for their commitment to our vision, their desire to practice NVC, their willingness to have patience with the process, and their comfort with creative chaos.

Harvests   It took a great deal of effort, patience, and time to lay the foundation for our school; now, after six years, we celebrate that we are living in an increasingly life-enriching way with each other. Some observations that confirm this for us are:

- Most of the children arrive at school early, stay late, and express their happiness to be at school; they play easily with all ages, boys and girls together.

• The number of conflicts between students has decreased dramatically since we opened; the children handle most conflicts that occur; and teachers spend very little time dealing with conflicts.

• Increasingly, students talk directly to each other when they don't like what someone is doing, with growing confidence that they will be heard in a way that will lead to mutually satisfying outcomes.

• We rarely experience resistance from the children because they know that we will listen to their "No" and will want to hear their needs. They now trust that we will not exert power over them and make them do things. This was not always the case.

• Academic achievement: Recent standardized testing for nine- and eleven-year-olds in reading, math, and English language show that our students are all performing at or beyond the expectations for their age. This is not a surprise to the teachers. It is, however, a big relief to parents who have wondered how their children could possibly learn skills when they're enjoying themselves so much.

• Our students are curious and love to learn. They can work alone and in groups. They are eager to learn from teachers and each other. We all learn from the wonders of the natural world surrounding us.

• The students have recently been asking to learn NVC. We teachers are now happy to teach it, trusting that it will not be learned as a formula or technique but as a truly life-enriching process, further enhancing our community.

Growing a life-enriching school is hard work; it is also very rewarding. When I see what has blossomed from our ongoing intention to meet needs and from the seeds of trust we have so carefully nurtured, and from all that we are learning together along the way, I'm joyful—as so many needs and dreams are met for me: for protecting the vibrant minds and loving hearts of children, for a caring community, for mutual learning, and for hope that we can create a compassionate and peaceful world.

CONCLUSION

In sharing this story, I want to celebrate the ability of one school to create a culture of peace; even more, I hope to elucidate what I believe is the key to their success: *the recognition that the culture we*

*want to create will not come about by imposing a new order but by liv-
ing a new paradigm.* If the Skarpnäcks teachers had tried to teach their students the
new partnership paradigm by just changing classroom structures,
routines, and curriculum, I doubt they would have been as successful. There have been, throughout history, many attempts to
create utopian cultures of peace by people with heartfelt yearn-
ings and lofty ideals. In most cases these were short-lived experiments because the processes they used to create the new order
were no different than those that supported the old order: Some
group of people determined what was right and then imposed the
so-called right way on themselves and others.

Gandhi admonished us to "Be the change you want to see in
the world." To create a culture of peace and partnership, we will
want to change our *internal culture of domination and violence:* to
shift from thinking in terms of *what* we are and what we *should* be,
to thinking in terms of our deepest needs and values. We will also
recognize that any demands we place on ourselves or others serve
to perpetuate the culture of domination.

The teachers at Skarpnäcks Free School set out to transform
the domination system existing within themselves so they could
relate to young people in ways that nourish and empower them to
create a culture of peace. They found in Nonviolent Communica-
tion^{SM} a technology powerful enough to bring about this transformation. These practical tools are accessible to everyone who
desires to create peace in themselves and in the world.

REFERENCES

Eisler, Riane. 1987. *The Chalice and the Blade: Our History, Our Future.*
San Francisco: Harper & Row.

————. 2000. *Tomorrow's Children: A Blueprint for Partnership Education
in the 21st Century.* Boulder, CO: Westview Press.

Rosenberg, Marshall B. 2000. *Nonviolent Communication: A Language of
Compassion.* Encinitas, CA: PuddleDancer Press.

————. 2003. *Life-Enriching Education.* Encinitas, CA: PuddleDancer
Press.

PART THREE

How Schools Would Be Different
in a Culture of Peace

EMPHASIZING VARIETY RATHER THAN COMMONALITY
Educating Young Children for a Culture of Peace

LISA S. GOLDSTEIN

F ear of differences—differences in religion, culture, ethnicity, race, nationality, language—is a fundamental strand in the complex web of problems causing the devastating international and cross-cultural conflicts featured regularly on the nightly news programs in nations around the world. Less violent manifestations of our fear of differences are a daily occurrence in our children's schools and classrooms—racism, classism, heterosexism, elitism, ethnocentrism, abilism—and bring harm to mainstream and minority children alike. The authors represented in this volume are working to create a culture of peace and to help young people develop caring, compassionate, and socially responsible attitudes toward others. To do this we must create an educational approach that dismantles fear of difference and promotes understanding, appreciation, and respect among all people.

Many current approaches to multicultural education in early childhood and elementary educational settings in the United States attempt to address fear of difference by highlighting the essential commonalities uniting all humans: We all love our families, we all dream of safety, we all wish for freedom. In this chapter I want to call this widely held and widely taught perspective into question, examining the ways in which this commonality view of human experience reinforces fear of difference and sows seeds of mistrust and violence.

The commonality viewpoint, although rooted in the best intentions, is deeply problematic and leads to the creation of classroom cultures that undermine efforts to build partnership and community among children. In place of the commonality view, I propose an approach to multicultural education that focuses on and emphasizes variety and difference. Examining and celebrating variety—in culture, language, ethnicity, race, religion, family structures, personal abilities, and so on—can serve as the foundation stone of an approach to diversity education for young children that leads to the development of a culture of respect, dignity, and peace.

FEAR OF DIFFERENCE

Children see differences among people. Research indicates that at ages as young as two years old children notice and comment upon differences in race, physical appearance, and other characteristics (Derman-Sparks 1989; Katz 1982; Van Ausdale and Feagin 2001). As children of the United States of America move through their daily lives, they often point out and ask questions about the differences they notice.

> That man has no legs.
> She's really fat.
> How come Rosie has a Mommy and a Mummy but no daddy?
> Wen-June's lunch looks weird.
> Why doesn't Jennifer have a Christmas tree?
> Why is Myesha's hair like that?

Generally speaking, adults squirm when children make these statements, particularly if they are voiced loudly within earshot of the person whose difference is being brought to public attention. Shush, we tell our children. That's not polite. It is rude to stare. Don't say that. We do our best to dodge these issues because of our own discomfort with them. Our responses, or nonresponses, to children's queries about difference often lead children to conclude that those differences must be very, very bad—so bad that parents or teachers won't even talk about them.

Adults' inability to talk about difference leaves children with no sources of reliable, constructive information about human variety. As a result, children are forced to develop their own theories about people they perceive as different from themselves. With little access to straightforward and honest information, children piece together their understandings of difference through guesswork; by collecting snippets of information from books, television, or other children; or by eavesdropping on adult conversations. Children rarely confirm or disconfirm their personal theories with the significant adults in their lives because they have repeatedly received the message that differences must not be discussed.

Children's self-created working understandings of difference are often limited, partial, and full of inaccuracies. Using this type of misinformation as their foundation for the consideration of human differences leads children to develop a host of troubling misunderstandings. Children grow to fear what they don't understand and to hate what they fear. When differences are to be hated and feared the seeds of violence are sown.

Well-meaning teachers often reinscribe and strengthen young children's growing fear of difference. An example of this linked to racial difference can be heard in a sentiment frequently expressed by teachers working in United States schools with highly diverse student populations: "I don't see color, I just see children." This statement appears to emphasize the equality of all children. However, an underlying message communicated to children is that color is so problematic that it must be ignored completely even though its presence is patently obvious.

It is easy to see how children of color could come to feel shame about their racial identities when the teacher has made it clear that their skin color needs to be erased. Less easy to see, perhaps, is that hearing a teacher say "I don't see color, I just see children" teaches white children that their identities are "normal," the standard against which their classmates of color will be judged. This color-blind viewpoint hurts all children.

Because of their commitment to treating all children equally, teachers who don't see color and just see children tend to favor approaches to teaching about personal and cultural diversity that emphasize the ways in which all people are alike. In multicultural educational programs featuring this commonality perspective, race, class, nationality, ethnicity, language, physical ability, religion, sexual orientation, and other differences are downplayed in order to foreground the fundamental biological and emotional experiences common to humans. Undergirding the commonality perspective is the assumption that awareness of the ways in which all other people are like themselves will help children to respect and accept others who initially appear very different.

Many multicultural education programs, children's picture books, and pedagogical practices common to early childhood and elementary education in the United States are rooted in this commonality perspective. Ideas such as "Christmas around the world" or "culture of the week" teach children to look at and appreciate other cultures by seeing the interesting ways in which *their* practices and experiences are similar to *ours*. Teachers using these approaches accept the premise that once children from mainstream North American culture can see that kids in Japan go to school like *we* do, and Mexican kids like to play soccer like *we* do, and African American kids like picnics like *we* do, and Jewish kids believe in the Bible like *we* do, then the differences between those cultures and ours won't seem so significant or scary to children.

Another assumption of commonality-based perspectives on diversity education is that minimizing attention to differences among children will lead naturally and easily to the development of a sense of community in the classroom. After reminding children that we are all the same underneath our different appearances, languages, and cultural heritages, teachers can emphasize students' similarities and connections to one another as a route to building community. If we are already equal partners in the human family, then it is easy to be equal partners in the classroom community.

One significant shortcoming of this assumption is that these practices do not address the differences that children see manifested in the human world around them. Instead, this perspective teaches children that the differences among people are insignificant next to the common bonds we share. When commonality is highlighted and focused upon, children's questions and concerns about difference are cast into the shadows and minimized. The silence around issues of human variety that characterizes this perspective sends the implicit message that differences are shameful and not to be discussed. Attempts to build a caring classroom community are undermined when differences are downplayed because certain children find parts of themselves rendered invisible, parts of their lives unspeakable, parts of their family culture unmentionable. Their differences are unwelcome additions to classroom life.

CELEBRATING DIFFERENCE

In direct opposition to the commonality perspective, a variety approach to considering human experience highlights and draws children's attention to the range of significant human differences. These differences are understood as a fundamental facet of human life and are represented within the variety perspective as strengths to be drawn upon. In this perspective, difference is examined and explored rather than ignored, and appreciated and valued rather than minimized.

By focusing on difference rather than on sameness, diversity education programs celebrating variety acknowledge the significant differences that children see among the people around them. Talking about these formerly taboo differences validates children's perceptions and addresses children's questions. Further, by giving children language for speaking respectfully and accurately about human differences, variety-centered approaches to diversity education break the cycle of silence, misinformation, and fear that characterizes commonality-based programs.

In classrooms functioning from a variety perspective, children move beyond acknowledging and understanding differences into the development of a worldview in which differences are considered to be strengths. Once this occurs, children can see the ways in which variety enhances and enriches the classroom community. Children who appreciate differences understand that the broader the range of languages spoken, of cultures represented, of perspectives shared, the richer and stronger the community: This approach teaches that *together we are better.*

Classroom communities rooted in a perspective that affirms and celebrates diversity are likely to be characterized by conflict and tension. "Because the basic values of different groups are often diametrically opposed, conflict is bound to occur" (Nieto 1998, 14); in variety-based classrooms, however, these conflicts are understood and accepted as an inevitable part of learning. Children encouraged to respect the viewpoints, needs, and attitudes of others will learn to manage conflict and negotiate workable solutions as a fundamental part of their classroom curriculum.

Teachers at the Washington-Beech Community Preschool, located in a public housing project in Boston, Massachusetts, have worked with tenants and the Committee for Boston Public Housing to implement and document an early childhood education program rooted in a commitment to appreciating differences and valuing diversity. Their program's goals are to create an educational context in which each child understands his or her own identity; respects and appreciates the identities and perspectives of others; sees how issues impact everyone in the community; and strives for justice and fairness in the community and the world (Wolpert 1999).

These goals could be fundamental to our vision of education for a peaceful future. Before developing educational programming around these goals, however, I think we must consider carefully the tensions and complexities within the goals themselves. For example, what does it mean for each child to understand his or her own identity? Does this mean children should understand and accept the oppressive interpretations of their identities currently circulating in mainstream United States culture? For example, should girls understand their gendered identities to include unnatural standards of thinness, low levels of intellectual capability in mathematics, and deferential behavior around males? Should boys understand their gendered identities to include avoidance of public displays of emotion, commitment to competition, and superiority to females?

Children surely should know about the various features that constitute their identities—their racial background, their ethnicity, their sex and gender, their family's religious orientation, and so on. But this alone is not sufficient to create a culture of peace. We must also teach children to question existing understandings and attitudes, to wonder why things are the way they seem, and to maintain a critical perspective on the range of cultural beliefs and attitudes influencing and coloring their identities.

Another goal of the Washington-Beech model, to help children learn to respect and appreciate the identities and perspectives of others, raises significant practical questions. Are all perspectives worthy of appreciation? Should children of color be taught that some people hold racist views and that those views are to be respected and appreciated? Must children learn to respect and appreciate perspectives that denigrate their own identities or that work to destroy community and connection?

An "anything goes" attitude of cultural relativism is not the goal of multicultural education approaches that honor difference. Teachers seeking to create a culture of peace cannot encourage children to accept and appreciate perspectives and beliefs that are hurtful and divisive. Even in a classroom that values difference and variety, some standards of acceptability must be determined, taught, shared, and reinforced. Awareness of the web of fundamental human rights and fundamental human responsibilities teaches children that justice and fairness must be shared equally among all people. Children educated in this manner will be able to envision new possibilities for a just and compassionate future.

SUGGESTIONS FOR EARLY CHILDHOOD TEACHERS

Given that so many of the multicultural programs and materials available emphasize commonality and sameness, how can teachers of young children work to celebrate difference and variety in their classrooms?

Choose Materials Carefully

There is a range of literature, music, video, and other materials for children that focus on multicultural education. Some of these materials highlight and emphasize sameness, some highlight and emphasize difference. Make thoughtful choices about the books you read with your students, about the music you play, the activities you select, the programs and field trips you plan. Be sure that the messages you are sending your students through your teaching materials are aligned with and support your moral goals.

Critique Materials with Your Students

Even the youngest preschoolers can see the difference between *we are all the same* and *we are all different*. Talk openly with your students about the distinction between these two points of view and help them see that balancing attention to commonality with attention to difference makes more room for people to be open and honest with each other and with themselves. When you encounter books that overemphasize commonality and disregard difference, encourage your students to create alternate versions of the story that would better support your classroom goals. Or work with your students to create class books that draw on each of their lives and their experiences and that depict vividly the beautiful differences found in your classroom.

Create Activities That Highlight Both the Unique Identity of Each Child and the Powerful Connections Within the Classroom Community

Emphasizing individual differences does not mean devaluing connection and relationship. Indeed, the richest and most remarkable communities can be formed when highly diverse groups of individuals comes together. We must be careful that a difference-oriented approach to diversity education does not lead to individualism and isolation. Just as children must be taught to appreciate the unique constellation of traits each individual brings to the class, they must also be taught to appreciate the ways that all of those strengths and gifts combine and blend together to create something powerful and beautiful. Creative teachers have developed all sorts of activities that teach this crucial lesson. Making class quilts out of fabric, paper, or other materials allows each child both to contribute something personal and unique to the project and also to enjoy the beautiful outcome of the community's shared efforts. Individually designed stepping stones offer a similar lesson: The individual stones are only truly useful when brought together to form a path that connects two points. Other activities along these lines could involve creating a class mosaic, a giant jigsaw puzzle, or a collage.

Have Conversations with Parents and Colleagues About Difference

Make an effort to model open communication about difference. Be vocal about your appreciation of variety. Fight against any discomfort you may feel in mentioning differences. This is likely to be hard work; the legacy of shame surrounding differences is very strong.

Teach Consciously

Most multicultural education materials highlight commonality. If you hope to teach your children to see and to appreciate difference, you will be swimming against the tide. As a result, you must commit and recommit to making a concerted effort to be true to your vision. If your school or district mandates participation in multicultural education programming that centers around commonality, find ways to affirm that party line and then move beyond that stance into a position of sharing the value of difference.

Remember to Appreciate and Respect Differences of Opinion

Sometimes teachers who value and appreciate differences among children are not so generous with their adult colleagues: What is seen as a difference to be celebrated in a child is often perceived as an annoying trait in the teacher next door. Remember that sameness and difference are both realities of human existence. You and your commonality-focused colleagues are working in the best interests of children and society in the ways that make the most sense to each of you. Do not use diversity education as a battleground or a site of divisive conflict. Work for peace, not for conflict.

REFERENCES

Derman-Sparks, L. 1989. *Anti-Bias Curriculum: Tools for Empowering Young Children.* Washington, DC: National Association for the Education of Young Children.

Katz, P. 1982. "Development of Children's Racial Awareness and Intergroup Attitudes." In *Current Topics in Early Childhood Education,* edited by L. G. Katz, vol. 4, 17–54. Norwood, NJ: Ablex.

Nieto, S. 1998. "Affirmation, Solidarity and Critique: Moving Beyond Tolerance in Education. " In *Beyond Heroes and Holidays: A Practical Guide to K–12 Anti-Racist, Multicultural Education and Staff Development,* edited by E. Lee, D. Menkart, and M. Okazawa-Rey, 7–18. Washington, DC: Network of Educators on the Americas.

Van Ausdale, D., and J. R. Feagin. 2001. *The First R: How Children Learn Race and Racism.* Lanham, MD: Rowman & Littlefield.

Wolpert, E. 1999. *Start Seeing Diversity: The Basic Guide to an Anti-Bias Classroom.* Boston, MA: Redleaf Press.

IF WE COULD REALLY FEEL
The Need for Emotions of Care Within the Disciplines
DIERDRE BUCCIARELLI

If we could really feel, the pain would be so great that we would stop all the suffering . . . If we could really feel it in the bowels, the groin, in the throat, in the breast, we would go into the streets and stop the war, stop slavery, stop the prisons, stop the killings, stop destruction . . . When we feel, we will feel the emergency; when we feel the emergency, we will act; when we act, we will change the world
— Julian Beck, *The Life of the Theatre*
[in Dworkin 1974, 91]

Helping students learn to seek the truth (or, for more progressive educators, the truths) is often considered one of the chief tasks of education and of schooling. And truth is often sought using the analytic tools of the disciplines of knowledge. In most schools in contemporary, industrialized societies, students spend a significant amount of the day's time learning the disciplines and the kind of understanding and worldviews they endorse.[1]

Traditional disciplinary ways of seeing and modes of analysis, often considered the primary route to intellectual truth and understanding, can be an obstacle on this path. These dominant ways of knowing, which are necessary to gain a critical distance, and whose elimination I do not call for, can also distort our vision and diminish our capacity to find the truth(s). They can, consequently, reduce our power to solve crucial human problems in a fully ethical way, in a way that demonstrates that we care about the needs of others. Traditional disciplinary methods employ a kind of abstract theoretical knowing, divorced from the real world, and their advocates pride themselves on that distance. Standing back from one's subject and not getting emotionally involved are supposed to enable one to think critically. In order to use traditional analytic tools, the emotional and moral aspects of a problem are typically disregarded as irrelevant and are thought to get in the way of an adequate solution. Thus, as we gain critical intellectual distance on a subject of inquiry, we can also become more removed from our feelings and the pain and suffering of real human beings, much to our collective human detriment.

But, there is another kind of disciplinary understanding that does not demand such distance. Feminists and other scholars have identified a relational understanding or "connected knowing" that seeks to make emotional connections with its subjects of investigation, and, in essence, demands that we think morally within the framework of the disciplines (Belenky et al. 1986; Collins 1991; Gilligan 1982; Keller 1983; Martin 1994; Stanfield 1985; Noddings 1984). This is fortunate because if we aim to educate for peace and partnership and to fully understand an issue, we must get closer to the concerns of others and nurture emotions of caring that extend beyond our immediate circle to encompass the world. These emotions and values need to be part and parcel of the kind of thinking that students learn as they study the disciplines; the emotions and values need to be cultivated therein. The conceptualization of disciplinary understanding that is adopted can make a difference in what is fostered in education and can ultimately have an effect on the way that students view the world, the kind of persons they become, and the world they create. Connected thinking is one tool, although not the only one, that can help us create a culture of peace in our schools and our world.

TRADITIONAL AND "CONNECTED" DISCIPLINARY KNOWING DEFINED

Disciplinary understanding does not consist of just a bunch of unconnected, Trivial Pursuit® facts. Nor does it mean simply knowing how to use particular techniques, such as addition and subtraction or calculus formulas. It is thought to be composed of a *structure* or *network* of concepts, theories, methods, and evaluation criteria that are related to each other in a systematic way.[2] Acquiring disciplinary understanding, then, means more than amassing a large number of discrete facts, concepts, and procedures. As contemporary teaching-for-understanding advocates tell us, learning the disciplines means learning "particular modes of thinking or interpreting the world" (Gardner and Boix-Mansilla 1994, 202). Attaining disciplinary understanding means learning to think about the world in new ways, in ways that transform or replace one's earlier or naive ways of understanding with those that enable one to *see with disciplinary eyes*. A major purpose of learning to think or see in disciplinary terms is to obtain a more veridical view and a deeper understanding of the world.

What does it mean to see with disciplinary eyes? What are students supposed to understand deeply? How are students supposed to *think* about the world? What are the key features of disciplinary *modes of thinking or interpreting the world* that students are supposed to learn?

Before I respond to these questions, it is important to understand something that is not always fully realized: The disciplines did not always exist; they have a history. The disciplines, which furnish us with intellectual tools, were created by human beings for the purpose of solving an array of complex problems. But the disciplines, as we know them in the West, were historically developed by particular groups of human beings (primarily rich white males) to respond to problems that had special relevance in their lives using modes of thought that made sense to them. This is not to say that all of the problems they examined were only problems for them, but it does mean that their experience took center stage and their dilemmas, ways of knowing, and methods of solution became—and still largely represent—the dominant disciplinary model.[3] For example, although it is changing, medical and biological theorizing was based on androcentric assumptions and health research centered on male physiology and problems (Bleier 1984; Hubbard 1990; Keller 1985; Rosser 1994; Schiebinger 1989). Other groups, with a different set of experiences—in this case, women—were largely excluded from the identification of problems and the creation of disciplinary knowledge and tools of analysis.

Problems that may have had significance in their lives often went unseen, and hence unaddressed, at least in the context of the disciplines. At other times, applying a male perspective to women's concerns may have had drastic consequences in women's lives (in the area of healthcare, for example). Once we appreciate that the disciplines do not have a rarefied existence apart from human lives and concerns, it becomes easier to see how it is possible for there to be different kinds of disciplinary understanding and different methods of inquiry.

Because I think that the conceptualizations and terminology of Mary Field Belenky, Blythe McVicker Clinchy, Nancy Rule Goldberger, and Jill Mattuck Tarule[4] help to capture the essential distinction between traditional Western modes of disciplinary understanding and the more recently identified (at least in the West) connected methods of knowing, I will borrow from their work.

Belenky and her colleagues speak of "separate knowing" as representative of traditional disciplinary modes of thinking, seeing, or understanding the world. Separate knowing means that when one "sees with disciplinary eyes," one adopts a perspective that attempts to extricate or separate the self from the object under investigation. Since emotions are thought to cloud or distort one's thinking, separate knowers strive to understand issues they confront with the use of reason or abstract critical thinking, remaining as aloof as possible from all concrete particulars. Each of the disciplines has its own set of critical thinking devices or technical problem-solving tools that can be used to help one achieve this impersonal or transcendent view. Such a dispassionate approach is thought to enable one to be nonbiased or objective and to give one an accurate view of the world.

For an easy-to-understand example of separate knowing in use, let's look at Jake. Jake is an eleven-year-old who relies on the techniques of traditional knowing to solve Lawrence Kohlberg's[5] now classic moral dilemma about a man named Heinz. Heinz cannot afford a drug that will save his wife's life because a druggist refuses to sell it to him at a reasonable price. In response to the question, "Should Heinz steal the drug?", Jake is confident from the start that Heinz should because "a human life is worth more than money." Jake has no difficulty accepting the terms of the dilemma that precisely delineate the dichotomous options: to steal or not to steal. As is typical of separate thinking, Jake does not contemplate the consequences of his decision. He also does not consider any other context-specific factors, such as what might happen to Heinz's wife if he gets caught and is put in jail (might she be worse off without his constant care?); whether to make a direct appeal to the druggist's sympathy; whether to nego-tiate a payment plan with the druggist; whether to raise or borrow the needed funds; whether to consult his wife, other family mem-bers, or friends about what to do, and so on. As Sara Ruddick notes, he also does not—nor is he meant to—challenge the con-text within which the dilemma is situated. He does not need to ask about the "socioeconomic system that sanctions a druggist's greed, a medical establishment that makes exaggerated claims for a drug's effectiveness, [or] a family system in which one individual husband is finally responsible for his spouse's health" (Ruddick 1989, 94). All of the above particularities would be considered irrelevant or inessential to understanding the problem when using the skills of separate thinking. Jake's abstract, decontextualized, either-or thinking helps him to simplify the complexities of the problem, to reduce it to its basic terms, and to deduce the general principle that life takes precedence over property.[6] For Jake, who is reasoning correctly according to the parameters of separate thinking and seeing only the formal aspects of the dilemma, Heinz, his wife, and the druggist are abstractions, not real people. He could as easily substitute the letters X, Y, and Z for their names and his solution would be the same. He uses deductive reasoning to solve what he sees as a problem in moral logic. As Jake puts it, it is "sort of like a math problem with humans" (Gilligan 1982, 26). He has seen the problem with traditional disciplinary eyes.

Instead of abstracting from the immediate context and standing at a distance to gain a deeper understanding, Nobel prize winner Barbara McClintock uses a type of connected thinking to get close to her object of inquiry, her corn plants (Belenky et al. 1986, 143–44). McClintock comments to her biographer, "I know every plant in the field. I know them intimately, and I find it a great plea-sure to know them" (Keller 1983, 198). "I actually felt as if . . . these were my friends" (Keller 1983, 117). Like separate knowing, pas-sionate connected knowing[7] (akin to that used by McClintock) is directed to achieving an objective vision, one that does not impose one's own personal meaning upon the world. However, unlike separate knowers, when connected knowers see with disciplinary eyes, they *use* the self as a tool of understanding, attempting to integrate both concrete and abstract, emotive and rational, subjective and objective knowing, giving equal status to both. But although both forms of knowing are valued equally, connected knowing, in contrast to traditional knowing, is rooted in everyday experience, intuitions, and feelings. Sara Ruddick, a feminist philosopher and peace scholar, whose thinking is noted by Belenky as an example of connected knowing, states, "Instead of developing arguments that could bring my feelings to heel, I allowed feeling to inform my most abstract thinking" (Belenky et. al. 1986, 143).

Connected knowers do not use just any type of feeling to enlighten their thinking. Since their goal is connection, not separation from the self and the object of study, they try to cultivate feelings that are empathic. In fact, the capacity for empathy that entails "opening up to receive another's experience" (Belenky et al. 1986, 122) stands at the core of the practice of connected disciplinary knowing. Connected knowers are "attached to the objects" they seek to understand; "they care about them" (1986, 124). A major way in which such connection and understanding is achieved is through attentive listening (as McClintock "listened to" her plants) and asking empathic questions of the object of study (as Amy does below). Contrary to a separate way of seeing that is "based upon impersonal procedures for establishing truth," with a connected view, "truth emerges through care" (1986, 102).

To understand how connected knowing works, let's look at how Amy reasons through the same dilemma as Jake. In reply to the question, "Should Heinz steal the drug?" Amy vacillates. She responds, "Well, I don't think so. I think there might be other ways besides stealing it, like if he could borrow the money or make a loan or something, but he really shouldn't steal the drug— but his wife shouldn't die either" (Gilligan 1982, 28).

Unlike Jake, she does not give an unqualified answer. She appears evasive and unsure of what to do. But, as Carol Gilligan explains, this is not because she doesn't value life more than property, rather, it is because she sees the problem differently than Jake. Jake sees it as a problem in moral logic (with only two possible solutions: to steal or not to steal); Amy, on the other hand, sees it as a failure of communication and as fracture in the web of human relationships. Amy considers not just the formal structure of the dilemma but the concrete details that could make a difference in its solution. Amy uses her "self" to imagine Heinz's real-world situation, his actual predicament. In evaluating the dilemma, she, in essence, asks the empathic questions, What are Heinz and his wife going through? How can their pain be lessened or eliminated? How can (further) harm be prevented? Since she cares about Heinz and his wife and the possible consequences that the theft might have on them, she looks for a different remedy. Amy believes that "if Heinz and the druggist had talked it out long enough, they could reach something besides stealing" (Gilligan 1982, 29). Amy's empathic approach takes her beyond the either-or thinking of Jake and allows her to consider other possibilities.

Before concluding this discussion, it is important to note that although the connected or emphatic method discussed here has been heard more frequently in the voice of women, it is hardly exclusive to women. John Nicholls, the late educational psychologist, believed that an empathic (or intentional) perspective is useful, not only for understanding another person or an object of study, but also for prediction of action and accomplishment, his domain of study in psychology (Nicholls 1989, 82–84). In the following passage he tells us that conventional disciplinary ways of seeing do not permit empathic modes of inquiry, and he notes that another psychologist besides himself uses this so-called taboo method of understanding. He asserts, "among academic psychologists, empathy has not been approved as a perspective for understanding people let alone rats. Yet John Garcia (1981) owns that 'I always use anthropomorphism and teleology to predict animal behavior because this works better than most learning theories. I could rationalize this heresy by pointing to our common neurosensory systems or to convergent evolutionary forces. But, in truth, I merely put myself in the animals' place'" (Nicholls 1989, 82–83).

We have now seen that, at least some of the time, disciplinary scholars use alternative techniques for understanding the world, techniques that to some extent conflict with dominant disciplinary approaches. But how do these different forms of disciplinary knowing matter to what students are learning in school, and what difference do they make to our ultimate goal of creating a culture of peace? The following examples help to illustrate some of the problems of traditional disciplinary thinking and suggest that connected disciplinary ways of knowing can help us overcome some of these disadvantages by focusing our understanding on the needs and plights of others.

PROBLEMS WITH TRADITIONAL DISCIPLINARY UNDERSTANDING

Noted Harvard psychologist Howard Gardner employs an example from the Gulf War of 1991, commonly referred to as "Desert Storm," to indicate how disciplinary understanding is applicable on an everyday basis, to show what an individual can do with her or his disciplinary understanding, and to demonstrate what an educated student should understand about various aspects of this war. Gardner seeks a traditional kind of disciplinary understanding:

> An individual with political or historical understanding of the region would be able to predict which kinds of outcomes were likely or unlikely to occur following the completion of the battle—including the unlikelihood of a permanent alteration of the *ante bellum* state of affairs. An individual with understanding of the principles of physics could indicate how to aim a Patriot missile so that it would intercept a Scud missile in flight; and to make some kind of prediction about how the resulting debris was likely to distribute itself upon the earth. Finally, an individual who understood the principles of economics could anticipate the effect on the United States economy (and on other economies) of an unanticipated large expenditure of money. It is probably fair to say that the highest degree of understanding was evinced with respect to the interception of Scud missiles; and it may not be coincidental that the necessary calculations were carried out by computers. (Gardner 1993, 188)

Gardner finds it distressing that "few adults in our society" possess the disciplinary knowledge that would allow them to understand the Gulf War in the ways he has indicated (1993, 189). He tells us that even individuals who have received their educations at "redoubtable institutions like MIT and John Hopkins" do not have this kind of understanding (1993, 188).

Notice that the concerns highlighted here regarding students' lack of understanding are related to technical issues within the disciplines of politics, history, physics, and economics. Gardner wants teachers to help students understand how their physics knowledge can be applied to the aiming of Patriot missiles and the distribution of resulting debris; he wants teachers to help students use their political and historical knowledge to predict the balance of power in the region; and he wants students to be able to use their knowledge of economics to understand the effect on the United States and other economies of the unexpected large-scale expense of the Gulf War. Nowhere in his example or in his article as a whole does he mention the moral considerations of embodied people. This is a troubling issue associated with the use of conventional disciplinary techniques of investigation and it can be a hindrance to full understanding.[8]

Although it cannot be debated that conventional disciplinary understanding is certainly better, even essential, for certain purposes—for example, programming a computer to aim a Patriot missile—of what use is this information in our daily lives in understanding the Gulf War? Why does the average citizen need to be able to understand how the principles of physics could be utilized to aim a Patriot missile or to predict how the resulting debris from the missile could distribute itself upon the earth? Most importantly, are the issues Gardner focuses on surrounding the Gulf War the most significant ones? Does such understanding, in this case, give us a better understanding of our world and help to make the world a more humane place?[9] If teachers discuss the Gulf War with their students, should they devote the bulk of their attention to the kinds of issues Gardner emphasizes or would doing so distract them from what many consider the most important issues? In other words, what are the consequences of seeing primarily with traditional disciplinary eyes?

Let me reiterate that I'm not arguing that traditional disciplinary understanding is never useful. Nor do I think that students should not learn it. But because of Gardner's treatment of the Gulf War as a technical disciplinary problem, problems surrounding the war are removed from the concrete world of human experience and concerns. Once such a disciplinary revision of experience is enacted, exigent human problems get translated into abstract, theoretical questions of politics, history, economics, military strategy, and physics. Using physics by itself, as a lens with which to view the war permits one to disregard the real Iraqi people whom "the resulting debris" would fall upon as well as overlook the psychological effects upon the U.S. soldiers aiming the missiles and fighting the war. And viewing it as a traditional history, political science, or economics problem allows one to neglect the effects on the real people who directly felt the pain and loss of the war.

Gardner never investigates questions about the purpose of the war; he never explores issues related to the "need" for this (or any other) war; he never examines the problems of violence and misery caused by a war. Gardner has framed a real-life issue involving human life and suffering solely in disciplinary terms; he has conceptualized the Gulf War as a classic disciplinary problem needing classic disciplinary solutions. But as with most social and human problems, the issues surrounding the Gulf War are not only technical disciplinary ones that can be solved by the application of correct disciplinary understanding and methodology. They also have pervasive normative, moral, and political dimensions that impact the lives of real people and that typically get overlooked with a standard disciplinary perspective. With such a disciplinary orientation, students are first taught how to carve up the question before them into different disciplinary areas and bring the critical thinking or argumentation from each discipline to bear on specialized aspects of the issue. Then, when their understanding is sufficiently advanced, they are taught how to unite different disciplinary perspectives. And while students are learning how to combine views from different disciplines, they are also learning to separate themselves from their fellow human beings. Connecting multiple disciplinary perspectives will be of little help in solving actual problems in the human and social realms since all these views approach or see a problem from a distance, separated from the cares of real people. Thus, instead of being the "best means available" for understanding and resolving problems that confront us in our lives, traditional disciplinary thinking stands in the way of full understanding in the human and social realms and in this way can even serve to reduce our humanity.[10]

It is important to realize that our understanding of human and social concerns is hindered, and moral issues, as they apply to the considerations of real people, are ignored precisely because this is characteristic of standard disciplinary analysis. It is not simply a failing of particular individuals to take these interests into account. In order to use these disciplinary tools of thinking, normative and moral aspects of a problem that matter in people's lives are typically disregarded as extraneous. The reason physicists qua physicists, historians qua historians, political scientists qua political scientists, economists qua economists, and other disciplinary efforts exclude these issues from their analysis is because they are considered irrelevant to investigation in their disciplines.[11] Now we can begin to see more clearly how limited understanding may result from excluding concrete moral concerns in the human and social realms.

Jane Roland Martin, whose work has been instrumental to my understanding of this issue, has examined the structure of traditional disciplinary thinking and raised questions about the purpose (and morality) of critical thinking in the disciplines (Martin 1988, 1992, 1994, 1996). As an example of the problems engendered by an exclusive reliance on separate or traditional disciplinary thinking, she relates a story told by Robert Coles. Martin reports,

> While sitting in the officer's dining room in a Mississippi air force base, he watched a crowd of blacks gathering on the beach . . . [who in] the early 1960s . . . were protesting segregation. But Coles knew that beach. And he said to himself, "Why do they bother? The water's too warm. There are no dunes. If it were Cape Cod, it would be a different matter, for that is gorgeous. But this beach is nothing." (Martin 1992, 163–64)

Martin feels that Coles' disciplinary analysis of the problem, which allowed him to distance himself from his subject matter and "from their hopes and fears," led him to the conclusion that the beach wasn't worth the effort of a demonstration because it wasn't aesthetically pleasing anyway. His disciplinary thinking authorized him to overlook the moral dimensions of the issue in relation to the human suffering caused by the segregation.[12] Martin asserts, "Transforming a real-life problem of racial segregation and oppression into a theoretical issue of aesthetics, he made it easy to solve. He also made it easy for himself to sit there in the air conditioned dining room and watch the action down below" (1992, 164). Although Coles doesn't cast the problem in exactly

the same terms as Martin, he agrees that his intellectual and emotional distance from the real people involved prevented him from
recognizing the moral significance of the issue.

Challenging the unquestioned superiority of conventional disciplinary understanding for solving human problems, Martin also
points to "public policy discussions on nuclear war where hawks
and doves alike transform a problem of the fate of life on earth
into questions of military technology and strategy about which
they exercise their considerable powers of critical thinking"
(1992, 164). She continues, "It is to be found also in discussions
of medical ethics where expert physicians and philosophers turn
real cases of birth and death that bring catastrophe into the lives
of family members into abstract questions of 'the patient's best
interest'" (1992, 164).

In a different but related context, Parker Palmer points to a case
from his own educational experience that can be seen as support
for Martin's view. He recounts how, when learning the history of
Nazi Germany he was taught "the statistics and the facts and the
theories behind the facts, but . . . at such objective arm's length . . .
that it never connected with the inwardness of my life. . . . All was
objectified, all was externalized" (Palmer 1997). As a consequence,
he felt that "somehow all of that murderousness had happened to
another species on another planet" (1997). Putting this in the
terms of my analysis, I would say that the disconnected methods of
traditional disciplinary learning required such distance and objecti-
fication from him. It is not astonishing that, as a result of this kind
of education, he failed to make connections with his own inner
emotional life and with the pain and suffering of real human beings.

It seems that not much has changed in certain quarters since
Parker Palmer had this experience. A young graduate student of
mine, not long out of high school, recently told me a similar story.
She stated, "I remember reading about the Holocaust in my history class in high school from the textbook. Yet it was not until [I
read] a book on someone's experience about the Holocaust . . .
that I actually began to sympathize with what happened and was
outraged. I remember reading about certain instances and having
to stop because my tears were clouding my vision." I would say
that her tears, or actually the emotions she was feeling, were per-
mitting her to connect with the real people who had undergone

such suffering. Through her tears, she thus developed a more complete vision and a deeper understanding of their experience.

It may be surprising to know that the emphasis on learning traditional disciplinary ways of thinking in school starts early. The following dialogue between a teacher and a kindergarten child named Danny is an illustration of this early learning process. Danny has brought a piece of lava to school to present to his classmates during sharing time.

> The teacher asks Danny, "Where did you get it?"
>
> Danny responds, "From my mom. My mom went to the volcano and got it."
>
> The teacher then inquires, "Is there anything you want to tell about it?"
>
> Danny replies, "I've always been, um, taking care of it . . . It's never fallen down and broken." (Wertsch 1991, 113)

Notice that Danny's remarks thus far are centered on the personal relation he has to the rock through his emotional connection to his mother.

> Next, the teacher shifts the focus and asks Danny, "Is it rough or smooth? . . . Is it heavy or light?" (Wertsch 1991, 114).

Deborah Tannen, a sociolinguist, who is concerned about the negative effects of valuing either-or analytical thinking more than relational modes, interprets the above student-teacher interaction in the following way. She comments,

> The teacher reframed the children's interest in the rock as informational. . . . She also suggested they look up *volcano* and *lava* in the dictionary. This is not to imply the teacher harmed the child . . . but the example shows the focus of education on formal rather than relational knowledge—information about the rock that has meaning out of context, rather than information tied to the context: Who got the rock for him? How did she get it? What is his relation to it? (Tannen 1998, 267)

Of course, Danny should learn to use standard forms of disciplinary thinking. But as his years in school accumulate, if there is an exclusive focus on conventional disciplinary tools, as is usually the case, Danny may also learn to become disconnected from his feelings and the feelings of others while he learns that emotions do not have a place in the disciplines. Sadly, in our patriarchal society, he may also learn to denigrate such concerns or come to view them as of secondary importance.

WHAT CAN TEACHERS DO? GUIDELINES FOR EDUCATIONAL PRACTICE

What can teachers do to overcome the imbalance given in education to traditional disciplinary approaches? How can teachers help students learn to see in a morally engaged way, in a way that generates a deeper, more holistic understanding of the world and its people? In other words, how can teachers help students learn to analyze problems with connected disciplinary tools of analysis?

Although I offer no definitive strategy to help with this process, I propose a set of closely related, overlapping guidelines for critical connected thinking. To assist students in putting these guidelines into practice in the analysis of a problem, I have, in addition, included some procedural questions that can be used to channel their thinking. Both the guidelines and questions are derived from the conception of connected knowing and my foregoing theoretical analysis. It is important to understand that my list is not exhaustive and that all of the questions will not necessarily be relevant to every inquiry.

To use connected disciplinary methods to both conduct our own investigations and to analyze the studies and projects of others, we must take into account:

• *What the subjects of our inquiry are telling us* (whether corn plants, as with McClintock; a poem; or human beings). This requires paying close attention to them and not imposing one's own predetermined interpretation(s).

Questions for attentive listening: What is this problem, topic, trying to say to me?

• *The real-life concerns, relationships, and concrete circumstances of those affected by our investigations.* This calls for heightened sensitivity to contextual details including the possible consequences of different approaches and solutions to a problem.

Context-dependent questions about consequences: What are the likely consequences of adopting a particular research perspective or of analyzing this problem/issue in this way? What outcome might result from this choice? Who is most/least affected by it?

How are they affected? What difference does it make? What is the possible effect on the web of relationships?

Questions for finely tuned awareness of additional contextual details: Whose experience or perspective is represented here? Whose is excluded? Why is it included/excluded? In whose interest is this study conducted, this project undertaken? For whose benefit? Who is speaking in this analysis/text/narrative? Whose voice is at the center? Toward what end is this research undertaken? For whose purpose? For whom is this a problem?

• *Concern for the needs and plights of others.* This entails culti-vating students' imaginations and feelings of care and empathy

Empathic questions to connect with others' plights: What is the other person (who I am researching) going through? What are you/they going through? How does the other feel about this? Are needs being met? Whose needs? Whose needs need to be addressed? Why are they suffering this predicament? How can the suffering be pre-vented, lessened, or eliminated?

Now let's look at how these guidelines can actually be applied in the classroom. Although this is not a detailed example exploring the range of possibilities for transforming the curriculum, following are concrete ideas for how the guidelines can be used to help students bring critical connected thinking skills to bear on issues and topics in the current school curriculum. These ideas demonstrate the potential of connected inquiry to facilitate deeper understanding.

Suppose students are studying rivers and/or water power in a science class.[13] One of the topics they encounter is dams. They learn that dams help to control the flow of water and are built for several reasons. Students typically investigate engineering ques-tions pertaining to the siting and construction of a dam. In some classes, they engage in experiential learning activities or "real-world" problem solving and actually construct their own dams, which helps them to see how certain scientific concepts work firsthand. In addition, students are sometimes asked to consider the negative consequences of diverting the flow of a river to build a dam and to weigh the positive and negative effects on people and animals in the path of this development. At times they also contemplate the impact on the land and the river itself. Even today's textbooks will briefly touch upon the economic, social, and environmental costs incurred from the building of a dam. Such discussion, when it occurs, is encouraging. However, since discussion of normative issues is usually given short shrift in the typical science classroom, since the emphasis is usually on learning standard disciplinary concepts and techniques, and since students spend a significant amount of time building a dam, the implied message that students receive is that the benefits of dam building generally outweigh the costs. Although this may be true in *some* circumstances, it is hardly universally true. Unless the discussion is given serious treatment and is of a certain type and depth, it will be far from adequate. It may miss crucial details and fail to uncover the full human meaning of the dam project, misleading students about the complexity of the issues involved.

What type of discussion is adequate if we want to teach students to develop a more complete understanding? How can the guidelines for connected thinking help us? It's no surprise to those who've read this far that discussion of the pluses and minuses of how, where, and whether to build a dam must not remain at an abstract level. The inquiry must not only examine the consequences of dam building in general; it must address specific situations and specific lives. Of course, students should understand the scientific concepts and principles involved in the issue of siting and constructing a dam, but they should also learn that much more is at stake.

If our goal is to encourage a deeper, holistic, morally engaged understanding, we should have students investigate the multifaceted aspects of problems as they occur in the real world. To consider the full context of human lives, we must help students situate their understanding in an ethic of care. Drawing on the guidelines for connected thinking, students must learn to ask such moral questions as: From whose perspective do the benefits outweigh the costs? In whose primary interest is the dam being built? What will lives be like as a result of the dam project? Who will suffer or gain the most? the least? Why? What will those individuals who are most adversely affected be forced to bear? What will they go through? How does it feel to be displaced, to have one's home lost to a dam? What kind of consequences will befall animals and plants in the path of the dam? What will the environmental impact be? Do all affected have a voice in deciding whether the dam should be built? Whose voice do we hear the loudest? Why? What will those building the dam experience? Unless we teach students to consider these kinds of questions, they're not truly exploring real-world problems and they aren't likely to develop full understanding.[14]

If students learn to look more closely, from the perspective of all those directly affected by an issue, they should get a different picture and a different solution to a problem might emerge. For example, when a group of engineers and environmentalists considered the full impact of, as well as the need for, the gigantic Three Gorges Dam on the upper Yangtze River in China, they proposed that several other options could solve the problems the dam was meant to solve without the concomitant disasters. Unfortunately, they have not prevailed and there will be much suffering caused by this project. Other contextual questions students should consider now arise: Who makes the decision to build a dam? Who has the power to make the decision? Why do some people have more power than others? What can we do to further democratic decision making?

These questions and those above can play an important role in facilitating an understanding that most real-world problems cannot be solved apart from human social life. However, unless students are directly affected by what they are studying, they may not always feel compassion toward the larger human community. An effective way to cultivate emotions of care and to enable students to feel what others are going through is to call on student imagination. Having students read stories or view documentary or fictionalized film accounts that pertain to the issues they are examining can help to accomplish this purpose.[15]

A cinematically beautiful movie that addresses some of the human and social problems surrounding dam siting and construction is The Emerald Forest, directed by John Boorman (1985). Although this film is not without certain normative difficulties of its own (another opportunity for student discussion and growth), it has many redeeming qualities, the most significant of which is that it enables students to imagine the concrete situations of others and to emotionally reach beyond their own immediate concerns. The Emerald Forest is loosely based on a true story. Its plot revolves around a U.S. engineer who has no qualms working on an enormous dam that will submerge part of the Amazon, until his teenage son (who has become fully integrated into an Amazonian Indian group that abducted him ten years earlier at his father's job site) needs his father's help protecting his home, which is now the rainforest.

Near the beginning of the movie, viewers sympathize with the engineer who has lost his son while just "doing his job," but eventually come to appreciate, with the engineer, the effects the dam has on the inhabitants of the forest. The film is another mechanism that can be used in the classroom to discuss the need to promote a socially and morally responsible science. When we do not treat moral discussion as tangential and as a distraction from the task of understanding disciplinary concepts and principles, we help students realize the importance of seeing in connected ways.

CONCLUSION

Although traditional disciplinary tools can have profound adverse consequences because of the intellectual and emotional distance demanded from them, my goal has not been to replace one correct disciplinary method with another; traditional disciplinary understanding does have its uses. But it also has serious limitations. Such understanding, by itself, is not always helpful in responding to questions that have a normative or moral dimension as most questions in real life do. By ignoring such considerations, traditional disciplinary argumentation and modes of thinking may be an obstruction to the solution of crucial human problems and may lead us into darkness. Furthermore, since traditional disciplinary understanding sanctions a distanced "ivory tower" view of the world, there is a danger that the kind of person we create who dons disciplinary lenses to experience the world may, at times, condone inaction in the face of injustice, as the earlier example of Robert Coles indicates.

When students learn disciplinary ways of thinking, they should not be limited to only one way of understanding the world, as is usually the case in most schools. Our goal is to make sure that students also learn to see the world with eyes that allow for a connected vision. To allay reservations about using connected modes of analysis, it might be helpful to remember that the disciplines are tools used to serve human interests and purposes. We must teach students to feel, not to excise feelings from their thinking. Instead of only developing the mind, we might also advance a model of understanding that supports the "opening of the mind and the heart to embrace the world" (Belenky et al. 1986, 141).

Nonetheless, thinking alone won't change the world, even "connected thinking." To change the world, we must act. We will be more motivated to act, as the passage from Julian Beck at the outset of this chapter states so movingly, "if we could really feel." For Nel Noddings, too, "human affect [is] at the heart of ethical-ity" (Noddings 1984, 3).

Instead of cutting us off from all feelings, as traditional disciplin-ary thinking requires, we must, as connected modes of knowing, rooted in an ethic of care demand, learn to elicit and connect with feelings of concern and empathy toward others while displacing feelings of indifference and hostility. Without feelings of compas-sion and care, students are unlikely to be motivated to overcome intolerance or apathy and inhumane behavior is not likely to be subverted. If we teach students how to see in a deeper, more holis-tic, morally engaged way, to "enlarge their circle of concern," as J. R. Martin (1992) expresses it, we have a better chance of helping them act to create a more peaceful, caring, partnership-oriented world. And "when we act, we will change the world." Connected thinking is one tool, although not the only one, that can help us accomplish this vital task.

NOTES

1. Advocates of the current "teaching for disciplinary understanding" movement in education would say—as their 1960s "structure of the disciplines" predecessors said—that this is more a goal than a reality. These critics claim that the subjects that students study in school are often only a resemblance of the disciplines, they are not the disci-plines themselves. Nonetheless, even if it is true that most students do not learn to fully think in disciplinary terms, the analytic thinking that students are taught to use in school is not radically different from the kind of abstract thinking employed in the traditional disciplines, as I will show. The push to standardize education through heavy reli-ance on standardized tests, which I oppose, is often seen as contrary to the movement to teach for disciplinary understanding, as it is at variance with a partnership approach to education.

2. For examples of early (and still current) work defining disciplinary understanding, see Bruner 1963; Hirst 1972; Peters 1967; Phenix 1964; Schwab 1964.

3. Accepting this view does not mean that there was some kind of intentional conspiracy on the part of dominant groups nor does it mean that women as individuals never participated in the construction of these knowledge forms. For arguments in support of this view, see, for example, Harding 1991; Harding and Hintikka 1983; Keller 1985; Martin 1988; Merchant 1980; Minnich 1990; Schiebinger 1989.

4. In the late 1970s, Mary Field Belenky, Blythe McVicker Clinchy, Nancy Rule Goldberger, and Jill Mattuck Tarule (1986) began a study of women's cognitive development that extended over several years. Based on in-depth interviews with 135 women of varying ages, life circumstances, and backgrounds, they discovered that women face special cognitive challenges as they try to negotiate their way through a male-dominated culture. Their major finding was that women know and view the world from epistemological perspectives that differ from dominant male views. Belenky and her colleagues refer succinctly to these perspectives as "women's ways of knowing," which is also the title of their book discussing this research.

5. Lawrence Kohlberg was a developmental psychologist who used moral dilemmas, such as the Heinz dilemma, to develop his well-known theory of moral development, which was subsequently criticized by Carol Gilligan (see Gilligan 1982; Kohlberg 1981).

6. Of course, Jake is right that life is worth more than property (his orientation can be called a "moral minimum"). However, he also misses crucial dimensions of the problem because of his either-or thinking. This limits the solutions he can envision and perhaps even distorts his understanding of the problem. As several feminists note, it is necessary to go beyond the "moral minimum" to achieve a full understanding and a caring perspective. In the next section, I explore in detail the consequences of limiting one's thinking to traditional disciplinary or separate thinking.

7. Passionate connected knowing is a highly developed form of connected knowing, also called "constructive knowing" by Belenky and colleagues. See Belenky et al. (1986), 141–44.

8. I will ask one critical question here, however. Why does Gardner believe that the highest degree of understanding was displayed by someone with an understanding of physics? Does he consider mathematical-scientific inquiry superior to problem solving in other domains? Does he place physics at the top of a hierarchy of disciplines? He never states his reasons for this assessment.

9. Gardner seems to think that disciplinary understanding, as he puts it, "could be useful around the world and might even help to bring

countries of the world and their peoples closer together" (Gardner 1991, 261). He feels so strongly about this that he advances a "single criterion for effective education—*an education that yields [disciplinary] understanding in students*" (1991, 145, emphasis in text). I argue that disciplinary understanding is not sufficient to accomplish these purposes and it should not be the primary goal of education. Education needs to encompass more holistic ends.

10. Gardner claims that "the ways of thinking—the disciplines—that have developed over the centuries represent our best approach to almost any topic" (Gardner 1999, 18). Of course, the ways of thinking he has in mind are traditional, "separate" modes of disciplinary thinking.

11. Even traditional philosophical and theological disciplinary approaches that address moral and ethical matters normally treat social and human concerns in an abstract manner. Utilitarianism, for example, calculates the greatest good for the greatest number, while Kantian deontology attempts to uniformly apply universal principles, derived from the categorical imperative, to all (presumably) "equivalent" situations. And, whereas neo-Aristotelian or "virtue ethics" is anchored in everyday affairs, it is guided by the behavior of moral exemplars who establish the criteria that every individual in the community should follow and be judged by, rather than being directed by, an ideal of caring, for instance, that comes to fruition in interaction with those affected by a situation and that warrants a differential response depending on each unique circumstance. Thus, moral agents, operating or seeing with conventional disciplinary eyes, do not even need to know the real people involved or much about them to arrive at a solution to a moral dilemma; their needs are irrelevant to the problem; they are not treated as unique and concrete individuals but as abstractions. As a matter of fact, if disciplinary thinking has been used correctly—in a disinterested, distanced manner—some moral philosophers believe that all moral "experts" should come to an equivalent solution, rendering a "correct" moral judgment, no matter what the context.

12. While I maintain that traditional disciplinary tools can have serious negative effects, I believe, with J. R. Martin, that we must also guard against too much closeness to one's object of study for one's area of inquiry can be developing bombs (Martin 1996, 592–93). The main issue for advocates of partnership and peace is not just closeness to one's subject matter, but closeness to the lives and concerns of real people, and I believe that connected disciplinary modes of analysis—because of their methodological use of emotions of care and connection—are more likely to promote this. Our goal in understanding should be to be close enough to see *and* feel the real-world concerns that affect embodied people.

13. For an example of how connected thinking is used in a current events and a mathematics class, see Apple and Beane 1995, 14–15. For an example of using connected thinking in an elementary mathematics class, see Putnam, Lampert, and Peterson 1990, 102–13. These authors don't use the term *connected thinking*, but they do, indeed, present examples of how to analyze problems in a connected way.

14. Students can bring connected thinking questions to bear on *real* real-world problems in their own communities. This approach can generate connections with students' lives outside school and motivate them to be more engaged in learning. Thus, rather than learning about dams in the abstract, since there are literally thousands of federal, state, local, and private dams all across the United States, students can investigate historical and contemporary issues surrounding actual dams in their own vicinities. They may be surprised to find that there are many social and environmental issues, regarding already-built dams, that still need to be addressed and that environmental organizations are currently working on.

15. Of course, as educators we don't want to manipulate students' emotions, but we do want to promote empathic feelings. As we help our students critically scrutinize real-world problems, we should also teach them to develop a critical sensibility with novels and cinema. Students can ask themselves, How am I affected by this presentation of the issues? Do my feelings lead to a distortion in a particular direction, especially in a direction that leads to hate or intolerance of an individual or group? Or are my feelings helping me to care and connect with the web of human relations? We should also help students understand the *importance* of developing care, concern, and compassion (the "three Cs" as Jane Roland Martin [1994]calls them) for the larger circle of concern.

REFERENCES

Apple, M. W., and J. A. Beane, eds. 1995. *Democratic Schools*. Alexandria, VA: Association for Supervision and Curriculum Development.

Belenky, M. F., B. M. Clinchy, N. R. Goldberger, and J. M. Tarule. 1986. *Women's Ways of Knowing: The Development of Self, Voice, and Mind.* New York: Basic Books.

Bleier, R. 1984. *Science and Gender: A Critique of Biology and Its Theories on Women.* New York: Pergamon Press.

Boorman, J., director. 1985. *The Emerald Forest.* Screenplay by R. Pallenberg, distributed by Metro Goldwyn-Mayer, USA.

Bruner, J. S. 1963. *The Process of Education.* New York: Vintage Books.

Collins, P. H. 1991. *Black Feminist Thought.* New York: Routledge.

Dworkin, A. 1974. *Woman Hating.* New York: E. P. Dutton.

Gardner, H. 1991. *The Unschooled Mind: How Children Think and How Schools Should Teach.* New York: Basic Books.

———. 1993. *Multiple Intelligences: The Theory in Practice.* New York: Basic Books.

———. 1999. *The Disciplined Mind: What All Students Should Understand.* New York: Simon & Schuster.

Gardner, H., and V. Boix-Mansilla. 1994. "Teaching for Understanding in the Disciplines and Beyond." *Teachers College Record* 96 (2): 198–218.

Gilligan, C. 1982. *In a Different Voice.* Cambridge, MA: Harvard University Press.

Harding, S. 1991. *Whose Science? Whose Knowledge? Thinking from Women's Lives.* Ithaca, NY: Cornell University Press.

Harding, S., and M. B. Hintikka, eds. 1983. *Discovering Reality: Feminist Perspectives on Epistemology, Metaphysics, Methodology, and Philosophy of Science.* Dordrecht, Holland: Reidel.

Hirst, P. H. 1972. "Liberal Education and the Nature of Knowledge." In *Education and Reason,* edited by R. F. Dearden, P. H. Hirst, and R. S. Peters, 1–24. London: Routledge, & Kegan Paul.

Hubbard, R. 1990. *The Politics of Women's Biology.* New Brunswick, NJ: Rutgers University Press.

Keller, E. F. 1983. *A Feeling for the Organism: The Life and Work of Barbara McClintock.* San Francisco: W. H. Freeman.

———. 1985. *Reflections on Gender and Science.* New Haven, CT: Yale University Press.

Kohlberg, L. 1981. *Essays on Moral Development.* Vol. 1. New York: Harper & Row.

Martin, J. R. 1988. "Science in a Different Style." *American Philosophical Quarterly* 25 (2): 129–40.

———. 1992. "Critical Thinking for a Humane World." In *The Generalizability of Critical Thinking,* edited by S. P. Norris, 163–80. New York: Teachers College Press.

———. 1994. *Changing the Educational Landscape: Philosophy, Women and Curriculum.* New York: Routledge.

———. 1996. "Aerial Distance, Esotericism, and Other Closely Related Traps." *Signs* 21 (3): 585–614.

Merchant, C. 1980. *The Death of Nature: Women, Ecology and the Scientific Revolution.* San Francisco: Harper & Row.

Minnich, E. K. 1990. *Transforming Knowledge*. Philadelphia, PA: Temple University Press.

Nicholls, J. G. 1989. *The Competitive Ethos and Democratic Education*. Cambridge, MA: Harvard University Press.

Noddings, N. 1984. *Caring: A Feminine Approach to Ethics and Moral Education*. Berkeley and Los Angeles: University of California Press.

Palmer, P. 1997. The Grace of Great Things: Reclaiming the Sacred in Knowing, Teaching, and Learning. Keynote address presented at the Spirituality in Education conference, Naropa Institute May 30–June 3. http://csf.colorado.edu/sine/transcripts/palmer.html. File: Full Transcript (accessed 4/02/02).

Peters, R. S., ed. 1967. *The Concept of Education*. London: Routledge & Kegan Paul.

Phenix, P. 1964. *Realms of Meaning*. New York: McGraw-Hill.

Putnam, R. T., M. Lampert, and P. L. Peterson. 1990. "Alternative Perspectives on Knowing Mathematics in Elementary Schools." In *Review of Research in Education*, edited by C. Cazden, vol. 16, 57–150. Washington, DC: American Educational Research Association.

Rosser, S. 1994. *Women's Health: Missing from U.S. Medicine*. Bloomington, IN: Indiana University Press.

Ruddick, S. 1989. *Maternal Thinking: Toward a Politics of Peace*. Boston: Beacon Press.

Schiebinger, L. 1989. *The Mind Has No Sex? Women in the Origins of Modern Science*. Cambridge, MA: Harvard University Press.

Schwab, J. J. 1964. "Structure of the Disciplines: Meanings and Significances." In *The Structure of Knowledge and the Curriculum*, edited by G. W. Ford and L. Pagano, 6–30. Chicago: Rand McNally.

Stanfield, J. H. 1985. "The Ethnocentric Basis of Social Science Knowledge Production." In *Review of Research in Education*, edited by E. W. Gordon, 12, 396–413. Washington, DC: American Educational Research Association.

Tannen, D. 1998. *The Argument Culture: Changing the Way We Argue and Debate*. London: Virago.

Wertsch, J. V. 1991. *Voices of the Mind: A Sociocultural Approach to Mediated Action*. Cambridge, MA: Harvard University Press.

DANDELIONS AND DEADLINES
The Preservation of Childhood
as a Temporal Location

CHIP WOOD

"Teach Peace" says the now-familiar bumper sticker, but the speed of technology, the strain on our schedules, and the ever-increasing pace of our lives constantly compromises our ability as teachers to remain true to this slogan. Often, despite our best intentions, we model for our students and colleagues hurry, anxiety, and worry.

"How are you?" someone asks, and, without thinking, we answer, "Busy!"

"Hurry up, children," we say, "we have to stop now, it's time to switch for math. We'll finish this when you come back." But it gets increasingly harder to do.

The space between our work, our families, the needs of our friends, and our service to the broader community seems increasingly compressed. Rather than teaching peace, we may be doing the opposite. The spiritual writer Thomas Merton spoke of this paradox nearly forty years ago when he wrote of the tension between the "rush and pressure of modern life" and our "inner capacity for peace" (Merton 1966, 93).

"Educating for a culture of peace" requires that we examine and confront the issue of time in our lives and in the lives of the students we seek to teach. The time and rhythm of the life we seek to care for is not fixed, but determined by our experience of it. Even children's experience of time, which has been understood as unfolding in a gradual developmental pattern, is now being attacked on every side by demands on that time that threaten or violate healthy patterns of social, cognitive, and spiritual growth. Caring for life as caretakers of the educational environment requires us to pay special attention to the temporal environment of the young.

At the turn of the twentieth century, one of the great pioneers in child development, Arnold Gesell, wrote: "The best measure of the civilization of any people is the degree of thoughtful reverence paid to the child," (Gessell and Gesell 1912, viii). The Greek root for the word *school* is *scholē*, which is literally translated as *leisure.* Teachers who seek to dedicate themselves and their classrooms to a pace that is right for children, a pace that encourages investigation, contemplation, completion, and community, must help parents and policymakers understand that learning and development take time. Unfortunately, policymakers are deciding for the teachers that increasing amounts of time are to be used to test what children are learning. The theory is that tests will show us what children do not know and we can address these areas more efficiently and effectively by, essentially, teaching to the test. However, the more time spent on testing and preparing to test, the less time there is for real teaching.

A good example of pressure to teach to the test appeared recently in our local paper. Reporters highlighted the poor performance of high schoolers on new state exams based on new standards. In another article on the very same day, teachers and administrators at the local high school indicated they were proposing dropping "block scheduling" (longer class periods that allow the exploration of curriculum content in more depth) because they would not be able to adequately cover the breadth of the material that would be on the test. The change was driven by the need to perform well on the test, taken at the expense of in-depth learning.

Lost in this accountability approach is any sense of balance about the value of what we are testing. Elliot Eisner once remarked that "we measure what we most value" (Eisner 1988). By emphasizing accountability, the highest value is placed on what an individual child can "bubble in" on a test form. What matters most is your individual achievement and rank among your peers, not who you are. Helping a friend learn the answer to a question, teaching someone else how to solve an equation, learning by watching someone else paint a picture—these abilities carry no market value. They are referred to as "fluff" in the educational jargon;

they are nice if we have time for them, but clearly not essential. The tests do measure individual academic progress, but they are purely objective tests; they provide no measure and indicate no value for social or ethical knowledge. We choose not to measure social growth. There is no test for kindness, no assessment for the development of a sense of right and wrong.

We often talk about "the best and the brightest." But the brightest, those who excel on standardized tests of academics, are not always the best if viewed from an ethical perspective. High achievers ran the savings and loan industry into their own pockets, poured PCBs into rivers until they became sewers of death, passed weapons technology around the globe in their own self-interest, and destroyed the rain forest.

What will be the outcome if we continue with so much emphasis on standardized tests? Karl Hertz, president of the American Association of School Administrators, wonders:

> What if we found that the great measure of American worth, namely our sense of goodness, was lost in the regimen that was demanded to achieve the easily measurable success of an efficiently scored test? Wouldn't it be strange if we got the highest test scores and then found that our employers were less pleased with their employees than they were in 1998? What if they were then saying that the people in their businesses were quite literate, but unimaginative, poor at innovating, and unlikely to solve problems? (1998, 44)

When standardized tests become an end unto themselves, the value of investigation, creativity, and positive social interaction is diminished.

PLAY

"What's recess?" asked five-year-old Toya Gray, interviewed for an article by *The New York Times*.

The city of Atlanta, according to the *Times*, has "eliminated recess in the elementary schools as a waste of time that would be better spent on academics." The policymakers in Atlanta have moved forward with their plan, even though some parents and educators are duly concerned. Olga Jarrett, professor of child development at Georgia State University, asks, "When do kids learn to interact with kids? We have so many latchkey kids who go home and lock the door until their parents get home. Now if they can't mingle with other kids at school or at home, how are they going to resolve conflict with their peers?" (Johnson 1998, A1).

In the professional development model I helped to develop, known as The Responsive Classroom® approach, we teach that it is only through practice that social skills can be learned. Just as we expect the budding pianist to practice daily, just as we sit our children down to practice the spelling list for the week on Thursday night before the Friday test, we must give children many regular opportunities to practice their social skills before they have to use them in life-and-death situations. School is the one place in contemporary American society where these skills can be practiced on a daily basis. Without significant practice, children can no more learn social skills or develop ethical character than they can learn to spell or learn how to play the piano. This practice requires time and patient tending. Recess is one of the most significant places where this can be learned both through careful modeling and monitoring by adults, as well as through children's own spontaneous play.

ATTENTION

In 1995 there were two million children estimated to show behavioral symptoms labeled ADD or ADHD.[1] This represented about 5 percent of the school-age population, according to Russell A. Barkley in his groundbreaking book *Taking Charge of ADHD* (1995, 3, 80). Most of these children were boys and most children who were formally diagnosed were being treated with a stimulant drug, Ritalin. Recent figures show that 80 to 90 percent of Ritalin produced is used in the United States, and that the number of children diagnosed with ADD who are being treated with Ritalin rose fivefold between 1989 and 1998. If the numbers continue to increase at the same rate, fifteen percent (eight million) of all children in our country will be on Ritalin within the next few years (DeGrandpre 1999, 18).

There have always been children whose attention spans and activity levels don't fit traditional classrooms. When I started teaching thirty years ago, these children were termed *hyperactive*. When treatment with Ritalin was first initiated, it was used in conjunction with behavioral programs. Today, in our fast-paced, quick-fix culture, many children whose behavior indicates some trouble with attention and impulse control are simply prescribed Ritalin without any thought of changing the expectations or schedules of their environment. We wish, hope, and expect a drug to fix what's wrong without looking at other factors that affect the problem.

In *Ritalin Nation: Rapid-Fire Culture and the Transformation of Human Consciousness*, psychologist Richard DeGrandpre (1999) argues that ADHD has more to do with changes in time expectations in our society than better diagnosis of a physiological problem. I see children who exhibit ADHD behaviors as suffering from temporal trauma. Sadly, they are serving as canaries in the cage of time, especially in our schools, where their failure to thrive should tell us something about their environment.

School schedules speed up year after year, putting more and more pressure on children to manage a world filled with more transitions, extended curricula, less predictability, and less time to accomplish more. It's tough on all children, but for these so-called canaries who have a heightened sensitivity to time pressures, it's impossible. Our society and schools are faced with two possibilities. One is medicating more and more children in an effort to decrease their sensitivity to our ever faster, less regulated pace of life and education. Another is making changes in the structure and pace of school life to reduce temporal trauma for all of our children.

WAREHOUSING

The occupational demands on the time of adults over the past forty years has resulted in parents being increasingly absent from their children's lives. Fear for children's safety and the inability to be with children before and after school has compelled parents to find surrogate caretakers or care programs. Children come to school for breakfast and go home as late as six in the evening following after-school programs. They average ninety minutes more a week at school than they did in 1981, according to a University of Michigan report (Vobejda 1998). Their free time *after* going to school has diminished as well, from 40 percent in 1981 to 25 percent today, according to the researchers. Children's time is programmed in formal activities supervised by coaches and instructors. Gone is the spontaneous neighborhood association, free play, and fantasy play in sandlots or open fields. In structured programs, all the rules are predetermined. Much of children's fantasy world is presented to them in video games, computer simulations, and cartoons. Children end up in one-way conversations with video screens—the screens doing the talking.

We know that whatever time parents do have with their children is precious and essential to their development, learning, and ethical judgement. Several studies of reading achievement have documented the importance of parents' reading to children at home. Recent studies are also noting that parents' conversation with children contributes to the development of reading skills (Snow, Burns, and Griffin 1998, 1–16). When talking with their children, parents are also likely to provide messages of morality— the cultural transmission of right and wrong. The screens carry so-called viruses of violence and target younger and younger audiences as product consumers.

SAFETY

In too many classrooms, students don't feel safe enough to share an opinion, risk a guess, formulate a hypothesis, speak individually to the teacher, befriend an unpopular classmate, or cross racial or gender lines when choosing classmates for academic project partners. Ridicule, peer pressure, teasing, bullying, exclusion, and ostracism are familiar experiences for many students.

Increased neglect and widespread domestic violence are powerful influences on the young and affect their behavior. Violence and neglect, it can be argued, are consequences of a society giving insufficient time and attention to the moral values found in faith traditions and the law. Even in school, the busyness of teachers and other caretakers often means they can be too preoccupied with the demands of curriculum and testing to notice what is going on socially or to take the time to deal with it. At about third grade, when boys and girls begin to segregate along gender lines, adult attention or inattention to children's social exchanges is key to ethical growth. Boys begin their taunting, crude dirty jokes, pinching, touching, punching, or worse. Girls move into cycles of meanness and exclusion, developing cliques that injure with petty gossip. This preadolescent and adolescent behavior is the proving ground for later adult functioning. Children test the limits to see where the limits are. When there isn't enough time given to enforce societal norms and to intentionally teach children what they are, succeeding generations are in grave danger.

TIME

Time is the major resource at the disposal of educators, and the most significant variable for the preservation of childhood in the school environment.

Children's first experience of time, of course, comes long before they enter school. Their understanding of time expands through their relationships with family and others around them as they grow. By age two, they are increasingly aware of time constraints and show their disdain for them with the emphatic "NO," so characteristic of the so-called terrible twos. Dawdling is a way to try to control time, as is fantasy play. "Hurry" is an unpleasant concept to toddlers because it has little concrete meaning in their overwhelming connection to the present moment. Think of the moments you have seen preschoolers absorbed in a puddle or blowing a dandelion.

Once in school, we teach children to pay attention to time cognitively by teaching them about hours and minutes, usually between kindergarten and second grade. But learning by rote that ten o'clock comes sixty minutes after nine o'clock does not necessarily provide the six- or seven-year-old with the knowledge of time she needs to navigate her world successfully.

As children grow, they begin to develop an understanding of present, past, and future—of what is called "diachronic thinking." *Diachronic* refers to children's developing ability to show their understanding of transformations over time, such as the growth of living things and changes in the weather. Children utilizing a diachronic approach in their thinking exhibit "a type of attitude or tendency of thought which consists of the spontaneous comparison of a current situation with its past and future states" (Montangero 1996, 80). This "tendency of thought," of course, develops over time.

By eight or nine years of age, children have a better sense of duration and comparative durations because they are now able to *conserve* concepts, holding more than one idea in their head at the same time. They can conceive of reforestation without human intervention and struggle with classic math problems such as, "If a train leaves the station on track one at 8:00 traveling at 40 mph and another train leaves at 8:30 on track two at 80 mph, what time will each train arrive at the same destination forty miles away?"

At eleven or twelve years of age, children's diachronic thinking and approaches to problem solving see a cognitive leap. This coincides with growth in other cognitive processes—such as more abstract reasoning, even about concrete problems—but we do not know exactly why. All this change seems to be the cumulative growth of cognition. Children can now see changes over time as successive states within an evolutionary process—such as growth of trees, thawing of ice, and the evolution of knowledge.

Children move from a quantitative understanding of changes over time to a qualitative one, a difference that allows understanding of not just *what* happened, but *when* and *why*. Mastering all the content standards requires diachronic thinking, not just core knowledge of words and concepts. The best use of time in school is to have the content of the curriculum more closely match the child's ability to struggle with age-appropriate concepts that help make meaning out of the content. This means that children need increasing amounts of time, not less, to plan out their learning strategies, to understand what is being asked of them. This means that children need time to work together in pairs and small groups, coming to understand different points of view about how a math problem might be solved, how a classmate thinks about a character in a book, how the teacher knows so much about science. They especially need time to reflect upon their mistakes, the very process of their learning. They need time for revision, through which they learn persistence when given the time to endure. For this to happen, educators must be willing to provide the time in school schedules and room in the curriculum to teach with greater depth, not greater breadth. Covering the curriculum can end up hiding truth under a blanket of facts.

In The Responsive Classroom® approach, mentioned earlier, attention is given to restructuring time. "Markers," described below, help adjust and regulate the experience of school to make it both more generally predictable and richer in content and context.

- *The first six weeks of school* provides ample time for introduction of expectations on the social and academic level, and content instruction is brought up to speed gradually (Denton and Kriete 2000).

- *Morning meeting* provides a structure at the beginning of the day during which children greet each other, share academic and social news, learn audience skills, and engage in literacy events. Morning meeting provides a living metaphor for the expectations for the rest of the school day (Kriete 1999).

- *Rules and logical consequences* are built on highly proactive strategies that accentuate the goals teachers and students have for learning and the means that will be needed to accomplish these goals, as opposed to setting up lists of "don'ts" that are designed to stop inappropriate behavior. In this discipline structure children are given the time to think about their behavior, to develop new strategies for problems they encounter, and to learn cooperative problem-solving techniques for the classroom.

- *Guided discovery* and *academic choice* also provide opportunities for students to engage in decision making around academic content and the use of materials, equipment, and supplies they will need in order to explore and represent their learning of that content. Such in-depth explorations require time structures in the daily schedule that can accommodate such practical activity.

Teachers who learn to use these and other structures and strategies will come to teach the key underlying skills of cooperation, assertion, responsibility, empathy, and self-control as cornerstones to academic and social success. Teaching at a pace that allows children to assimilate these skills through elementary and middle school requires a schedule that honors the need for careful work and thoughtful reflection throughout the school day.

DEADLINES

We are clearly asking too much. We are going too fast. We need to remember that children do not experience or understand time in the same way adults do. It is our job as teachers, administrators, and educational policy-makers to think carefully about how we expect children to negotiate the time of school itself. We need to assess the proper duration of instruction at different ages and the right amounts of outdoor time and quiet time. We need to decide how much time testing learning deserves in children's educational experience at different ages. We need to consider what are reasonable times for transitions, the proper balance of time for singing and playing as well as reading and writing, and how much time children need for silence.

I deeply believe that our schools can be better, our classrooms more purposeful, more disciplined, more generative. We can make the schoolhouse a joyful community of learning, a workplace of deep intellectual exploration and broad creative energy, a trustworthy place for social and emotional support.

With such change, children would have time in school to consider and reflect on what they were learning and time to care about and contribute to each other and their school. They would have time to ponder where their lives were headed. School would be a learning community, not a fact factory with only enough time to worry about the next test or homework deadline.

Peace is a state of time. Here is how one preadolescent described it:

Of Sleep and Elementary School
What happened to my unicorns?
They used to dance in my dreams
and prance along the borders of my page.

They held
the web
of hope
that I would call
my life
and my tears would collect on it
like dew drops and now
I am somewhere between
balancing and
falling
with no unicorns to keep me up.
                              —*Fleur Beckwith*

To educate for a culture of peace in our time will require us to slow down and attend to the children in their own good time.

NOTE

1. The behavior referred to here was called *hyperactivity* in the medical profession prior to 1989. Between 1989 and 1994, it was referred to as ADD. Currently it is defined as ADHD in the *Diagnostic and Statistical Manual of Mental Disorders* (see DeGrandpre 1999).

REFERENCES

Barkley, R. A. 1995. *Taking Charge of ADHD*. New York: Guilford Press.

DeGrandpre, R. 1999. *Ritalin Nation: Rapid-Fire Culture and the Transformation of Human Consciousness*. New York: W. W. Norton.

Denton, P., and R. Kriete. 2000. *The First Six Weeks of School*. Greenfield, MA: Northeast Foundation for Children.

Eisner, E. 1988. Keynote address, Conference on Developmental Education, Oakland, CA, March 23.

Gesell, A., and B. Gesell. 1912. *The Normal Child and Primary Education*. New York: Ginn and Company.

Hertz, K. V. 1998. "What If We Had the Highest Test Scores?" *Education Week* (May 13):44.

Johnson, D. 1998. "Many Schools Putting an End to Child's Play." *New York Times*, April 7, 1998.

Kriete, R. 1999. *The Morning Meeting Book*. Greenfield, MA: Northeast Foundation for Children.

Merton, T. 1966. *Conjectures of a Guilty Bystander*. Garden City, NY: Doubleday.

Montangero, J. 1996. *Understanding Changes in Time*. Bristol, PA: Taylor and Francis.

Snow, C. E., S. M. Burns, and P. Griffin, eds. 1998. *Preventing Reading Difficulties in Young Children*. Washington, DC: National Academy Press.

Vobejda, B. 1998. "Study Finds Children Reducing Time Spent at TV, Eating." *Washington Post*, December 2, 1998.

MUSIC
A Culture of Peace
RAFFI

How can music help foster caring relationships? Let's start at the beginning, with the basics, with what we know. Caring for life starts with families that care for and look after their children. Human cultures are made up of families; and we know that music plays a prominent role in every culture. The vast majority of people love their children, sing to them and with them, and enjoy the richness that music brings to life.

Look closely and you'll find that we live in a vibrational world, that we humans share the fundamental rhythms of our living planet with all of life. And caring for life means feeling part of and responding to this living world. In Mother Earth's playground, the sound of thunder or a woodpecker's call share the same vibrational principle as the light refractions that give the colors of a rainbow. So the music of the world is very much a part of us. From the day we are born, we are bathed in light and sound; some of this is within our perceptual field and much of it beyond.

A growing body of evidence suggests that our very capacity to perceive and distinguish between perceptions depends on not either-or but *both* the nature and nurture we receive. In other words, it's both heredity *and* social environment that shape our capacity to learn and, indeed, our very capacities as choice-making, imaginative, and creative beings.

This *response* ability, this capacity to choose, has everything to do with our ability to find peace within, from where we may exude that state outward. Peace is not an abstract idea; it is something to be cultivated from the youngest years, learned as a way of being—an experience of a largesse, of capacity. Being firmly grounded in the loving nature of our being, knowing our lovability and that very trait in others is a huge gift. Many in our culture

171

don't have it, and spend years and huge sums of money learning to love themselves.

How we listen to others, how we hear each other, how we listen to our own feelings, these are key early lessons in the musical life of peacemaking. Our own being is where we practice this art—whether engaged with others in dynamic harmony, or sorting through discord and conflict by which to learn and grow, to heal and regroup, to resolve anew.

RHYTHMS

Music is the inborn cry of the highly relational, highly expressive human species. A fundamental understanding and experience of music as a way of life, as a dance with life, is a key learning in the physiology of love and connection. The more connected we feel to creation and the more we sense our belonging, the less likely we are to despair and lash out, the more likely we are to find peace within. That's why cultivating musical expression and appreciation is a key part of education for a culture of peace.

From the first sound of heartbeat in the womb, we feel the pulse of life. Before we are able to see or move about, we are drawn to the voices of our caregivers, whose sounds we quickly remember. Such is the primacy of vibration in our sensory world. And we are kin to this life of vibration, the patterning wave of creation.

The cries of birther and birthed, the lullabies, the little song-rhymes of first weeks and months, birthday songs, and toddler tunes all help welcome a newborn to infancy and growth. Unless stunted through neglect or suppressed, singing is a way of being that can stay with us all our lives. Singing is the human signature, it comes naturally, often without thinking—a whole brain language, universal to all cultures. From tribal drum to folk dance to orchestra, music is a language of the human spirit and aspiration. It embroiders our lives from beginning to end.

Think of the sound of children at play, their spontaneous chants and melodies. For the very young, music is the welcome ring of belonging. Mother father, sister brother, family and community join in song. We know that in the first years of life language acquisition stimulates brain development. The same is true of music. Funny rhymes, pots and pans, favorite songs, flutes and gongs make the child's world a stage, expanding knowledge with mirth and whimsy.

In the impressionable time of the very young, in their dream-world of daring and discovery, every note and gesture of a little child's perceptions finds a reply in his or her surroundings. Whatever the reply—silence, a nod of the head, a smile, a reprimand, or encouragement—it shapes the possibility pool from which a child imagines life's contours and his or her place in the world.

Introduced early to the moon and stars, children can know the mathematical universe right from the start. They can learn that the measured cycles of existence—days, weeks, and months—are shared with a silvery moon that plays hide-and-seek with us. And what child doesn't know the sun? It's the most recurring image in children's art. Consider life as a musical merry-go-round, a cycling turn through rhythm and time. Celestial bodies dance with us as they make their way through the cosmos. The moon's pull on tides connects the continents and guides seafarers; it affects child's play on a sandy beach.

And songs, in their poetic structure, in their rhythm, and rhyme, meter, and cadence, offer a natural way to learn about the mathematical patterns that make up our world. Like a good children's story, a good song will have enough repetition (in the chorus) and enough novelty and adaptability to engage young listeners in a number of ways. The repeating chorus becomes a familiar assurance that they look forward to, a chance to "sing it again." The predictive process strokes memory and self-esteem, and when the chorus is shared in group singing it becomes a comfort for all to return to.

HEART SONG

Not having children of my own, I knew nothing about children when I started singing with them. From my wife, who taught kindergarten, and our primary teacher friends I learned that young children are not little adults, but whole people who deserve special consideration. And throughout my career, this became the core value of my work: respect for the child as a whole person.

And this compassionate view of the child defined every decision in my music making—in writing songs, choosing repertoire, adapting lyrics, and also in the playful tone of respect for my young audience.

From the start, my songs were not out to preach or even teach. There was no didactic agenda here, but rather a desire to share the joy of singing. A variety of song styles and rhythms expressed various moods from silly all the way to pensive. And in my playful way with the songs, I was without fully knowing it engaging the world of play that children inhabit, meeting them where they live. And here and there, I'd change a lyric just for fun, and sometimes for gender balance—for example, in "Baa Baa Black Sheep," "one for the little girl who lives down the lane."

There was a high degree of conscious choice applied to song selection and the imagery presented within each song. My musical colleagues and I took care to avoid imagery with gender stereotypes, violence, and humor at someone's expense. These choices reflected the values of caring and compassion—of joyful living. We wanted to celebrate life as joyful discovery, offering songs with which children could explore both the world around them and also the inner world of feelings and emotions. And songs that connected the listener to other children, and to the greater family of life on our "big beautiful planet."

"Baby Beluga" is a good example of a playful song designed to elicit wonder and caring about a magnificent sea creature. Though the beluga that inspired the song was one I met in an aquarium, in the song she swims wild and free. I knew that the positive image of a baby whale would be a far better offering to young children than a save-the-whales lament. Our young need life-affirming imagery that is awe-inspiring and that reflects the beauty and mystery of the natural world.

In my *Baby Beluga* album, the song "All I Really Need" was inspired by the UN's Declarations of the Rights of the Child. I wrote it in a way that would be true for every child, regardless of race, religion, or socioeconomic standing. In a way, I saw it as a song that protested consumer culture, focusing on the basic necessities for all growing children:

All I really need is a song in my heart, food in my belly, and love in my family.

And I need some clean water for drinking, and I need some clean
    air for breathing;
So that I can grow up strong, and take my place where I belong.

"Thanks a Lot," a song of thanksgiving and contentment, sings
praises of nature's gifts and of our inner and outer blessings.

Thanks a lot, thanks for the wonder in me; thanks a lot, thanks for
    the way I feel.
Thanks for the animals, thanks for the land, thanks for the people
    everywhere.
Thanks a lot, thanks for all I've got; thanks for all I've got.

HARMONY

Every child is a marvelous and unique unfolding of human potential. Paradoxically, that uniqueness is what we all have in common. No two faces quite the same, no voice exactly the same as
another. And in all cultures, young children have the same developmental needs, the same irreducible needs for respectful love,
nutritious food, and shelter. In this we have a unifying principle
that resounds at the heart of partnership education for peace.

Knowing what traits we have in common with people of different cultures, we are less likely to fear our differences and more
able to celebrate them. My song "Like Me and You" features the
names and countries of children from all continents, and its chorus celebrates the unity of this diversity:

And each one is much like another / A child of a mother and a
father / A very special son or daughter / A lot like me and you

In school assemblies, children dressed in colorful clothes and carrying flags of various countries have beautifully illustrated the
theme of this song.

In 1990, in response to the global environmental crisis, I recorded
Evergreen Everblue, an ecology album for older children and
adults. Songs like "Our Dear Dear Mother" and "One Light, One
Sun" pay tribute to the planet that gives us life, and to the splen-
dors that are for the whole human family to share, just as the sun
shines its blessings for all of us. *Evergreen Everblue*'s songs are now

used for environmental education in classrooms all across Canada and the U.S.

Sadly, since the 1992 Earth Summit in Rio, Brazil, despite some advances the overall state of our planetary systems has deteriorated; restoration efforts have fallen behind, and our biosphere now contains toxic chemicals that are also prevalent in our blood, flesh, and breast milk. This is not something easily addressed, let alone in song. And yet young children are the ones most vulnerable to the excesses of our polluted world, just as they are to the prevalence of domestic violence and corporate exploitation.

Responding to the current world—where children face unprecedented social, cultural, and environmental threats—I have, in recent years, promoted the integrative vision of a child-honoring society, one whose love for its children is evident in every aspect of its design and organization. (Such a society, as Riane and I have often noted, would very much be a partnership society!) The spirit of this vision is expressed in A Covenant for Honoring Children (unpublished paper), which sees our young as "the embodiment of life, liberty and happiness . . . original blessings, here to learn their own song."

To express "child-honoring" musically, I have written motivational songs to stir policymakers and caregivers to a renewed look at those in their care. "It Takes a Village," "Turn This World Around," and "Salaam Shalom, Side by Side" are three such songs.

Impressive evidence that early years' experience shapes a lifetime of behavior spurred me to write a song that not only draws attention to the early years but also states clearly that the work of raising children belongs to the whole community. No phrase or saying could have captured that point better than the African proverb "it takes a village to raise a child," from which the song got its name.

> . . . not just parents' love, not just love of the family . . .
> not just teachers who care, not just the care of doctors . . .
> how about the love of the farmers, how about the business people /
> how about the people who pass the law . . .

Nelson Mandela, certainly one of the twentieth century's true heroes, inspired the song "Turn This World Around" with his words at the launch of a Say Yes for Children campaign that he and child's rights champion Graca Machel led (in concert with UNICEF). Referring to the worldwide prevalence of preventable diseases, acute poverty, and child exploitation, Mandela said that we could no longer accept mere words and empty rhetoric from world leaders. It's time, he said, to turn this world around for the children.

> We heard it from Mandela, turn this world around
>   for the children, turn this world around!
> He's done it once before, and now we hear his call, for the
>   children . . .
>
> If every nation's leaders put their children first,
> Care and provide for every child.
> Each and every household would sing a song of joy
> And all 'round this planet a new light within it could
> Turn turn turn, turn this world around, for the children . . .

It takes courage to make peace. It takes heart to walk a new path. If not for our children, for whom would we do it?

Written and recorded in 2002, "Salaam Shalom, Side by Side" was born of a simple truth: Arabs and Jews have the same root word for peace: *salaam* in Arabic, *shalom* in Hebrew. Disturbed by the chronic Israeli-Palestinian conflict that traumatizes the region's children and troubles the world, I wrote a song to shed light on the children's experience of this ongoing tragedy. The song's instrumentation and Middle Eastern rhythm paint a picture of two coexisting cultures.

> Salaam shalom, salaam shalom, side by side we sing "salaam
>   shalom" . . .
> Mother father, sister brother, sing a new song, walk a new path,
> find a new dance, make a circle where we all belong—where we all
>   belong!

These motivational songs have been cheered as vocally as any of my children's songs. At conferences where I've been invited to sing them, people have joined in spontaneous rhythmic clapping and singing, and many have been moved to tears. But "Turn This World Around" and "Salaam Shalom, Side by Side" aren't for adults only. They are being downloaded from websites and sung at youth gatherings, children's choirs are adding them to repertoires, and school groups are choreographing dances.

VIBRATO

Instead of languishing outside curriculum, music deserves to be at the heart of learning, and central to education for a culture of peace. Music for children is not only a form of "math, their way," it is an early introduction to the patterns and cycles that underlie all life, the math that describes nature. The skills learned in playing an instrument engage whole brain memory, motor activity, and provide a lifetime of music making; they also teach the patience, perseverance, and discipline required for reaping later rewards.

As if to confirm the observations of child development experts that the arts are the essential learning mode of the very young, scientific research now shows the connection between music and learning, and music's role in stimulating brain development. As children benefit developmentally from engaging the arts, the arts become gateways for learning partnership, and for the lifelong work of peacemaking.

Singing is the first human art, the most compact, portable, and natural art form; and as such, it can be seen as a child's play of discovery and sharing. Singing is the inward-outward life expression that benefits individual, family, group, and village. Music, therefore, is essential art, essential to being human, to building community. Diverse human cultures have widely varying musical sounds and traditions and musical scales that are starkly different. And yet, it's the human voice, human hands, and human choirs and ensembles that sing and play as only humans can. To make music is to partake of a worldwide feast of feeling and expressing our humanity.

In music making, we also join other highly communicative animals—especially the birds whose songs fill the air and the whales whose symphonies span the oceans. But more importantly, we welcome our young children into music circles that can last a lifetime.

Song of the heart, food for the soul, music is a circle where we all belong. Blessed is the musical household, and the learning environment that's full of song. May the laughter of joyful singing comfort us throughout the day as we work and play. May we continue to share concerts that express and celebrate our deep humanity, that keep alive our cultural history. And may the respectful relationships within child-honoring families be their own sweet music—for our young and for ourselves, for fostering peaceful communities.

PART FOUR

Moving from Dominator
to Partnership Culture

FROM GLADIATOR TO MIDWIFE
Birthing "the Beloved Community" of Partnership in a Black Studies Classroom
PAULETTE PIERCE

Teaching has been the greatest joy of my life. When I stepped into the classroom as a teacher for the first time I felt more alive and connected to people than ever before. I had discovered my "bliss," Joseph's Campbell's eloquent term for realizing the true purpose of one's life. More than twenty years later I still feel the same intense energy and love whenever I am with my students. My passion for teaching, as well as my devotion to mentoring individual students, has earned me two university-wide teaching awards. Nonetheless, in recent years I increasingly felt a need to make radical changes in my approach to teaching. I wanted to bring it into agreement with the new vision I now hold in my heart. At the deepest level, this new vision, inspired by my discovery of Riane Eisler's work on "the partnership way," revived my long discarded faith in Dr. Martin Luther King, Jr.'s dream of "the Beloved Community."

The assassination of Dr. King was a life-changing event for me. I gave up on nonviolence and interracial unity as a teenager and embraced the militant Black Nationalist vision of Black Liberation. I learned to speak the new language of violent revolution. I quickly became a master at the art of verbal combat. I was then a student so the university served as my battlefield. I used words as weapons to attack anyone who held opposing views and always went for the jugular. I toned down my image as a Black militant as I advanced through graduate school but continued to hone my lethal intellectual abilities with the help of my professors. My superior performance landed me teaching jobs at two major white universities where I imagined my role to be intellectual gladiator, the defender of the dignity and rights of blacks and all oppressed peoples.

Then, about five years ago, Eisler's powerful persuasive vision of the partnership way revitalized my desire to work for peace and interracial cooperation and I became uncomfortable with my so-called successful teaching style. I could not ignore that my performance as the intellectual gladiator violated the most basic tenets of the partnership way of life: egalitarianism, mutual respect, democratic participation, and productive nonviolent conflicts.

While I certainly cared deeply about my students, I knew my traditional style of teaching did not model the qualities of partnership I most deeply desired to help actualize. As the fierce intellectual gladiator, I showed my students how to destroy the enemies of justice and equality. I dominated classroom discussions. I demonstrated how to mercilessly tear apart an opponent's ideas. I taught my students how to win, in the words of Malcolm X, "by any means necessary."

I most certainly had not enacted the ways of thinking, speaking, and, most importantly, relating to human beings that are necessary to create and sustain true partnership. Even more disturbing, I realized that I never had the opportunity to see partnership actually work, let alone experience it in my own life. I felt like I had hit a wall. How could I teach my students what I myself don't know? What could I point to in the world today to prove that the partnership way is more than a utopian dream?

Only last summer, a friend helped meet this urgent need when he introduced me to the method of nonviolent communication (NVC) developed by Marshall Rosenberg. I eagerly immersed myself in the teaching videos, tapes, and written instructional materials distributed through the Center for Nonviolent Communication. Almost immediately, I saw a near-perfect match between Eisler's partnership vision and NVC. Eisler is a theorist focusing on the grand historical pattern while Rosenberg is a practitioner concentrating on developing concrete tools and real-life application. In terms of basic precepts, Eisler and Rosenberg are almost indistinguishable in my thinking.

The partnership/NVC vision proposes nothing less than a revolutionary paradigm shift: It requires a decisive break with any form of coercion, unilateral control, or competitive structure that pits us against one another. It invites us to connect with our true feelings and to speak from the heart, to get in touch with what is alive in us and to express it. It assumes that we have life-affirming needs and that we cannot safely or fully satisfy our needs at the expense of others. Finally, it assumes that we only want others to meet our needs if they do so from the heart—a genuine desire to give—in which case we all gain.

Nevertheless, I found it hard to imagine how I could use NVC to teach Black Studies. My subject matter (the horror of the middle passage, the brutality of slavery, centuries of rape, decades of lynching, and so forth) is painfully charged. I could not yet visualize myself teaching this material without *deliberately* invoking and fueling powerful moral outrage in my students.

I felt vulnerable as I tentatively started to practice NVC with "safe" individuals, close friends and family members. The more public arena of my life was then out of the question. I was afraid that partnership and NVC required me to unilaterally disarm while my enemies remained armed to the teeth! Then, someone reminded me that this was precisely what Dr. King insisted upon and the civil rights movement trained people to do.

A sense of conscience pushed me to take bolder action. Thirty years after the collapse of the Black Power Movement, it was painfully obvious to me that the violence I once championed did not work. Worse still, the force of its angry, destructive, and self-defeating wake has reached a new generation, the hip-hop generation. It is their unfocused rage and profound cynicism about politics and the possibility of progressive change that most worries me. I felt responsible to show them a better way. As the start of the fall term drew closer, I wondered what would happen if I taught my students how to connect with the real needs that underlie the hurt and pain they seek to express through the outrageous, in-your-face styles that are the hallmark of hip-hop.

To my own surprise on the first day of school, I felt compelled by an intense life-serving energy to drop my gladiator armor and share my new vision of partnership/NVC with my new students. Trembling on the inside, I tried to look completely confident as I described how it would be possible to communicate in such a manner to make everyone feel safe and comfortable. Of course, we would have different opinions, at times even conflicts. Yet, I predicted, if we listened with our hearts, tried hard to imagine what *motivated* the speaker instead of who was right or wrong, and always showed respect to each other the class would be far more interesting. More important, we might also discover new liberating ways of thinking and being and amicably resolve our conflicts.

My hope, I confided, was to midwife a caring community that would support the highest actualization possible of each student's inherent, perhaps previously unrecognized, intellectual and creative potential. Referring to *Emotional Intelligence* by Daniel Goleman (New York: Bantam Books, 1995), I explained that intelligence is expressed in many different ways that traditional schooling overlooks. I invited them to come up with their own projects to highlight their unique passions and strengths that I would gladly use as alternatives to exams and papers to grade. I would be thrilled if they created poems, dance routines, or music, for instance. The job of a midwife, I explained, is to assist rather than control a woman as she gives birth (in the way she has chosen) to the new life ready to come forth from inside of her. Similarly, I hoped to work with them to help them to bring forth their innate potential in ways that best work for them.

This new partnership approach to education, I observed, ironically would require we unlearn the ways of thinking and acting that are rewarded in traditional classrooms. I strongly urged them to work cooperatively, for example, form study groups, share class notes, and team up for research projects. I would not allow, I promised, any statements, body language, or behavior intended to make any member of our class feel inferior or not welcome. I made sure to include myself and urged them, "Please! Please! Let me know if I inadvertently say anything or write comments on papers that hurt your feelings. My goal in giving feedback will always be to promote your growth." To dispel possible questions about race preference, I added I was always delighted when white students enroll in my Black Studies classes.

Given the large class size I asked that we wear name tags to facilitate a sense of intimacy and we frequently break into small groups for discussions. The goal was not, I emphasized, to decide whose view is right but to try to understand the experiences that have led individuals to see things as they do. Looks of surprise, disbelief, and relief showed on their faces as I finished explaining what I called "our group process and ground rules" by saying I hoped we would always respect each other and use our emotions to enhance the learning process. An awkward silence followed. I reassured them that I recognized how unfamiliar and perhaps difficult it might be to embrace a new noncompetitive, mutually empowering way of interacting in the classroom. I dismissed class with a proclamation of encouragement, "We can do this!" Elated and frightened I looked forward to an exciting quarter that did at times push me to the limits of my creativity, flexible, and resilience. It was time to "walk my talk."

Challenging learning opportunities appeared immediately. Monique constantly raised her hand to make long comments. I called on her to speak several times but soon asked her to try, with little effect, to shorten her remarks so that others might also share. I then ignored her waving hand to give others an opportunity to speak. Monique slouched in her chair, rolled her eyes, and audibly sucked her teeth. Deliberately not looking at her, I explained to the class that I wanted to encourage those who had not yet spoken to join the discussion, so I requested that all speakers be conscious of our time constraint. Class discussion resumed with new and former participants. I called on Monique when she again raised her hand. Again, she talked much longer than others and showed no sign of trying to wrap up so I requested she "please be brief." Later, when she claimed to have made a perfect score on the SAT a group of students started to murmur and then challenged her in a tone of mocking disbelief. I assumed they were angry at what they saw as her grandstanding and used this chance to "get her." I quickly stopped what I saw as an attack. In order not to appear as if I were ridiculing anyone I waited a few minutes before I said, "I hope we will always consider the possible negative impact our words can have on people before we speak. Remember, our goal is to empower each other, never to hurt or offend because this doesn't serve human development. Hopefully, with practice, we will find positive ways to communicate improvements individuals need to consider."

This tense class session proved to be decisive. After this, I never had to stop a discussion because I saw it as unproductive and/or hurtful. Instead, I had numerous opportunities to flag especially nurturing exchanges that occurred.

Not surprisingly, I had to check myself at times. Saniosa regularly came to class late. One day I made a smart remark when she "waltzed in" twenty minutes late. She is a very shy young woman and this public shaming obviously hurt her. Seeing her pain I quickly apologized and explained to the class that my remark had been thoughtless, hurtful, and, most importantly, unnecessary. I was hurt by what I interpreted as Saniosa's disrespect for my class, I confessed. "It would have been better if I had privately inquired what was motivating her tardiness and explored with her the possibility of a mutually satisfying solution to the problem." The class appeared surprised and appreciative that I would humble myself in this manner. Ironically, I found the experience quite liberating. My sarcasm had been a throwback to my days as the armored gladiator defending against real and imagined insults.

We were clearly becoming what one student described in a written class evaluation as "a community of love." Several shared this student's assessment: "I really love this class because there is no right or wrong answer and we can all share our experiences. Dr. Pierce has taught us how to listen . . . before we jump to respond." White students wrote about their initial feelings of vulnerability in a predominately black class, but noted they soon felt "safe, accepted, and respected, like I'm in the company of friends." They frequently remarked to the class that a whole new world had opened up for them. The following written comment sums up this experience: "Not being black, I've learned things I could never have otherwise either through history classes or reading books. The topics we discuss are so powerful and extraordinarily meaningful."

Near the end of the quarter, a group of students swamped me in the hallway before class. They were furious about a racist article in the student newspaper. With total confidence they said, "We just know we are going to discuss this in class!" I agreed but worried about how the white students would react to their intense anger. I prayed the black-white class bonding we had achieved could sustain us in this moment of crisis. Patrice read aloud the inflammatory article. Reactions came fast and furious from several black students. Krisha, a large black woman with a penchant for blunt expression, sat quietly boiling with rage. Finally, she blurted out, "I want to kill white folks!" However, no sooner then the words were out her mouth, she reassured the white students she did not mean them. Fighting back tears, she said, "I'm so sick of my people always being portrayed as wild animals or criminals. The sh-t just never stops!" A deep silent empathy seemed to enfold her.

Tangible evidence of our enduring bonding came when the students agreed to take action. Three white students—Karen, Libby, and Pamela—volunteered to work with several black students, including Krisha. Just one week later, they led a highly successful silent protest march attracting roughly one hundred people. My students were thrilled. I was delighted that their organizing method embodied so many of the tenets of the partnership/NVC vision: honest discussion of feelings, identification of their needs (in this case to be heard and respected), shared leadership, direct but nonconfrontational protest, and interracial cooperation.

Looking back over the academic year, I see two major areas where I am still uncomfortable using the partnership/NVC approach in the classroom. The first concerns the risks involved in forming bonds of trust and caring among oppressed people who carry layer after layer of pain inflicted by society. Who knows what will happen when those who have been schooled in silence with little access to societal resources respond to the invitation to speak from their tortured hearts? I want to believe partnership/ NVC will help blacks, women, and others to more effectively express and fulfill their humanity. Yet in the absence of adequate campus services to meet their real needs, I fear I will be left with an impossible task or feel guilty for not trying. How do I not get overwhelmed by their personal problems? How can I turn away when I know what they are going through? What, moreover, is my responsibility if I help them connect to formerly repressed feelings and needs? Is it enough simply to offer empathy when they are in psychological crisis or physical danger if I know support services on campus are grossly inadequate and many students are, in any case, unwilling to go?

The questions are not abstract. One woman confided that her live-in boyfriend was beating her and owned a gun. Another used a class assignment about rape to uncover her rape as a child by an uncle—something she had heretofore kept buried. I cried uncontrollably as I read her paper and fell into a brief depression because I too am a rape survivor. As I write, I am very fearful for her because these feelings are now alive in her and she has rejected my recommendation that she seek counseling.

The second problem area involves my responsibility for improving the academic skills and knowledge of my students and grading. How, I wonder, do I balance these traditional and essential aspects of the teacher's role with my desire to help students give birth to more holistic selves? This academic year I clearly favored their development of emotional and social skills and bringing forth creativity. At this, we were stunningly successful. Unfortunately, traditional exams and research papers painfully revealed just how deep their need of basic reading and writing skills is. In this regard, I am saddened to say I did little to assist them. Next year I plan to first brainstorm with students about how improving their basic skills would help them achieve their professional and personal goals; second, to explore with them new ways to weave instruction and practice of these skills into partnership/NVC approaches such as peer tutoring, small group instruction, and creative writing exercises.

I was terribly conflicted as I determined their course grades: I looked for ways to reflect their truly impressive development of partnership/NVC skills but in the end I gave much more weight to their exams and papers for which I had numerical and letter grades. I still do not know how I will "measure" or grade the intangible partnership/NVC skills in the future but I firmly believe these crucial skill are equally as important, if not more so, as traditional academic skills for my students' future happiness and success. Moreover, I am convinced our collective well-being and, perhaps, survival foremost depends on effectively teaching students the partnership way of life.

My journey along the partnership/NVC path has been difficult, even painful at times. There are also obstacles ahead. Nonetheless, I feel freer and more energized now that I have surrendered my heavy armor as the gladiator and picked up my new midwife bag to assist in the birthing of "the Beloved Community" I yearn for.

STRATEGIES FOR TEACHING CARING AND EMPOWERMENT

Drawing from African American, Mexican American, and Native American Traditions

LINDA BYNOE

E ducational scholars and community practitioners committed to the socialization of children of color and to the ideals of peace and love for humanity and the earth must first teach youth to love themselves. Loving themselves requires an acceptance of who they are, how they look, how they speak, their history and cultural heritage. Learning about love starts in the womb. As children grow they associate love with acts of caring, affection, and attention. Love is understood by most children as those good feelings they have when they are treated as though they matter. Unfortunately, the reality is that some parents never learned to be loving parents (hooks 2000). How then do we socialize youth to love themselves, and care about others and the earth? African philosophers have stated and westerns have learned to quote "it takes a village to raise a child." Haki Madhubuti reminds us that:

> Most children are born into the world at the top of their game, genius level. The culture that receives them will either nurture or develop the genius in them or silence their minds before they reach the age of six. (in Shujaa 1994, 6)

Many youth of color and most people throughout the world experience their nuclear family as merely a small unit within a larger unit of extended kin. Teachers, parents, businesspeople, politicians, social movement organizations, and community leaders must build partnerships that sustain life and that socialize youth to be knowledgeable, caring, empathic, and loving citizens. Through mentoring programs and community involvement opportunities,

189

youth learn to bring service to their communities, use their voice to evoke leadership and activism, and speak with knowledge and compassion.

Many educators see knowledge as a social construction that uses implicit cultural assumptions, perspectives, and a cultural lens to frame the evolutionary process of learning. Knowledge based in experiences attracts youth and promotes an understanding of the power of language and of the language of power. Although many adults fail to understand or to decipher the words of rap music, few educators would dismiss the power of the rap (hip-hop) genre to express the experiences of youth in pop culture. Yet the outcomes of these messages can and sometimes are hurtful and harmful to women, children, and others. Multicultural and multigenerational community youth programs must critically edit, respect, and understand the language of pop culture before they can assist youth in developing antidotes to the language of materialism, gangster posturing, and misogyny.

Paulo Freire (1990) suggests that the oppressed can teach only the oppressed and, for that matter, the oppressors, for those in power have the essential nature to construct and maintain power models. Therefore, I propose that leaders of community youth programs elicit as facilitators people of color who relate generationally, culturally, and spiritually with youth. It is imperative that community educators motivate youth to enlarge their worlds as they deconstruct status models. It is vital to the success of any community-based program to understand that youth will not learn immediately everything they are taught. Enlightenment begins with exposing youth to different ideas, situations, and relationships. It is through exposure that youth learn their amazing potential, a practice of ethics for their future, and perspectives and recognition for other's kindness, thus developing within themselves a loving, compassionate, and humanitarian attitude. To produce caring leaders who are critical thinkers, knowledgeable, confident, and articulate, community leaders must first show that youth matter. Riane Eisler writes:

> If we prepare today's children to meet the unprecedented challenges they face, if we help them begin to lay the foundations for a partnership rather than a dominator world, then tomorrow's children will have the potential to create a new era of human evolution. (2000)

EDUCATION FOR A PARTNERSHIP CULTURE

In the context of this chapter, youth of color are those children of Mexican, African, and Native American ancestry, who share in their cultural heritage marginalization, exploitation, cultural invasion, powerlessness, and violence (Young 1990). Youth of color in the United States are socialized to accept their marginal status through educational systems that emphasize individual rewards. But these youth can become leaders for a healthier culture that combines individual rights with a sense of community responsibility and service if they are taught to understand and use the cultural heritage of African, Mexican, and Native Americans linked to models of cooperation, consideration, and community collaboration (Mbiti 1970; Takaki 1993; Hill 1972). This chapter draws on these traditions as a rich source of education for a culture of partnership and peace.

Knowledge of one's cultural mores builds self-confidence and orients youth of color to a broader understanding of society. Cultural heritage, as described by Anita DeFrantz,

> is not based on pigmentation, hair texture, and physical features; these mark us phenotypically. What constitutes our heritage is much deeper than that—it has to do with our worldview, our systems for survival, our spirituality and interconnectedness, and interdependence with the earth. (DeFrantz 1995, 136)

To transform education and to create a partnership culture, the visions, experiences, and goals of people of color require the active participation, collaboration, and organization of many community educators—parents, teachers, politicians, private industry leaders, professional and social movement organizations, and other adults who benefit from youth's education. They must become actively involved in teaching. Communities need youth programs that undergird youth's social development and learning rather than optional activities or projects based on public relations. It is not enough to require academic excellence; as community educators we must understand the culture of youth if we are to deconstruct existing educational systems and provide youth of color experiences that question social systems while strengthening their self-concept, self-image, and self-confidence. We must expose youth to the essence and teachings of their cultural heritage and to learning strategies endemic to building a partnership community.

The three main elements of this cultural ethos most similar, familiar, and representative in African, Mexican, and American Indian cultural heritage are deference for generational reciprocity, spirituality, and activism. Modeling this cultural trilogy supports social transformation and may serve to groom youth of color in their journey toward building community partnerships for peace.

GENERATIONAL RECIPROCITY

Youth of color may be taught to access their cultural memories and to understand how generational reciprocity has historically served their communities well. The premise concerning generational reciprocity begins with a shift in perception and implies that generations of ethnic groups live in greater harmony when respect for knowledge, wisdom, and traditions are valued. In developing community partnerships, youth must learn to focus on relationships moving away from individualism and specialization. One of the first steps to this transformation is realizing that they are part of the natural world, where all life is interconnected and interdependent. Since the values and behaviors of adults may not always demonstrate the best role models for youth, it is imperative that adults who work with youth of color actively listen, encourage, and support honest dialogue. John S. Mbiti (1970) explains African relationship as:

> vertical in that it includes the living and the dead and those unborn, and horizontal in that it includes all living persons in the tribe even though they are in different family units. (48)

The biological cross-pollination of the Mexican, Native American, and African peoples throughout the United States possess familiar cultural characteristics. African Americans do not always function as horizontal communities today, yet prevailing in urban areas is the higher population of African American communities. Segregated rural and urban Mexican communities contrast with communities of the dominant society. Mexican Americans continue to live in barrios and family-oriented neighborhoods similar to the community ranches established in Mexico. Some Native Americans live on reservations that are communal in nature and function as tribes have for centuries (Kitano 1995). The rationale for a vertical perspective of family has to do with the beliefs that the elders are the closest to the ancestors, the most wise and the transmitters of the cultures, values, practices, and community histories. The children are quintessentially humanitarians, not yet subsumed by adult knowledge and persuasions. Those yet to be born are the ultimate future of the community and must be honored and protected.

The pedagogical strategies for teaching an understanding of generational reciprocity are to expose students of color to role models who are charismatic ethical leaders. This process requires students of color to consider the position, power, and leadership of their role models and requires that youth learn to network, minimize biases, and maximize relationships. Generational reciprocity requires that youth engage their philosophical worldview or theoretical model of their heritage and cultural orientation as it is reflected in their contemporary life. The cultural commitment of Native, African Americans, and Mexican Americans is distinguishable by their respect for the knowledge and wisdom of their elders, ancestors, and the prominence of community.

The elders, many who are women, pass on generational reciprocity, also known as a community's spiritual history. Those deceased family members, as well as those yet to be born, are always acknowledged. Everyone within the community knows the history of his or her village, ranch, or tribe. Vine Deloria states:

> A most encouraging sign today is the number of young Indians who are coming to respect and learn the ancient tribal knowledge. Most discouraging, however, is the rate at which tribal elders who have this knowledge are passing away. These two curves may well intersect in the immediate future, leaving tribes considerably poorer in their ability to deal adequately with their natural resources and to continue their ceremonial life. (Deloria, Foehnr, and Scinta 1999, 65)

The height of the hierarchy in communal living (extended family) is the community; family is second; the individual last. The community's role is to ensure the welfare and health of the families. The family is responsible for the individuals within the family. The individual is expected to care for younger family members and listen to and learn from the elders so that individuals can replace community leaders through their natural demise.

Wade Noble (1986) suggests that generational reciprocity and spirituality are similar in that they are vitalistic, a sense of the visible and invisible, humanity, nature, and the ultimate power. This is illustrated in the ceremony of the Mexican Americans culture's "Day of the Dead" and African American and Native American cultures' burial praise to their ancestors. These traditions express common spiritual sentiments and show a level of deference for generational reciprocity. It is primarily the women in the family who ensure that devotion to tradition continues. Mexican American youth quickly praise their mother or grandmother's role in developing and maintaining family altars and other family rituals.

Spirituality

One of our problems in the United States is that youth have been sold a bag of secular individualism, one that encourages the worship of money and power. Youth can be taught to understand that spirituality is about the greater, larger picture of the universe. Community leaders can be spiritual guides who may provide a catalyst for our youth's spiritual awakening. Spirituality is not about a religion. Spirituality is based on our interconnection and interdependence with each other and the earth. This element of the trinity requires that we teach youth of color that ethical behavior is necessary to their spiritual foundations. Spirituality must not be taught as a good or evil religion, but as the basic good of the human spirit and how that spirit links to our humanism. Youth of color ought to be taught to appreciate and explore their talents, creativity, and intuitive knowledge in ways that evoke an understanding of their personal power as it relates to the greater spiritual power.

> It is a recognition within everyone that there is a place of mystery in our lives where forces that are beyond human desire will alter circumstances and/or guide and direct us. (hooks 2000, 76)

> Spirituality involves conscious relationship with the realm of spirit, with the invisibly permeating, ultimately positive, divine, and evolutionary energies that give rise to and sustain all that exists. (Hull 2001, 2)

Youth can be taught to appreciate those gifts or talents that they uniquely possess, and that by linking their talents they can develop relationships that cross ethnicities, class, and cultural barriers.

Through modeling, youth can learn to see beyond the daily details of life and be one with a larger whole. Spirituality requires educators and students to connect to their intuitive power and their heritage of combined ethnicities.

Activism

Activism requires a sense of courage to face our convictions and to follow our hearts. It also requires perseverance. Activism is based on cooperation, collaboration, organization, creativity, and leadership. Youth can be taught to think about subjects and situations from multiple perspectives and to speak from truth. It is through the teaching of activism that we draw on the other ethos of spirituality and generational reciprocity, thus incorporating all elements endemic to the cultural heritage of people of color. Through the teaching of cultural mores the voice of critical democratic pedagogy for self and social change occurs (Shor 1992). W. E. B. Du Bois (1973), expressing concern for the education of African Americans and their want of self-confidence, self-assertiveness, and self-knowledge, described the "Great Lack" that causes students who speak from a bicultural perspective to fear the presumption of inferiority, displaying a depressed performance level and a diminished public voice. Yet within their own communities, youth of color practice improvisations, call and response, poetic rhythm, and bicultural voice to represent their uniqueness and affirm their reality. These methods of performing are not so different from the girots of Africa, the shamans of Native people, and the Mexican folklorist. Antonia Darder gives us an understanding of the bicultural voice:

> The bicultural voice points to a discourse that not only incorporates the world views, histories, and lived experiences of subordinate cultural groups in the United States, but also functions to rupture the historical and institutionalized silence of students of color and the beliefs and practices that support such dehumanizing forms of silence in the first place. (Darder 1995, 40)

LEADERSHIP WORKSHOPS FOR YOUTH

Using the philosophies associated with the trilogy—generational reciprocity, spirituality, and activism—I developed community-sponsored youth leadership workshops and exercises to improve intercultural, intracultural, and intergenerational communications for middle and high school students of color. In these workshops, youth are taught to be critical thinkers and to use their voices in positive and constructive ways to promote unity, peace, and a caring attitude for their community. For example, the five youth programs discussed in this chapter were developed specifically for middle school and high school students of color who lived in low- to working-class communities. Eighty percent of the youth attending the programs were middle school students and fewer than 3 percent were from middle-class families.

In addition,

• Two summer schools were sponsored by a professional social movement organization in a large metropolitan area. The summer school programs lasted for four weeks and were composed of fifty-six students (thirty-two Mexican Americans, twenty African Americans, two Asian Americans, and two White Americans).

• A summer camp program was sponsored by an ethnic community center for a large metropolitan area and was specifically developed for middle school and high school youth from homeless shelters or near-homeless situations. This two-week camp was composed of twelve youth (five African Americans, three Mexican Americans, three White Americans, and one Native American).

• Two leadership workshops sponsored by a community center were developed for middle school and high school students from a small metropolitan community. These workshops were composed of thirty-five students, twenty-four Mexican Americans, five Asian Americans, four White Americans, and two African Americans).

BUILDING COMMUNITY AMONG YOUTH

Within the United States, racialization has produced arbitrary boundaries and exacerbated tensions among people of color, particularly those people of African, Mexican, and Native Americans ancestry. The term *race* disables all people but particularly people of color because it proposes a difference based on the amount of melanin in one's skin as a hierarchy of what is good, intelligent, and beautiful in humans. Youth of color learn at a young age to perpetuate these biases, stereotypes, and violence against other people of color, fulfilling the prophesies of colonization. Community partnerships that create community alliances across color hues, and/or with victims of institutionalized racism, have proved essential in reeducating youth about ethnicities, identities, cultures, and deferring violence against others. By relying on the teaching of cultural heritage and the diaspora, connection among people of color promotes an understanding of the interconnection and interdependence with other humans and the earth.

To link Native, Mexican Americans, and African Americans to each other and to their heritage, I stress the familiarity of having ancestors from continents that archaeologists found important to the history of human origin. Africans are essential to the humanity on several continents; their presence in the Americas did not begin with enslavement, segregation, or apartheid (Bennett 1988; Van Sertima 1976). Asians, the people who traveled the Bering Strait, were pivotal to the lineage of American people. Vikings and their genealogy of European, African, and Asian lineage are the vanguards of combined heritage. People of color in the United States of America have a spiritual connection based on these multiple ancestors. Building an understanding of this human connection offers youth a perspective about human rights as opposed to civil rights. I do not trivialize cultural differences nor do I promote the assimilation of people. I stress that knowing our common cultural heritage unites us as a people, teaches us to become cultural relativists, and can and should defuse animosities between ethnic groups.

THE PRACTICE OF GENERATIONAL RECIPROCITY

Communications between youth and elders have significant cultural implications. The leaders, educators, and elders of African American, Mexican American, and Native American communities are typically addressed by their titles, an expression of respect for their positions. To eliminate authoritarian models and connect to democratic models, youths are encouraged in some communities to call their elders and teachers by their first names. While I agree that teachers' role is that of change agents and organizers and that they are important facilitators of education expendable, I also maintain that youth of color connect with their cultural heritage and speak from respect when addressing elders who are their benefactors. This more formal manner of addressing adults in communities of color demonstrates a respect for self, a level of manners, and an understanding of the cultural heritage.

Strategies for teaching generational reciprocity require the use of historical videos and books that depict the resilience and resourcefulness of struggling people. A series of drama-based exercises using the traditional African method of call and response prompt students to participate in class. One exercise requires students to describe their oldest living relative. They role-play their relative's relationship within the family and his or her historical significance. This exercise allows students to creatively express their understanding of the elder's position and knowledge. Many of the scenarios developed by students are rich with metaphors, analogies, and parables learned from grandparents, aunts, uncles, and others.

Another exercise requires students to role play a scenario in which youth address an adult, a peer, and a younger sibling or relative about a community topic of their choice. Working within a group and individually, students identify the differences in their speech patterns, language, and mannerisms, when talking to adults versus a peer or a younger sibling. Several students acknowledged that when speaking to an elder they are conscious of their body language, vocabulary, and voice inflection in order to ensure respect for their elders, whereas when speaking to a peer or a younger sibling they are more interested in conveying a message.

THE PRACTICE OF SPIRITUALITY

A simple way to introduce spirituality to students is to connect them to their inner voice. For example, the facilitator guides students through a series of meditation exercises. They relax to soft background music and follow the facilitator's voice. The facilitator describes utopia, a world of nonviolence, love, and peace, in a caring world of humans, animals, and the earth. Students take turns facilitating this exercise for others as a way to stimulate interests in describing their own utopia.

For additional exposure to ways of respecting the inner voice, a Taoist was hired to teach one Tai Chi class to a group of mostly high school students. Several students expressed pleasure in how simplistic the exercise was. One fourteen-year-old student who lived in a stressful family situation said that the Tai Chi exercise was the first time she felt safe and secure in her own quietness, while she remained consciously aware of her surroundings. Other exercises helped students to connect with their personal talents and their own rhythm of speech and movement. "It is through rhythm, music, and voice that we connect with our personal talents and creativity, where order and harmonious balance is established between us and others" (Bynoe 1996).

The Dance

One of the more popular exercises, "The Dance" requires students to hold hands and dance to the rhythm of the music as they feel it. One person leads at a time. After a few minutes the music and the leader alternate roles. Students learn that leadership can be as simple as a dance among people. They also learn that each person has a different rhythm, talent, and style that can be followed when given special attention. (Rittenberg 1989, 32)

Students were encouraged to share their talents in daily presentations, at play and in ceremony. When youth of color learn to honor their personal talents, they are forced to connect with the spirituality of their ancestors and to use their talents to raise the status of others and the condition of the earth. Students learn to question where this talent comes from. Inspiring students to use their talents to express themselves, share their ideas, and promote cooperation and collaboration cross-culturally involves a critical evaluation of hegemony. The interconnection and interdependence of our humanity becomes clearer when energies and knowledge are central to our yearning for peace.

THE PRACTICE OF ACTIVISM

Activism requires creativity, a connection to people in the community, and respect for the work of our predecessors. Activism combines with the other ethos to broaden opportunities to build self-confidence. It is the feelings of rhythm and musicality when combined with thought and action that produce and affect soul (Noble 1986). Activism demands a sense of reality and a desire for idealism. Youth need to be hopeful that improvement is possible. In the pro and con exercise, students learn to test and accept different perspectives.

Pro/Con

The facilitator chooses a topic, e.g., homelessness/teen pregnancy. The student is required to give a one-minute speech about the pros (positive aspects) of a subject and then upon cue to vie on the con (negative aspects) of a topic. Each student is given a different topic (Rittenberg 1989).

A sixth grader demonstrated a level of wisdom when she expressed pro and con for the topic of farm laborer. The con included short sentences about the hard and torturous work in the sun, from sun up to sun down. She also included information about the instability of the job market, low pay, and poor housing. But the pro was a litany of prose about the beauty of the deep rich earth, the wonderment of the fruits and vegetables grown in very short periods of time. The value of this job, the youth stated, is knowing that many people are fed healthy and nutritious foods created by the hands of the farm laborer. She summed up her pro statements with an appreciation for her parents, both of whom were farm laborers and the most honest and loving people she has ever known.

Activism is taken seriously and time is allocated for students to develop projects and write proposals for the betterment of their communities. It is critical that community educators follow through, acknowledge, and celebrate the work completed by students. One of the groups in the summer camp program for youth from homeless communities developed a project to acquire toothbrushes, washcloths, and haircombs for people in shelters. They submitted a proposal to a local department store and were given fifty packages of hygiene-related products. Another group of seventh graders raised money for a senior citizen retirement center. They collected enough recyclable objects—cans, bottles, and paper goods—to give the center more than three hundred dollars for their Thanksgiving dinner.

Through a series of drama-based exercises and project development activities, students are empowered to lift their community as they advance in their personal knowledge. The mere practice of speaking to an audience using various techniques to develop dynamic use of voice, rhythm, concentration, enunciation, and articulation empowers students to be more confident and socially conscious. The students who attended these workshops, camps, and summer school programs experienced ways of seeing and thinking endemic to their cultural heritage. They learned to use their voices and talents to address community issues and to deconstruct existing educational systems and question society in ways that strengthened their self-concept, self-image, and self-confidence.

The issues raised by W. E. B. Du Bois' "Great Lack" must include the lack of experience and exposure. The young people who participated in these programs were exposed to many new social and educational experiences. The community involvement included guest speakers representing various cultures, ethnicities, and genders. I worked closely with sponsors to coordinate field trips including visits to community leaders' offices and businesses. Students toured the police department and held conversations with the chief of police, the mayor, city hall officials, judges, local computer company engineers, utility company managers, and higher education institutions' faculty and university students. Students had the opportunity to present their proposed projects at various civic locations such as community centers, city halls, the Chamber of Commerce, and at their program's graduation. I sought every opportunity to encourage students to practice speaking in public.

At the end of each day, there was an audit in which students reflected on the intellectual and emotional development gained through the cultural theme of the day. Ira Shor (1992) states that allowing students' themes, understandings, and cultural diversity to codevelop the curriculum is one democratic goal of dialogue between educator and student. We had ten themes: education, business, art, justice, civic duties, spirituality, ethics, manners, history, and activism. Students assisted in establishing the curriculum for the specific knowledge they were seeking. Many of the students wanted to know appropriate etiquette, for example, what silverware to use at formal dinners, how to greet people in person and over the telephone, and how to shake hands. Almost all were very interested in their legal rights, when and how to hire a law-yer, and levels of punishment for various misdemeanors. These lessons were added to the curriculum as the students requested them. A judge in the smaller metropolitan area developed a mock trial for the youth to role-play. The students were energetic and excited about this opportunity as they rehearsed their roles.

It is equally important for children from the dominant culture to recognize different cultures. A dangerous message is sent to white children when they fail to experience other cultures in their neighborhoods, schools, and social surroundings. Perhaps this lack of experience implies to white youth that other cultures and peoples are not important. Within two weeks students learned to engage in dialogues about cultural difference, they challenged the ideas of social construction, developed projects to correct social injustices, and became friends. Bonding between the students was enormous. They played games, shared personal and family stories, learned to accept their differences, explored and appreciated their talents and the talents of their peers, and continued their friend-ships long after the programs ended. Students learned to bond with other students from different backgrounds and ethnicities, and they learned to care for themselves and each other through the exchanges of ideas.

The results from the programs confirmed the need for these types of experiences for youth of color. I continue to receive emails with questions about future programs, electronic greeting cards, or progress reports about school or other activities the students are involved in. Young people of color are hungry for exposure to their community, for role models, and for support for their voices and their talents. I teach youth to respect our common heritage so that they may become agents for changing the poor race relations so ever-present in our communities and the larger society.

It is my hope that youth of color gain self-confidence, learn to express themselves with verve, and perform service to their com-munities as their ancestors have for centuries, in pursuit of equity, justice, and value for all people. Youth of color act out in negative ways sometimes because they do not know what to do about their hopelessness. Given hope, guidance, and assurance that they are important members of their community, tied to a heritage rich in leadership, and of a culture highly regarded for its ability to survive, young people can broaden their perspectives and enlarge their dreams. Youth who are exposed to the triad of generational reciprocity, spirituality, and activism may challenge the world of monotheistic, monolingual, and monopolist thinkers and strive for a pluralistic society that celebrates the ideals of a caring and peaceful existence.

REFERENCES

Berger, E. H. 2000. *Parent's Partners in Education: Families and Schools Working Together.* Upper Saddle River, NJ: Prentice Hall.

Bennett, L. Jr. 1988. *Before the Mayflower: A History of Black America.* New York: Penguin Books.

Bynoe, L. T. 1996. African American blues women contribution to womanist theory: an ethnographic educational study. Unpublished dissertation.

Darder, A.1995. "Bicultural Identity and the Development of Voice: Twin Issues in the Struggle for Cultural and Linguistic Democracy." In *Reclaiming Our Voices: Bilingual Education Critical Pedagogy and Praxis,* edited by J. Frederickson. Ontario, CA: California Association for Bilingual Education.

DeFrantz, A. 1995. "African & African American Educational Voice." In *Reclaiming Our Voices: Bilingual Education Critical Pedagogy and Praxis,* edited by J. Frederickson. Ontario, CA: California Association for Bilingual Education.

Deloria,V., K. Foehnr, and S. Scinta. 1999. *Spirit & Reason: the Vine Delorian, Jr., Reader.* Golden, CO: Fulcrum Publishing.

Dog M. C., and R. Erdoes. 1990. *Lakota Woman.* New York: Harper Perennial.

Du Bois, W. E. B. 1973. *The Education of Black People: Ten Critiques, 1906–1960.* New York: Monthly Review Press.

Eisler, R. 2000. *Tomorrow's Children: A Blueprint for Partnership Education in the 21st Century.* Boulder, CO: Westview Press.

Foster, M. 1997. *Black Teachers on Teaching.* New York: The New Press.

Freire, P. 1990. *Pedagogy of the Oppressed.* New York: Continuum Publishing Company.

Giddings, P. 1984. *When and Where I Enter: The Impact of Black Women on Race and Sex in America.* New York: Quill William Morrow.

Hale, J. E. 1986. *Black Children: Their Roots, Culture, and Learning Styles.* Rev. ed. Baltimore and London: The Johns Hopkins University Press.

Hill, R. 1972. *The Strengths of Black Families*. New York: Emerson Hall.

Hilliard, A. G. 1997. *SBA: The Reawakening of the African Mind*. Gainesville, FL: Makare.

hooks, b., 2000. *All About Love New Visions a Warm Affirmation That Love Is Possible*. New York, NY: HarperCollins.

Hull, A. G. 2001. *Soul Talk: The New Spirituality of African American Women: A Transformative Paradigm*. Rochester, VT: Inner Traditions.

Kitano, H. L. 1995. *Race Relations*. Upper Saddle River, NJ: Prentice-Hall.

Kozol, J. 1991. *Savage Inequalities*. New York: HarperCollins.

Mbiti, J. S. 1970. *African Religion and Philosophies*. New York: Anchor.

Meier, D. 1995. *The Power of Their Ideas*. Boston: Beacon Press.

Noble, W. 1986. *African Psychology: Toward Its Reclamation, Reascension and Revitalization*. Oakland, CA: Black Family Institute.

Olsen, L., J. Bhattacharya, M. Chow, A. Jaramillo, D. P. Tobiassen, J. Soloria, and C. Dowell. 2001. *And Still We Speak . . .: Stories of Communities Sustaining and Reclaiming Language and Culture*. Oakland, CA: California Tomorrow.

Rittenberg, M. 1989. *English Through Drama: An Introduction to Language Learning Activities*. San Francisco: USF Press.

Shor, I. 1992. *Empowering Education Critical Teaching for Social Change*. Chicago: Chicago Press.

Shujaa, M. J. 1994. *Too Much Schooling Too Little Education: A Paradox of Black Life in White Societies*. Trenton, NJ: Africa World Press.

Takaki, R. 1993. *A Different Mirror: A History of Multicultural America*. Boston: Little, Brown.

Van Sertima, I. 1976. *The African Presence in Ancient American: They Came Before Columbus*. New York: Random House Inc.

Young, I. M. 1990. *Justice and the Politics of Difference*. Princeton, NJ: Princeton University Press.

WHAT IS THE LANGUAGE OF CARE AND SOCIAL JUSTICE THAT WE USE IN SCHOOLS?

CARL A. GRANT
LAVONNE J. WILLIAMS

T he hope and promise of the future fidget in their seats in classrooms across the United States. They come to school needing to learn knowledge and skills, develop an appreciation for beauty and culture, and develop the attitudes and practice the behaviors that are necessary for productive citizenship and a good, happy life in the twenty-first century. Some come in search of havens from violence, from streets and homes where they are not safe. Many come with a nagging sense that the larger world around them is not safe, that they face an uncertain future. Others come from homes of privilege where they have learned consciously or unconsciously that they have certain entitlements based upon their wealth, skin color, or gender. And all come in need of caring, both receiving it and learning to give it.

Audrey Thompson states, "caring means bringing about justice for the next generation, and justice means creating the kinds of conditions under which all people can flourish" (1998, 533). In classrooms, this means that teachers must become personally knowledgeable and engaged with diverse perspectives, cultures, languages, relations of power, and interests that exist both within and outside U.S. borders. Also, in the post 9/11 period, it means that a caring classroom must not ignore religious and ethnic differences; instead, students must be taught to be more aware and to understand the rights and the responsibilities of U. S. citizenship. For this is a time when we can easily fall into the trap of sacrificing the values that define us for the sake of some understandable, but misguided, notion of national security (American Civil Liberties Union 2002).

The rights of citizenship for all Americans include freedom, diversity, property, privacy, human rights, and due process. The responsibility of citizenship includes justice and equality, adherence to authority when it comes from the people, participation in the democratic process, speaking the truth about all people, and patriotism in the democratic process (Butts 1988).

A CLASSROOM IN ANY TOWN U.S.A.

A class roster in some school districts may show that the students are all or mostly of one ethnic group and speak the same language, or that the students represent several different ethnic groups and speak several different languages. If we use data from the 2000 Census, a classroom in Any Town U.S.A. will show a multicultural population: there are thirty students (fifteen girls and fifteen boys), eighteen are white, five are African American, four are Hispanic (three Mexican Americans and one Cuban American), one is American Indian, one is second-generation Asian American, and one is an Arab American. Two of the African American students, one Hispanic student, and four white students come from families that live below the poverty line, while another four white students are from upper-income homes. The students' families vary widely: Only two students come from families in which the father, but not the mother, works outside the home, nine are from single-parent families (six of which live below the poverty line), and both parents of the remaining nineteen students hold or have recently held jobs at least part time. Most of the students grew up speaking English, but two of the Hispanic students speak Spanish at home, one white student speaks French at home, and the Arab American student speaks both and English and Arabic at home.

These students, regardless of their race, gender, socioeconomic status, or religion, come to school expecting to be loved and helped. Similarly, their classmates across the globe, regardless of their ethnic background or living conditions, have similar dreams and expectations. All of these children, wherever they reside, have become connected to one another because of world events and conditions, such as advances in technology, the interdependence of the global marketplace and the world's economy, and the impact of the greenhouse effect.

Paradoxically, such world conditions and events, which need cooperation and understanding between and among nation states to be resolved, are at the same time disrupting the opportunities for these students' connections to lead to better understanding and harmony. This is because violence, in its many ugly and varied forms, is ever present. Terrorism, ethnic cleansing, ethnic and religious profiling, and suicide bombers teach children to distrust or to hate those in their own age group and others who are not of the same ethnic and religious background. Poverty, racism, sexism, religious intolerance, and homophobia, which abound in many of our nation's states, teach children that some people within our nation and in other nations are better than others, and social justice is for a very select few.

On the playground, in the school, and in the neighborhood—those private places reserved for living and acting as kids and teenagers—violence in the form of gangs, drugs, suicides, religious intolerance, and the massacre of classmates has become too commonplace to attract and sustain any attention outside of the immediate school community. Human tragedies are often handled by assigning counselors to work with students until they feel better, holding discussions about the tragedy in classes and at student assemblies, by establishing a zero-tolerance policy, and encouraging students to contact school authorities if they know about an upcoming act of violence. While we applaud these efforts for dealing with violence, we are concerned because they are not systemic and are not constructed to eliminate or prevent such events from happening again. They are, for the most part, reactions to mainly local problems, conditions, and events, instead of being preventive, systemic, and national in design and effort.

Also, such school responses do not make clear that the purpose of education is to promote the growth and development of students to become healthy, caring, well-rounded, and grounded individuals who accept and advocate social justice and equity for all people. Furthermore, such reactionary responses do not allow schools to be seen as places where students' purposes, anxieties, and relationships are not ignored in the service of making students competent in academic skills (Noddings 1992).

In many classrooms throughout the world, students face violence of a different sort: testing and accountability. Here the focus of schooling is "excellence," defined by a passing score on a standardized achievement test and how well-prepared students are to enter the workforce. Our argument is not against accountability per se, but the excesses in the accountability movement as defined in policies, practices, and language from the bully pulpit at the state and national level. For example, the high-stakes testing movement has created a school climate where discussions about the purpose and value of an education are narrowly defined, and those in charge of defining the purpose of education are a select few. In this context, the voices of educators—teachers and principals—are mute. Students fear if they don't pass the standardized exams they will be failed, which can lead to being pushed out of school. Teachers know if their students are not successful they will not receive any rewards or incentives and may be professionally humiliated, and principals know if their school does not perform at a certain level they may be fired.

Obsessed with high-stakes testing, discussions of education as a way to make life rewarding and satisfying, to provide the wherewithal to make intelligent decisions about our natural resources, to work with other peoples of the world for human betterment, to more effectively use our leisure time, to more effectively deal with psychological tensions, to more effectively accept and affirm diverse cultural and demographic groups, and to make bolder strides to achieve democracy and social justice for all, are receiving very little attention, or attention mainly in the context of standardized testing.

The testing and accountability movement also disrupts teachers' abilities to actualize the reasons they entered the profession. Love for and wanting to help students has been replaced with preparing students to pass tests. Linda Darling-Hammond argues, "as teachers prepare students to take tests their teaching focuses on recognition of answers in artificial formats rather than the production of idea, solution, designs, or analyses" (1997, 58). Also, she states, "Evidence from many studies demonstrates that when high-stakes decisions are attached to scores, tests can be expected to exert a strong influence on what is taught, how it is taught, what pupils study, and what they learn" (1997, 58).

Teachers know that students come into the classroom with a wide range of interests and abilities and with multiple intelligences, as Howard Gardner suggests (1983). For some students, their interests and strengths may be in written literary forms of communication; for others, in one or more of the performing arts. A caring classroom acknowledges, values, and promotes the strengths and interests of each child and considers artistic expression and communication as valuable as other forms of expression. Art is essential to men's and women's well-being, but in the testing and accountability movement, the voices of those who represent the arts in education are excluded.

The importance of the arts in the education and overall lives of students is for the most part silenced, ignored, or minimized, tantamount to declaring it a frill in the curriculum. Kerry Freedman disagrees with such a contention, arguing that art should no longer be thought of as a curriculum "extra," tacked on to meet the therapeutic activity needs of students taking dull, academic school subjects. Beginning in elementary school, art should be at the center of a curriculum on culture because understanding the characteristics of artifacts, ceremonies, costume, and other aspects of visual culture is fundamental to understanding human existence (Freedman 2001, 237).

Similarly, Julia Koza (2001) contends that music is often considered a nicety, but not a necessity. She argues the struggle to have music in the curriculum is a commentary on the values of those who decide what constitutes worthwhile knowledge, usually resulting in the marginalization of music. Honoring curriculum areas other than the traditional "basics" is an acknowledgment that there are many ways of knowing. Valuing music, as well as other arts, invites more pluralistic and diverse views about what it means to be intelligent. Valuing music education is a valuing of the affective component of living, of the emotional aspects of life often dismissed as feminine and, therefore, inconsequential (2001, 246). In conclusion, Koza states, "valuing music and other subjects that may not necessarily lead to gainful employment help send the message that material wealth is neither the only nor the most important of life's treasures" (2001, 246).

Recently, Sonya Ross (2002) an Associated Press writer, reported that President Bush said, "the nation's educators have a responsibility to challenge the status quo, but that burden is not borne by educators alone—government, parents, and business leaders must rise to the occasion too. All of us must assume responsibilities if we expect the best for every child" (Ross 2002). Apparently, the larger communities served by schools are—consciously or unconsciously—left out of the president's remarks. By *community* we mean the people, agencies, and organizations in the area that the school or school district services. We argue that the community should be involved because we believe that citizen participation is, theoretically and practically, fundamental to American democracy, and that without community involvement, power is dominated by government and business more so than by the people who are closer to the schools (Grant 1979). In addition, Manuel Montano states,

> The most productive approach to improving education for students of color has been a school-community partnership. In this partnership, the community's contribution is to help define and illuminate the interests and needs of their children. The school, representing both the dominant culture and the education profession, then contribute to problem solving abilities. The coequality of school and community can strengthen school-community relationships and can reveal problem areas which have escaped previous identification and consequently impeded progress. (1979, 152)

Furthermore, government and business do not have a good record of including those who are not white and male. Consider, for example, the racial makeup of the United States Senate. Through 2002, there have been only two African American senators, the number of the other senators of color has fluctuated between two and four, and the number of women senators are thirteen. In the 107th Congress there are 435 congresspersons, 8 percent African American and 3 percent Hispanic. There are fifty-nine women in Congress (13.5 percent). In the business world, as of 1995 most female workers were concentrated in low-paying "pink collar" jobs, with 14.2 percent in administrative positions as compared to 40.3 percent in technical, sales, and administrative support positions, and 15.83 percent in service occupations (U.S. Department of Education 1996).

And so, the curious minds, the faces with big smiles, the expectations to learn knowledge and skills and to develop the attitudes and practice the behaviors necessary for productive citizenship and a good life in the twenty-first century are seriously challenged and even in some cases stopped because of oppression in its many forms, before, during, and after school.

In a world filled with multiple forms of oppression, and with schools caught up in the accountability mania, teachers ask, What can we do? How can our love of children and our desire to help them learn remain our focus when so many state and national policies and global events seek to cause us do otherwise? Of course, there are no simple answers to this question, no silver bullets or magical formulas. Some argue that educators must maintain commitment and stay the course, that without dedicated, compassionate teachers life for children will become much worse. Others argue that in order to establish learning environments where students and teachers can feel good about what they do, teachers and other educators need to reintroduce themselves and students to the "ethic of care." Teachers should, with student involvement, establish caring classroom communities.

We, too, would argue that any social or academic hope for children lies within their homes, neighborhoods, and schools. At the state, national, and global levels, we need to inculcate an ethic of care that is both preventive and systemic. However, in a world where concepts and application of ideas are often devalued because they are not clearly articulated, or discussed without reference to professional literature or best practices, or defined according to one person's or groups' narrow background or bias, it is particularly important that we address and clarify the "ethic of care" that we have in mind.

OUR LANGUAGE OF CARE AND SOCIAL JUSTICE IN SCHOOLS

What is the language of care and social justice that teachers use with students? Robert Chaskin and Diane Rauner identity caring as an umbrella concept that encompasses and connects a range of concrete subjects such as empathy, altruism, prosocial behavior, and efficacy. Also, Chaskin and Rauner contend, caring involves mutuality and connection to others and is constructed on attention to reciprocity in human interaction rather than self-interest. With such a definition, Chaskin and Rauner argue that caring offers solutions to moral problems that go beyond a moral framework of the ethic of justice, so the context of relationships and commitments in any situation is taken into account.

Caring should expand the moral framework to one that supports and advocates for race, gender, class, ablism, sexuality, and religion. The establishment of care should include an understanding and analysis of the interlocking systems of oppression—racism, poverty, sexism—that prevent equity and social justice. Unfortunately, there is a popular history of and definition of care that places it almost solely in the context of missionary zeal, tolerance, bootstrap help, welfare, public assistance, helping out, and compassion for the infirm and grieving. David Purpel supports our observation when he describes how schools have defined care in past decades:

> The schools have traditionally encouraged the concept of caring in a variety of ways: organizing food drives for the needy; arranging for ways to comfort classmates who are ill or have suffered family loss; encouraging concern for others when the safety and well-being of others are involved, such as conduct in the cafeteria, hallways, and auditorium; and in the emphasis on caring as a positive value in the context of academic classes. (1989, 40)

While these notions of care are significant, especially to those immediately involved, they are nevertheless ineffective when dealing with the demands for care brought on by interlocking social oppression and injustices. That schools advocate a tolerant and benevolent notion of care is not surprising—the same is true with how multicultural education is advocated in schools. The tolerant and benevolent notion of multicultural education is the one most selected by teachers and other educators (Haberman and Post 1990; Sleeter 1992). A benevolent or tolerant interpretation of care mutes or silences discussions of power, privilege, and oppression, and leaves the discourse on care unproblematized. Furthermore, based upon a cursory examination of the 184 books in education published since 1995 that include care in the title and description of the publication, very little attention is given to race, class, gender, sexuality, and religion within the context of caring, nor are interlocking systems of oppression that may cause the need for care to be rendered discussed and analyzed to any extent.

Care in any societal institution must address the influence of race, gender, class, sexuality, ablism, and religion, and schools must address these issues of care in both the official and hidden curriculum, and in school policies and practices. To omit such an analysis supports existing social paradigms that do not actively challenge personal and institutional inequities. In addition, in order to implement the ethic of care, caregivers must first examine their own biographies, interrogate their own belief systems, and not take for granted that behaviors and attitudes support an ethic of care that embraces social justice.

Arthur Jersild reminds us that "an essential function of good education is to help the growing child to know himself (and herself) and to grow in healthy attitudes of self acceptance" (1955, 13). Therefore, in order for a good education to take place, Jersild states, "a teacher cannot make much headway in understanding others or in helping others to understand themselves unless they are endeavoring to understand themselves. If they are not engaged in this endeavor, they will continue to see those who they teach through the bias and distortions of their own unrecognized needs, fears, desires, anxieties, hostile impulses, and so on" (1955, 14).

The concept of care that we support mostly comes out of the black and Latina feminist literature. The black and Latina feminist theoretical conceptions of care include societal issues, including the concept of the ethic of care. The people, the *others* that are often the objective in standard discourses on care, are seen as individuals who are whole, and their race, gender, class, sexuality, religion, or physical or mental ability are seen as assets. Also, black and Latina feminism serves as a useful lens for examining how multiple oppressions such as racism, sexism, classism, and homophobia are constituted and fortified by elaborate interlocking justifications the dominant group maintain to continue their dominance.

Blacks and Latinas give a great deal of attention to social justice, affirmation of culture and language, and interlocking systems of oppression. Issues of race, gender, class, sexuality, and religion are concerns that scholars of color examine because surrounding such issues is the denial of equality in the school setting. Audrey Thompson states,

> Black feminist theories have paid close attention to the issue of race, and whereas color-blind theories of care tend to emphasize the innocence, Black feminist ethical theories emphasize knowledge.

Indeed, an almost defining feature of Black feminist ethical theory is that, characteristically, it is referenced to Black culture as experienced, interpreted and reproduced by Black women and "womanish" girls. (1998, 532)

Also, Thompson points out that the education literature on caring assumes a color-blind posture. She contends that most theories of care are limited and biased. In contrast, she argues the black feminists' theories pay great attention to race, and address race issues with an emphasis on the lived experienced and knowledge (1998, 532). In addition, Thompson argues that most black feminists find that most theories of care fail to address issues of power within a caring relationship, the essentialism of attribution of an ethic of care to women in general, the deficit assumptions inferring that children of color come from uncaring homes, and the disregard for the politically oppressive purposes to which caring have been applied (1998, 532). Thompson argues that for black theorists, *care* includes the emotional, political, physical, and intellectual labor needed to help all African Americans survive racism without the loss of integrity (1998, 533).

Angela Valenzuela argues that many traditional concepts of care are racist and authoritarian; students are expected to support a school and curriculum that holds their culture, language, and community in disrespect and is dismissive or derogatory (1997, 24–25). Valenzuela's definition of care includes having concern for the high values Mexicans give to interpersonal relationships, such as respect and honor for others, and that which is embodied in the Spanish word *educacion*. She explains that two types of caring are found in school, aesthetic and authentic. She claims that aesthetic caring is not good for Latino students' academic achievement and personal growth. To Valenzuela, aesthetic caring is found in nonsupportive school relationships, policies, and organizational structures that serve to diminish Mexican American students' culture and weaken their identities, which prevent supportive and nurturing social ties from existing and eliminate resources critical to students' academic achievement. Although aesthetic caring is intended to help students achieve, in reality this type of caring is *subtractive* in that aesthetic caring reduces Mexican American students to English-speaking, monolingual, ethnic minority students who are not identified with Mexico and are not equipped to operate competently with mainstream students.

On the other hand, authentic caring "expands on caring theory to include a pedagogical preoccupation with questions of otherness, difference, and power that resides with the assimilation process itself" (1999, 25). In addition, Valenzuela argues that difference is perceived as positive and a resource, and authentic caring affirms and embraces students' cultural and linguistic knowledge and heritage to create bicultural, bilingual competent youth (1999, 11).

Other black feminists and scholars of color have contributed to the literature on care. They have related caring to community, teachers' attitudes, language and voice, understanding of students, and curriculum. Lisa Delpit (1998) claims that in the black community a teacher's power and authority stems from the ability to establish meaningful interpersonal relationships that earn students' respect and the belief that all students can learn, with a demonstrated commitment to push students to achieve standards.

Geneva Gay states that caring is concern for the person and performance; is multidimensional responsiveness; is action-provoking; and prompts effort and achievement. She also notes that teachers' attitudes and expectations are paramount to the caring classroom. Gay argues that care is shown through teachers' attitudes, their expectations, and their behavior concerning students' human value, intellectual capability, and performance responsibilities. Teachers demonstrate caring for children as *students* and as *people*; teachers who really care about their students honor their humanity, hold them in high esteem, expect high performance from them, and use strategies to fulfill these expectations (2000, 45–46).

Language and voice play a major role in communities of color. The way parents and significant others talk to one another and to their children, and the voices they use in these conversations, is a major feature in demonstrating regard, care, and concern. June Gordon (1998) supports this observation. She claims that voice is communication based on trust, praise, and respect. Teachers don't intimidate—they talk real with the students. For example, caring teachers let students know the hard facts of life and that there are consequences for their behaviors, especially behavior thought inappropriate or disrespectful. Also, Gordon argues that caring teachers strive to gain understanding and knowledge of their students. Acquiring such knowledge, she contends, means extending oneself beyond the perimeters of teaching and the classroom. This means going to community events or activities and mingling with students and family members, or it may mean stopping a lesson to inquire into the start of a problem or recognizing and celebrating an event in a student's life.

Caring, to Gordon, is intervention into a student's life, speaking about or implementing action that facilitates the student's life opportunities. It is helping the students acquire the intellectual and behavioral tools that allow them to compete for their place in the system and to work to change the system to benefit those who are locked out. Simply put, caring in the classroom means that a teacher is responsive to the whole child—not only their achievement, but also the student's life situational factors, such as the stress of poverty (Foster 1995).

The curriculum is often described as the lifeblood of the school. It presents the past and prepares students for the future. It is crucial for students of color, gay and lesbian students, and students who are not Christian to be represented in the curriculum, for this is a form of caring. Thompson believes that to be a caring place, the classroom needs to encourage and respect the viewpoints of students of color and it needs to foster an antiracist curriculum, which she contends will help students to understand the political, social, and economic ramifications of race, racism, and racial relationships (1998, 544).

CONCLUSION

Care and caring are powerful medicines in the battle against oppression and for social justice. Schools need to have caring classrooms; teachers and students need to learn to be caring people and to advocate for the ethic of care. Care and caring are much, much more than benevolence, tolerance, or compassion. Care and the practice of caring must affirm one's race, gender, sexuality, and religion, and must illuminate how race, gender, class, sexuality, and religion construct how care is conceived and distributed. In addition, care must take into account how the interlocking systems of oppression serve to silence or mute how the care discourse is reasoned and addressed. Finally, students of color, poor students, students who are physically and mentally challenged, students who are gay and lesbian, and students whose religion—while old to the world may be new to the school—face oppression in multiple forms; care and caring can help them, but it must be of such a nature as to first accept and affirm them.

REFERENCES

American Civil Liberties Union (ACLU). 2002. Correspondence. New York.

Butts, F. 1988. *The Monthly of Democratic Citizenship: Goals for Civics Education in the Republic's Third Century.* Calabass, CA: Center for Civic Education.

Chaskin, R., and D. Rauner. 1995. "Youth and Caring: An Introduction." *Phi Delta Kappan* (May, 1995), 667–74.

Darling-Hammond, L. 1997. *The Right to Learn: A Blueprint for Creating Schools That Work.* San Francisco: Jossey-Bass.

Delpit, L. 1988. "The Silenced Dialogue: Power and Pedagogy in Educating Other People's Children." *Harvard Educational Review* 59(3): 280–98.

Freedman, K. 2001. "The Social Reconstruction of Art Education: Teaching Visual Culture." In *Campus and Classroom: Making Schooling Multicultural,* edited by C. A. Grant and M. L. Gomez, 225–38. Upper Saddle River, NJ: Merrill.

Foster, M. 1995. "African American Teachers and Culturally Relevant Pedagogy." In *Handbook of Rresearch on Multicultural Education,* edited by J. A. Banks and C. A. M. Banks, 570–81. New York: Macmillan.

Gardner, H. 1983. *Frames of Mind: The Theory of Multiple Intelligences.* New York: Basic Books.

Gay, G. 2000. *Culturally Responsive Teaching: Theory, Research, and Practice.* New York: Teachers College Press.

Gordon, J. 1998. "Caring Through Control: Reaching Urban African American Youth." *Journal for a Just and Caring Education* 4(4): 418–40.

Grant, C. 1979. "Partnership: A Proposal to Minimize the Practical Constraints on Community Participation." In *Community Participation in Education,* edited by C. A. Grant, 116–33. Boston: Allyn and Bacon.

Haberman, M., and L. Post. 1990. "Cooperating Teachers—Perceptions of the Goals of Multicultural Education." *Action in Teacher Education* 12(3): 31–35.

Jersild, A. 1955. *When Teachers Face Themselves.* New York: Teachers College Press.

Koza, J. E. 2001. "Multicultural Approaches to Music Education." In *Campus and Classroom: Making Schooling Multicultural,* edited by C. A. Grant and M. L. Gomez, 239–58. Upper Saddle River, NJ: Merrill.

Montano, M. 1979. "School and Community: Boss-Worker or Partners?" In *Community Participation in Education,* edited by C. A. Grant, 150–61. Boston: Allyn & Bacon.

Noddings, N. 1992. *The Challenge to Care in Schools: An Alternative Approach to Education.* New York: Teachers College Press.

Purpel, D. 1989. *The Moral and Spiritual Crisis in Education: A Curriculum for Justice and Compassion in Education.* Granby, MA: Bergin & Garvey.

Ross, S. 2002. "Bush Touts Education Reform." *Washington Post,* May 6, 2002. www.washingtonpost.com/wpdyn/articles/A40009-2002.

Sleeter, C. E. 1992. *Keepers of the American Dream.* London: Falmer Press.

U.S. Department of Education. National Center for Education Statistics. 1996. *The Condition of Education 1996.* NCES 96-304 by Thomas M. Smith. Washington, DC: U.S. Government Printing Office.

Thompson, A. 1998. "Not the Color Purple: Black Feminist Lessons for Educational Caring." *Harvard Educational Review* 68(4): 522–54.

Valenzuela, A. 1999. *Substractive Schooling: U.S.–Mexican Youth and the Politics of Caring.* Albany: State University of New York Press.

CONTRIBUTORS

Dee Bucciarelli, coeditor of *Partnership Education in Action,* teaches in the Graduate School of Education at Rutgers University and at Goddard College. She has experience developing curriculum and teaching courses and workshops in various subjects, where she has given special attention to multicultural and gender issues and to uncovering the structural roots of racism and sexism.

Linda Turner Bynoe is a professor at California State University, Monterey Bay. She teaches culture and equity courses, including The Sociology of Multicultural Education, American Cultural Heritages, and Culture and Cultural Diversity. Dr. Bynoe presents leadership workshops for youth of color in Salinas, San Jose, and Oakland, California. She is currently investigating programs that effectively utilize the cultural differences in the listening, speaking, and language skills of African American youth, and how these differences relate to reading abilities.

Doralice De Souza Rocha is the author of *Schools Where Children Matter,* published by the Foundation for Educational Renewal (2003). She completed her doctoral work in education at Harvard University, where she pursued research on holistic approaches to education. She has returned to her native Brazil to continue research on holistic education and to teach in universities there.

Riane Eisler is a cultural historian and systems/evolutionary theorist best known as the author of *The Chalice and the Blade: Our History, Our Future,* a reevaluation of 30,000 years of human cultural evolution published in eighteen foreign languages. In this book and in *Sacred Pleasure,* Eisler develops her influential cultural transformation theory, most recently applied to personal development in *The Power of Partnership* and to the field of education in *Tomorrow's Children: A Blueprint for Partnership Education in the 21st Century.* She is cofounder and president of The Center for Partnership Studies, has taught at UCLA and Immaculate Heart College, is a fellow of the Academy of Art and Science, and serves on many boards, commissions, and advisory councils. Eisler has been named in *Macrohistory and Macrohistorians* as one of twenty major macrohistorians, along with Vico, Hegel, Marx, Adam Smith, and Toynbee.

Lisa S. Goldstein is the author of several books, including *Teaching with Love*, and numerous journal articles on the role of caring in the education of young children, in teacher education, and in research on education. She is assistant professor in the Department of Curriculum and Instruction at the University of Texas at Austin, where she teaches in the early childhood education and curriculum studies programs.

Thomas Gordon, the author of *Parent Effectiveness Training* (1970) and *Teacher Effectiveness Training* (1974), was a faculty member in the Department of Psychology and at the Counseling Center of the University of Chicago; an organizational consultant; and a private practitioner as a client-centered therapist. He was the founder of Gordon Training International, an international human relations training organization that distributes his programs for parents, teachers, managers, youth, salespersons, and couples. More than one million persons in twenty-four countries have taken his training. His other books include *Group-Centered Leadership* (1955), *P.E.T. in Action* (1976), *Leader Effectiveness Training* (1977), *Discipline That Works* (1989), *Sales Effectiveness Training* (1993), and *Making the Patient Your Partner* (1995).

Carl A. Grant has written or edited twenty books or monographs in multicultural education and/or teacher education, including *Global Constructions of Multicultural Education: Theories and Realities* (with Joy L. Lei, 2001): *Multicultural Research: A Reflective Engagement with Race, Class, Gender and Sexual Orientation* (1999); *After the School Bell Rings*, second edition (with Christine E. Sleeter, 1993, 1995); *Making Choices for Multicultural Education* (with Christine E. Sleeter, 1994); and *Dictionary of Multicultural Education* (with Gloria Ladson-Billing, 1997). He has also written more than 125 articles, chapters in books, and reviews. Several of his writings and programs that he directed have received awards. Dr. Grant is Hoefs-Bascom Professor, chair of the Department of Curriculum and Instruction, and professor in the Department of Afro American Studies at the University Wisconsin–Madison.

Sura Hart is coauthor, with Victoria Kindle Hodson, of *The Compassionate Classroom: Relationship Based Teaching and Learning* (Center for Nonviolent Communication 2003). She has taught young people and adults, in and out of schools, for the past twenty-five years. She is a certified trainer for the Center for Nonviolent Communication (CNVC) and for the past two years has served as director and coordinator for CNVC's Education Project.

Rachael Kessler is the director of The PassageWays Institute (www.passageways.org), author of *The Soul of Education: Nourishing Spiritual Development in Secular Schools* (ASCD 2000), as well as coauthor of *Promoting Social and Emotional Learning: Guidelines for Educators* (ASCD 1997). Described by Daniel Goleman in the *New York Times* as a "leader in a new movement for emotional literacy," Rachael has spent more than twenty years as an educator, author, speaker, and consultant on issues concerning the need for emotional intelligence, social competence, and spiritual meaning in our classrooms, our workplaces, and our everyday lives.

David Loye is a social psychologist, futurist, and developer of moral transformation theory, evolutionary action theory, and a new triadic theory of evolution. His many books include *The Healing of a Nation, The Leadership Passion, The Knowable Future, The Sphinx and the Rainbow, Arrow Through Chaos, Darwin's Lost Theory of Love,* and, with Riane Eisler, *The Partnership Way*. Currently, he is completing the seven-book Darwin "Better World" Cycle including *The Great Adventure: Toward a Fully Human Theory of Evolution* (SUNY Press 2004). A former member of the psychology faculty of Princeton University, Loye was a professor for nearly a decade in the research series and was director of research for the Program on Psychosocial Adaptation and the Future at the UCLA School of Medicine.

Ron Miller is a leading author and publisher in the field of holistic education. A historian of American culture and education, he has written or edited seven books on educational alternatives, including *What Are Schools For? Holistic Education in American Culture* (Holistic Education Press, 1990) and most recently *Free Schools, Free People: Education and Democracy After the 1960s* (SUNY Press, 2002). He founded Holistic Education Press, the Foundation for Educational Renewal, and the journals *Encounter* and *Paths of Learning*. He teaches at Goddard College in Vermont and was a cofounder of an independent school near Burlington, Vermont.

Paulette Pierce is an associate professor in the Department of African American and African Studies at the Ohio State University, where she won the Distinguished Teaching Award in 2000. Previously she taught in the Sociology Department at Queens College, CUNY, where she also won its Outstanding Teaching Award. Her published work focuses on Black Nationalism in the 1960s and black feminism.

Raffi is an internationally acclaimed children's troubadour, composer, and author. For more than twenty-five years, his award-winning music has included hundreds of sold-out concerts and sales of millions of albums, videos, and children's books based on his songs. A passionate champion for children and ecology, Raffi is the recipient of the UN's Earth Achievement and Global 500 awards. *A Covenant for Honoring Children*, Raffi's poetic declaration of our responsibilities to the very young, is circulated widely through child development and environmental health groups. His autobiography, *The Life of a Children's Troubadour*, was published in 1999. Raffi is also president of Troubadour Music, a private company with a "triple bottom line" vision and mission. He is a Member of the Order of Canada, and founder of Child Honoring, an integrated philosophy addressing children's personal, cultural, and planetary needs.

LaVonne J. Williams completed her doctoral work at the University of Wisconsin–Madison in 2002. Her research interests include multicultural education, teacher education, educational equity and social justice, and caring classroom communities that promote student achievement. Her publications include "The Social, Economic, and Political Climate in the United States and the Education of People of Color" in *Combating Educational Disadvantage: Meeting the Needs of Vulnerable Children*, edited by T. Cox (2000).

Robert A. ("Chip") Wood has written the books *Time to Teach, Time to Learn: Changing the Pace of School* and *Yardsticks: Children in the Classroom Ages 4–14*. He is a teacher and teacher educator with thirty years of experience in K–8 education. He is a cofounder of the Northeast Foundation for Children and of the Responsive Classroom approach to professional development for educators. He has also taught child development and education courses at the high school and college level and is on the adjunct faculty at Fitchburg State College in Massachusetts. He is also a facilitator for the Courage to Teach program based on the work of Parker Palmer.

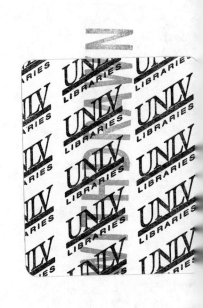